GEEKY PEDAGOGY

jessamyn neuhaus

GEEKY PEDAGOGY

A Guide for Intellectuals,
Introverts, and
Nerds Who Want to Be
Effective Teachers

WEST VIRGINIA UNIVERSITY PRESS
MORGANTOWN 2019

ISBN
Cloth 978-1-949199-05-5
Paper 978-1-949199-06-2
Ebook 978-1-949199-07-9

Library of Congress Cataloging-in-Publication Data
Names: Neuhaus, Jessamyn, author.
Title: Geeky pedagogy : a guide for intellectuals, introverts, and nerds who want to
    be effective teachers / Jessamyn Neuhaus.
Description: First edition. | Morgantown : West Virginia University Press, 2019. |
    Series: Teaching and learning in higher education | Includes bibliographical
    references and index.
Identifiers: LCCN 2019010278| ISBN 9781949199055 (cloth) | ISBN 9781949199062
    (paper) | ISBN 9781949199079 (ebook)
Subjects: LCSH: College teaching. | Effective teaching.
Classification: LCC LB2331 .N424 2019 | DDC 378.1/25--dc23
LC record available at https://lccn.loc.gov/2019010278

Book and cover design by Than Saffel / WVU Press

Grade me. Look at me! Evaluate and rank me. Oh, I'm good, good, good, and oh *so smart! GRADE ME!!!*

—Lisa Simpson, "The PTA Disbands," *The Simpsons*

CONTENTS

ACKNOWLEDGMENTS

IN P. G. WODEHOUSE'S short story "The Man Upstairs," the main character is a young woman struggling to become a professional songwriter. She has to teach piano lessons to support herself, and her students "were at once her salvation and despair. They made life possible but they also made life hardly worth living." Almost every college teacher has had this feeling at some point. Many of us set out to be academics because we wanted to be scholars, not because we wanted to be teachers. Fortunately, most of us discover that teaching has its own abundant rewards, and of course, we couldn't do this without the students. So, to all my students, thank you for the privilege of helping you learn and for the amazing gift of meaningful work. A couple of you were jerks and a few of you broke my heart but every single one of you—one way or another—always inspires me to keep learning how to do my job well.

I am indebted to the SUNY Plattsburgh history department for giving me the tenure-track opportunity to teach topics I love to a student population that matches my professorial strengths. My sincere thank you to the committee of the whole who hired me in 2004: Sylvie Beaudreau, Vincent Carey, Wendy Gordon, Jeff Hornibrook, Gary Kroll, Jim Lindgren, Jim Rice, Doug Skopp (1941–2018), and Stuart Voss. And because even the best teaching job in the world can become hell on earth if you're trapped in a dysfunctional department, I am additionally grateful to all my current department members, including Ryan Alexander, Mark Richard, Connie Shemo, Richard Schaefer, and secretary Nicole Jarvis, for their commitment to collegiality and for supporting my work as a teacher-scholar. Special thanks to Jeff and Connie for their encouragement at key points in the creation of *Geeky Pedagogy*, and also to my department and the SUNY Plattsburgh administration for a semester sabbatical that allowed me to complete this book.

I have learned so much about teaching from other professors during informal conversations, by reading published scholarship, and attending teaching conferences, especially the annual Lilly Conference on Teaching and Learning in Bethesda, MD. Thank you, one and all.

My teaching career began several years before my adjunct gig at Case Western Reserve University but my career as a reflective and effective teacher began when I consulted Mano Singham, then director of the CWRU University Center for Teaching and Innovation. Getting his insightful, generous advice was the first step on the SoTL road that led me to this book.

The vote of confidence that Tom Moran gave me when he nominated me for the SUNY Chancellor's Award for Excellence in Teaching in 2012 had a profound impact on how I perceived my teaching career. Receiving that award changed my professional life, and I will be forever grateful.

Although I'm a mediocre mindfulness student, I'm sincerely grateful to Luis F. Sierra of ADK Yoga for his illuminating and practical guidance on the practice of being present, and also for modeling teaching authenticity, expertise, and a sense of humor in every class. Thank you, Luis, for always saying to your students "It's good to see you"—and meaning it.

Working as a teaching fellow at SUNY Plattsburgh's Center for Teaching Excellence with Director Becky Kasper (1963–2019) transformed my understanding of teaching and learning, and planted the seed that grew into *Geeky Pedagogy*. For this opportunity, and for her abiding belief in my ability to be an effective teacher, I will always be deeply grateful to Becky. She was a consummate educator and a good friend.

The anonymous reviewers at West Virginia University Press and series editor James M. Lang gave me constructive, inspiring feedback that helped me significantly improve this book. Director Derek Krissoff's assistance and support was also invaluable. Charlotte Vester patiently answered all my formatting questions, Abby Freeland ably facilitated *Geeky Pedagogy*'s marketing, and Allison Scott provided expert copyediting. My heartfelt thanks to all.

Kelly Douglass is the person I most trust to listen when I need to belly-ache about the frustrating parts of teaching. Because she's always there for me, and because I know that she knows that occasionally griping about students does not cancel out being a caring and effective college teacher, and because her #grading tweets always make me laugh—thank you, Woman. Thank you also to the Douglass-Sullivan family for the Harry Potter references.

Today everyone seems to know about introverts but back in 1995 it was a revelation to me to learn about this fundamental personality trait. It explained so much and I want to thank the person who showed me the way: Stephanie Vader, fellow introverted professional whose job requires extrovert skills. Thank you for shedding some necessary light.

For cheering me over the finish line, thank you to Liz Mang, Marcia Ochoa, Dana T. Payne, Mark Payne, and Nan Brandenbergerpayne.

As described in the introduction, my first student was my sister, Alison Neuhaus, but she's taught me far more than I could ever teach her about acceptance, family, love, and doing the work that's given to you. Thank you, A.

My husband, Douglas Butdorf, and our son, Solomon Neuhaus, are neither geeks nor introverts nor nerds. Living with them is a master class on the differences between nerds and normals, and understanding those differences in my home led directly to understanding those differences in my classroom, which led directly to this book. Sol, I love everything about you that makes you completely different from me. Thank you for being my most important teacher, and I'm not just talking about the pick and roll. Doug, thank you for dragging me into the twenty-first century: geekypedagogy.com and @GeekyPedagogy would not exist without your know-how. Your unwavering support for this book is just one of the innumerable ways you are, and always will be, my rock. I am grateful beyond words every day and in every way for NeuBut Inc. (est. 1991).

Finally, this book is dedicated to my parents John Neuhaus and A. Lori Neuhaus—educators, introverts, and the biggest bookworms I know. For passing on the bibliophile and wordsmithing genes that made me a professor, and for the unconditional love and support you've given me every day of my life, thank you, Mom and Dad.

"STRANGE, SPECIFIC STUFF"

Just because you know a lot about something
doesn't mean you can teach it.

—Anonymous 1998 student evaluation
I received after teaching my first college class

———

IT'S HARD to write a catchy statement of teaching philosophy. Required by many hiring and promotion committees, these nebulous documents tend to sound pretty much all alike. When I was applying for college teaching jobs, I tried to liven up and personalize my teaching philosophy statement with this true anecdote:

> Learning how to read in first grade was the best thing that had ever happened to me. I still vividly remember the moment the words on the page started to make sense, and the feeling it gave me of unlocking a secret door and entering a wonderful new world. Afire with my discovery, I decided that my sister Alison, a kindergartener, should learn how to read too. After several weeks of sitting together and poring over books, Alison learned to read a year before her classmates and my career as an educator began.

Cute story and a good way to introduce myself as a teacher, right? I know at least one search committee thought so because during my interview for the tenure-track job I eventually landed teaching US history and popular culture at the State University of New York Plattsburgh, one of the department's most esteemed teachers complimented me on it.

There's just one little problem with framing my philosophy of college teaching through the lens of this particular childhood story: it illustrates the very worst assumption many of us make about teaching at the college level, namely, that sheer love of a subject inevitably leads to effective teaching and student learning. In my story it's not a desire to teach that makes me a teacher but instead an all-consuming passion for reading. There's no need for me to learn *how* to teach someone else to read because purely through some mysterious alchemy conferred by my own mastery of reading skills and adoration for books, I'm able to impart these skills to another person effortlessly. This is the problematic premise of college teaching because earning an advanced degree is the main criteria for most college teaching jobs, usually with no additional formal preparation for teaching required. But as the reality check given to me by my first student evaluation of teaching pointed out, although it's a necessary precursor, knowing a lot about a subject doesn't automatically mean that you can effectively teach other people how to do things in and with that subject matter.

Yet many advanced degree programs offer little meaningful professional teaching development for their students. Instead, graduate students spend years immersed in their own research, experiments, writing, or art, and completing a dissertation, which literature professor Jay Parini calls "the worst possible preparation for teaching."[1] If grad students do get classroom experience as teaching assistants, programs often send them into the teaching fray with the unspoken supposition that any teaching they have to do will be the grunt work that (partially) pays the bills and thus allows them to continue their *real* work—the work of the mind. This isn't the case at every institution, and the growing presence of teaching and learning centers on campuses and increased attention to pedagogy as part of graduate school is a hopeful sign that more students are finding support for developing their teaching skills.

However, the basic model remains firmly in place, and many people teaching college classes today followed this process. Step One: Spend at least a decade grappling with an erudite subject and proving how smart you are to other smart people who know a massive amount about said erudite subject and who, like you, believe the erudite subject is incredibly important and have devoted their professional lives to it. Step Two: If the stars align and you are fantastically lucky, obtain a job teaching college classes in the erudite subject. Step Three: Realize that many students believe the erudite subject is pointless and boring and seem to be unwilling or incapable of learning anything about the erudite subject. This book is for everyone teaching college classes who has reached Step Three and wants to successfully move on to Step Four—become an effective teacher.

The premise of *Geeky Pedagogy* is that those of us who have reached this moment often have another important thing in common. People teaching college classes are usually intellectuals and frequently some combination of introvert, nerd, and/or geek. Although they bring some hefty baggage with them, "geek," "nerd," and "introvert" are not necessarily pejorative or inherently derogatory terms. Emulating other writers and commentators today who are proudly self-identifying as geeks and nerds, expanding the definition of geek culture, and challenging negative stereotypes about nerds, I use these words as a wry, occasionally self-deprecating, but also affirming and celebratory way of describing certain characteristics we in higher education often share and which have an impact on teaching. For ease of reading, I'll refer to geeks, introverts, and nerds as GINs, and I presuppose that identifying college teachers as such is not in any way to criticize nerdiness, denigrate geekdom, or decry introversion. I am all of those things myself and, in fact, these are qualities that make many of us scholastically successful during our own education.

However, many GINs have neglected to figure out how these particular qualities may enhance but also may impinge upon our ability to teach effectively. If we want to be effective teachers, recognizing and embracing these characteristics and learning how to deploy them strategically in the classroom and during interactions with students is essential for those of us with advanced degrees in our own specialized scholarly subjects but little formal training in pedagogy. I argue that effective teaching is fundamentally an intellectual activity, an endeavor to which we brainiacs in higher education are particularly well suited, but as introverts who may be more practiced at studying than at peo-pling, we also have to understand and prepare for all the important ways that teaching and learning are social and emotional interactions that require clear verbal and nonverbal communication. In the following introduction, I will briefly unpack the terms "geek," "introvert," and "nerd," and explain why I see them as a useful way to describe college instructors and to frame our work as teachers. I will also set forth my conceptual framework of five general categories—awareness, prepa-ration, reflection, support, and practice—for organizing the activities which effective teaching encompasses. Finally, I will summarize what *Geeky Pedagogy* adds to the scholarship of teaching and learning (SoTL).

"Geek," "introvert," and "nerd" all have their own etymology, with introvert being perhaps the least debated. Coined by Carl Jung in the 1920s, "introversion" and "extraversion" are now accepted as measur-able personality traits by social scientists and psychologists.[2] Though often mistakenly equated with being shy, an introvert is not perforce someone who is awkward in social settings or has trouble connecting with other people. These things may frequently go together, at least according to #introvertlife tweets, but being introverted just means that you need time alone to recharge your mental, physical, and emo-tional batteries. You draw energy from time by yourself. In contrast, extroverts draw energy from interacting with other people, explains journalist Michael Godsey, who writes that introverts are those "who are energized by quiet space, introspection, and deep relationships and are exhausted by excessive social interactions" while extroverts "are energized by social interaction and external stimulation and tend to be bored or restless by themselves."[3] Whether you only slightly tend towards introversion or whether you are an off the charts "I" on the Myers Briggs, you almost certainly already know this about yourself. There's an obvious divide between those who favor social situations over solitude, and those who need more time by themselves and find socializing tiring.

For example, when he was only a year old, I took my son to his first playgroup. The moment we entered the community center teeming with shrieking toddlers and parents I'd never met, I felt a wave of ex-haustion. My extroverted child, on the other hand, lit up as if he'd seen the Promised Land and immediately began trying to wriggle out of my arms, eager to plunge into the seething mass of other tiny noisy people. He'd been looking for this his whole life! Instantaneously energized just by being surrounded by other people—that's an extrovert for you. Fifteen years later, he expressed genuine dismay when his summer job with a landscaping company required him to spend time by himself mowing grass and painting fences. "What am I supposed to *do* all day?" he lamented in real outrage. "Be *alone* with my *thoughts*?!" There's no better definition of what it means to be an introvert. If "being alone with your thoughts" is something you regularly seek out, if that sounds pretty good to you, you belong on Team Introvert.

In academia, there are some major benefits to being an introvert or having introvert qualities because "being alone with your thoughts" is the essence of doing intellectual work. Introvert qualities are what enable many of us to undertake successfully the hours of concentrated, mostly solitary mental labor required for research and for writing. Due in large part to the 2012 publication of Susan Cain's *Quiet: The Power of Introverts in a World That Can't Stop Talking*, many Americans seem to be increasingly recognizing that introverts' introspection and thoughtfulness is a valuable quality in a world ever more chaotic and noisy.[4] Twitter humor about our social awkwardness aside, introversion as a descriptive term about individual people does not for the most part conjure up highly problematic stereotypes.

In contrast, the words "geek" and "nerd" are historically thickly layered with meanings in popular media as well as people's lived realities.[5] A high level of intelligence is the common denominator in all iterations because the one agreed upon attribute of nerds and geeks is that we're *smart*. The debate begins when trying to define just what other aspects of personality and personhood constitute a nerd or a geek and to make value judgments about those qualities. Both terms gained traction as demeaning descriptors about certain kinds of studious men beginning in the early to mid-twentieth century, but some of those at the receiving end of the slang embraced and repurposed "geek" and "nerd" in order to claim membership in a self-defined subculture, marking the beginning of a discursive and embodied struggle about the meaning of these words which continues to this day.[6]

"The nerd" remains in many ways a negative stereotype in our culture and in our visual media, depicted as an overabundance of intellect, a sad lack of social and physical skills and other sexually desirable traits, and perhaps most notably, a man whose repeated failure to fulfill masculine ideals makes him the hapless victim of jocks, bullies, and attractive women. The stock figure of "the nerd," gendered as male, also reinforces the stereotype that intellectual superiority, with all its potential advantages and social drawbacks, is raced white (and, in the early 1900s, as Jewish).[7] Similarly, popular usage of the term "geek" equates being geeky not only with being obsessed with and good at technology but also regularly assumes a white, male identity that falls short of masculine norms.

However, in contemporary culture, numerous commentators, feminists, and writers reject the derogatory meanings of "geek" and "nerd," including any attendant assumptions about gender and race. Instead, online and social media users such as Nerds of Color, Black Nerd Problems, and Geeks of Color celebrate qualities such as science fiction fandom, insisting that we geeks and nerds exemplify what *Star Trek*'s Spock called "infinite diversity in infinite combinations," and although they're still rare, a few fictional characters on television illustrate increasing diversity in popular representations of nerds.[8] Another significant development in diversifying the image of "the nerd" in popular discourse is the ascent of the "blerd"—the black nerd—online, in media, and in real life.[9] Successful black performers who've declared themselves proud nerds include Keegan-Michael Key, Jordan Peele, Donald Glover, and W. Kamau Bell, and fictional representations of black nerdiness are increasing as well.[10] Though criticized by some African Americans, the assertion of blerd identity poses an important challenge to stereotypes about both black Americans and nerds.[11] Many people find "blerd" an empowering term, and this is especially true for black women because, as Jamie Broadnax, creator of Black Girl Nerds, points out: "Black women [nerds] face twice the scrutiny. A lot of folks have an idea of what a nerd is—and it's that they look like a white dude."[12]

Broadnax's observation about gender and race assumptions holds true among certain groups of white men who position themselves as nerd victims in a culture war.[13] For these trolls and flamers, being a geek or nerd entails elaborate patrolling of just who gets to do/read/play/say what, and who doesn't. Such "policing" of geek identity has reached a frenzy pitch in contemporary society with the blurring of subculture and mainstream culture entertainment, when comic book superheroes are today's most profitable film franchise juggernauts and *Game of Thrones* is an HBO megahit.[14] Some self-identified male nerds and geeks resent such mass-market intrusion into *their* carefully curated and proscriptive subculture. People of color like Broadnax who identify as nerds additionally confront this subculture about issues of representation and diversity, but at the same time they face what self-defined nerd Erika L. Sánchez describes as being "doubly ostracized": "We don't fit in mainstream white culture and our Latino communities often shun us because of our bizarre ways, interests, and beliefs. Many times we're accused of 'acting white,' whatever the hell that means."[15]

Sanchez's summary of this double ostracism, of "acting white," also evokes a crucial point for GINs in the academy and in the classroom. When we're women, people of color, and/or queer, being a scholar means fighting stereotypes outside *and* inside geekdom and academia, having to continually proclaim and prove ourselves as knowledge producers and our authority as teachers. Whether cosplaying at a Comic Con or teaching English 101, GINs of color and "female nerds" challenge the stereotype of the hyper-smart nerd as a white male—a stereotype that has real-life consequences. Stereotypes about nerds and geeks contribute to sociocultural factors that discourage girls from entering and women from flourishing in STEM fields where a "brogramming" culture still dominates.[16] And while some observers of youth culture suggest that stereotypes about geeks no longer doom studious teenagers to ostracism, others argue such hierarchies remain firmly in place and nerds are still at the bottom.[17] There are still popular kids and the guy playing D&D all weekend is still probably not going to be crowned prom king (or whatever the equivalent is for cool kids these days, maybe number of "likes" on Instachatface).

However, that guy *is* much more likely to become a professor. If you are teaching an academic college-level class of any kind, from remedial community college course to rarified Ivy League seminar, chances are good that you are at least a little bit of an intellectual, egghead, wonk, or some combination thereof. Even those of us in academia who never think of ourselves as nerds or geeks—because of the terms' negative, stereotypical associations or because we don't read comic books and eschew popular sci-fi—nonetheless almost invariably possess a few nerdy and geeky qualities. Certainly many students, in keeping with the contemporary usage of "geek" and "nerd," will readily define their college professors as such. No matter how with-it we are, no matter how tattooed or adept at social media, the fact is that many nonacademics and numerous students describe anyone with an advanced degree who's teaching college classes as a nerd, not as a demeaning insult but rather simply as an aptly descriptive noun. Student perception often becomes teaching reality, so it behooves all of us in higher education to consider how we might use geekiness and nerdiness to our pedagogical advantage.

Indeed, there's significant overlap between an "academic," that is, a person who has single-mindedly pursued years of original research and participates in the production of knowledge with a community of other scholars, and "nerd" or "geek" as defined by a variety of contemporary writers, commentators, and social scientists. Read their descriptions of "nerds" and "geeks" but replace "nerd" or "geek" with "academic" or "scholar," and you'll see what I mean:

- "The essence of being a geek is the unrestrained passion we have for the most esoteric things."[18]
- A nerd is someone who "pursues an unfashionable or highly technical interest with obsessive or exclusive dedication."[19]
- "To be [a] geek is to be engaged, to be enthralled in a topic, and then to act on that engagement. Geeks come together based on common expertise on a certain topic."[20]
- Geeks are "those with a passionate enthusiasm that may eclipse other life activities. . . . It is a subculture in which enthusiasm, knowledge and skill are appreciated and prided over good looks and attendant popularity."[21]
- Nerds have "an obsession with every inane detail of our interests."[22]
- A geek is "a person who is wildly passionate about an activity, interest, or scientific field and strives to be an expert in said vocation."[23]

- Nerds "obsess over things that are purposefully complex." "When it comes to our topic of interest, the "studying never stops." We are "protective of our knowledge" and "before we allow others to claim they are just as smart or have the same acumen, we're going to test that claim. If someone does not measure up or surpass us, we're going to inform them of this and seem like pompous, elitist jerks."[24]
- "Strange, specific stuff. That's what makes a nerd a nerd."[25]

The same enthralled engagement with complex topics and the perpetual studying of those topics that defines nerds and geeks apply equally well to many of us academics.

Scholars are actually sort of über-geeks because we've taken our obsessive individual interests and surpassed even the most dedicated hobbyist or fan: we've turned our devotion to a specific subject into our adult workplace and professional identity. We've embraced scholarship as our employment because we love "strange, specific stuff" so much we want to study it *forever*. Michael Flachmann describes this trait, arguing that professors who are effective teachers are "hopelessly, profoundly, inextricably invested in their areas of expertise":

> They drone on at cocktail parties about the inherent evils of defor-estation; they scribble obtuse mathematical formulas on napkins at their daughters' soccer games; and they haunt out-of-the-way book-stores in hopes of discovering a long-lost tome on some obscure sev-enteenth century German physicist. They go to sleep dreaming about Piaget and wake up thinking about him.[26]

This is the overlap between "nerd" and "scholar": a passionate fascina-tion with our chosen subjects that distinguishes us from other people at cocktail parties and soccer games. My own intellectual obsession is prescriptive popular discourse. As a historian of gender and culture, I am endlessly fascinated by old cookbooks, classroom instructional films, advertising, and marital advice manuals and how they reinforced sociocultural norms at different points in the US past. I've spent a zillion of the happiest hours of my life reading, studying, and writing about these everyday texts and ephemera. Please let me tell you *all* about them, in exhaustive, heavily annotated, detail![27]

In *Geeky Pedagogy*, I contend that people like us who truly love their field and devote themselves to knowing as much about it as possible, and who are determined to keep learning about that subject for their entire lives—we academic nerds and scholarly geeks—bring some noteworthy qualities to the work of teaching and learning. Yet SoTL has not previously addressed the fact that a significant number of us in higher education—regardless of our rank, salary, place of work, publication record, current position, and other aspects of our individual identity—are nerdy intellectuals and many of us are to some degree introverts. We who love "to be alone with our thoughts" are the ones generating knowledge, advancing understanding, and shepherding the next generation into the world because we know the most about the subjects we've studied. We are the *experts* in our fields.

But often we are not also experts at teaching students how to do things in and with those fields and all our expertise can in fact impede our teaching goals. Educational consultants Michele DiPietro and Marie Norman explain how college faculty's "expert blind spot" interferes with fostering student learning:

> Their disciplinary expertise allows them to operate easily and intuitively in their domains, but it also means they may fail to recognize the component skills within complex tasks and skip steps without realizing it. This proclivity, called "expert blind spot," is one of the chief obstacles to successful teaching. Because of expert blind spot, faculty often fail to teach or adequately reinforce key skills, routinely overestimate the abilities of students, and underestimate the time it takes them to complete tasks.[28]

We know *so much* about our topic, our brains are so wired with it and we are so adept at making connections and drawing on our previous knowledge that our expertise actually interferes with our ability to teach that topic. We routinely "fail to recognize" when students aren't getting what has become second nature to us. It can be hard for us to remember, let alone skillfully convey to others, the most basic first steps and foundational assumptions and intellectual practices of our discipline.[29] Effective teaching requires much more than subject expertise: it requires effective communication with students and knowledge of how to best foster student learning.

We are often woefully short on this vital pedagogical content knowledge. But GINs are a proud people and we don't like to let on that we don't know something. We love knowing stuff. We like to lord it over people too. Graduate programs foster this mindset, whereby admitting you don't know something is tantamount to lying down and exposing your vulnerable underbelly to the Alpha Academic. Also, being a scholar is mostly a solitary endeavor, with the rewards of grants, fellowships, and publishing meted out largely on an individual basis. So when we begin teaching, usually long after we've already made considerable progress in our scholarly work, we often erroneously assume that we'll be able to do it all on our own with little or no assistance or training. Our big fat brains have gotten us this far, haven't they?

In an essay about his own short stint teaching a writing class, memoirist David Sedaris describes how he imagined his class would go, contrasted with the harsh reality of the first class meeting. He captures how many of us with vast knowledge of a subject but little understanding of effective teaching and learning envision our future classrooms, and our subsequent struggles:

> I guess I'd been thinking that, without provocation, my students would talk, offering their thoughts and opinions on the issues of the day. I'd imagined myself sitting on the edge of the desk, overlooking a forest of raised hands. The students would simultaneously shout to be heard, and I'd pound on something in order to silence them. "Whoa people," I'd yell. "Calm down, you'll all get your turn. One at a time, one at a time." The error of my thinking yawned before me. A terrible silence overtook the room, and seeing no other option, I instructed my students to pull out their notebooks and write a brief essay related to the theme of profound disappointment.[30]

"Profound disappointment" is right: disappointment in yourself, in your students, and in all of academia, during that "terrible silence" when it dawns on you for the first time that teaching is not going to be an easy, natural extension of your scholarly expertise. The first time you realize that faced with a classroom of students, you're going to have *do* something because lo and behold, they don't seem as besotted with your subject matter as you are. Because you're reading *Geeky Pedagogy,* you've already distinguished yourself as one of the astute GINs who has faced this moment and accepted this fact and now you possess the single nonnegotiable quality of effective teachers—you *want* to be an effective teacher and you want your students to learn how to do things.

Here is where our huge GIN advantage comes in. Being an effective college teacher requires first and foremost *learning how* to be an effective teacher and then repeatedly *relearning* how to be an effective teacher. And as every nerd knows, we are "enthusiastic about learning."[31] Before we were teachers, we were students. Fantastically good students! That doesn't always mean getting good grades, though many of us did, but it does mean that out of all the things we might have chosen to do with our time, energy, and lives, we chose school. And more school. Really insane amounts of school. We can never get enough! Then we painstakingly built our expertise article by article, experiment by experiment, analysis by analysis, extensive footnote by extensive footnote. What we almost certainly didn't get along the way was commensurate knowledge in how to teach other people to use some of the intellectual tools we now possess, and how to speak at least a little bit of the specialized language in which we are now fluent.

Fortunately for us, decades of SoTL prove that acquiring pedagogical content knowledge and engaging in effective teaching is an intellectual activity.[32] Teaching offers us an infinite number of puzzles, problems, and research questions, and an abundant SoTL offers us endless avenues for identifying, exploring, and discussing those questions and problems, enabling us to engage in teaching as intellectually demanding work. Scholars know that when we frame anything as brainwork, we will succeed. Don't ask me to play sports. Don't ask me to make small talk with random strangers at social gatherings or even to call my best friends very often. But ask me to problematize, hypothesize, research, and reflect? Give me a homework assignment? Yes. Yes, *please.*

We have to deliberately, systematically learn and keep relearning how to best help our students know and do some of the things that we know so well and do so naturally in our specialized fields because experts teaching college classes must be more than the privileged bearers of knowledge about our scholarly subjects: we have to share that knowledge with our students.[33] In other words, we have to foster a geek culture in our classrooms not of exclusion nor of hostile gatekeeping but rather of enthusiastic sharing. In his research on geek subcultures, communications professor Joseph Reagle identifies this point of view as "a more progressive and welcoming notion of geeks who share," contrasted to "geek policing" of who can and cannot claim the title of geek.[34] As professors, we must be like those geeks today who celebrate the diversity and plurality of geekdom rather than unilaterally deciding from our perch of superiority who belongs and who doesn't. We need to promulgate a geek culture of sharing.[35]

We must be more like actor Wil Wheaton, a triple-threat nerd because he 1) played a character on *Star Trek: The Next Generation*, 2) played an ultra-nerdy character on *STTNG,* and finally, 3) has also publicly celebrated nerdy things in real life. During a 2013 Calgary Comic and Entertainment Expo Q&A, Wheaton famously summarized what it means to be a nerd: "It's not about what you love, it's about how you love it. . . . The way you love it, the way you find other people who love it the way you do, is what makes being a nerd awesome."[36] As Wheaton suggests, being an expert about something does not have to mean deliberately excluding others or enforcing hierarchies of knowledge. Instead, we can foster a community of sharing and celebrating knowledge. Teaching our beloved scholarly subjects in our academic disciplines should not be about keeping people *out* but rather about bringing more and more students *in* and showing them how much we love something and why they just might find something to love in it as well.

We can't convert every student into a fully realized professional scholar like ourselves, but we can actively, persistently seek ways to translate effectively our enthusiasm for whatever it is we love with all our bookish, dorky hearts into things that our students will want to learn how to do. As introverts, this means constantly pushing out of our comfort zone (being alone with our thoughts) and conveying to students why they should care about and learn how to use the tools of our discipline. Simon Pegg, another celebrity with solid nerd credentials, defined being a geek as "all about being honest about what you enjoy and not being afraid to demonstrate that affection. It means never having to play it cool about how much you like something."[37] That's exactly what effective college teachers do in our classrooms and in our interactions with students: forget "playing it cool" and instead enthusiastically share our passion for our subjects with our students. As described by Flachmann, being "hopelessly, profoundly, inextricably invested" in our scholarly discipline can fuel effective teaching.[38]

A geek culture of sharing as pedagogy facilitates effective teaching because it underscores that we aren't teaching in order to show off our own laboriously acquired expertise. We are in the classroom in order to share with as many students as possible what we value most in our disciplines. Pedagogical scholar Robert Rotenberg advises:

> If you value the intricacies of the material, teach it in such a way that the students can directly appreciate those intricacies. If you value the give and take of discussion, create a classroom that fully supports the flow of ideas, getting out of the way when necessary. If you value the research side of your discipline, make that experience the core of your classroom. If you value the quiet contemplation of a problem or levels of a text, make journaling and writing reflection the basis of your class. If you cherish the quick and easy recitation of facts, give students tools for assimilating facts efficiently.[39]

Rotenberg asserts that as college instructors, we should, in today's common parlance, *nerd out* about those specific aspects of our academic studies that we most cherish, and find ways to bring them into the classroom and share them with our students.

These days there are plenty of geeks intent on keeping the posers and the normals completely out of the geek kingdom. But others like Wheaton argue that our love for our subject should motivate us to share it, not dismiss or demean others who don't know as much as we do. Sci-fi author John Scalzi writes:

> Many people believe geekdom is defined by a love of a thing, but I think . . . that the true sign of a geek is a delight in sharing a thing. It's the major difference between a geek and a hipster, you know: When a

hipster sees someone else grooving on the thing they love, their reaction is to say "Oh, crap, now the wrong people like the thing I love." When a geek sees someone else grooving on the thing they love, their reaction is to say "ZOMG YOU LOVE WHAT I LOVE COME WITH ME AND LET US LOVE IT TOGETHER." Any jerk can love a thing. It's the sharing that makes geekdom awesome.[40]

Similarly, while "any jerk" (well, any smart, self-disciplined jerk) can write a dissertation, it's the *sharing* of knowledge with students that makes a college professor an effective teacher. This is our task as GINs teaching college classes: to get our students "grooving on the thing we love," even when it forces our introverted selves out into the messy and complicated world of social interaction.

That can be really hard. Teaching can be bewildering, discouraging, and tiring. So let me be absolutely clear on this point: I know you deeply love the subject you teach but you don't have to love every moment of teaching students about that subject in order to be effective and to help students learn. Teaching need not fill you with the same kind of ineffable joy and contentment you experience when you write code or read poetry or track data or study policy or make music or collect bark samples or whatever your vocation. Some books about teaching imply or state outright that a quasi-religious fervor for teaching is a requirement for effective teaching.[41] But I take exception to any hint of a suggestion that effective teaching requires a specific kind of innate personal quality or emotional state, rather than being a set of skills, attitudes, actions, abilities, and a reflective, intellectual approach that can be learned, applied, and improved with effort by anyone who wants to be an effective teacher.[42]

Unquestionably, effective teaching requires a lot of time and effort. We have to work hard at it and we have to demonstrate to our students that we care about the subjects we're teaching and about student learning. However, there are many and diverse ways to achieve this, some of which align better with intellectual and introvert qualities and personalities than others, as we'll see in the following chapters. To be an effective teacher you do not have to be unceasingly agog with unfettered delight at the prospect of molding young minds. You don't have to bring extreme cheeriness or extraordinary inborn teaching prowess to the task. You don't have to be Professor M. Poppins magically making the learning medicine go down with a spoonful of supercalifragilisticex-pialidocious pedagogical sugar.

If the foundational myth of academia is that knowing a lot about something automatically enables you to teach, there's another wide-spread and persistent myth about teaching generally in our culture: that good teachers are born, not made, and the best teachers are so good at transferring knowledge that students learn effortlessly.[43] These educator paragons make learning continuously fun for everyone, no matter what. The power of their teaching excellence alone counteracts and overcomes any and all obstacles to learning—poverty, illiteracy, abuse, disinterest, disabilities, etc.—that students bring with them into the classroom. These teachers' preternatural love for learning transforms the life of every single pupil it touches. Utterly selfless, absolutely devoted, and practically perfect in every way, these Superteachers appear regu-larly in popular culture and are well and truly fixed in our collective consciousness.[44]

Oh, how I hate them.

That's why this book is about *effective* teaching. I use that word deliberately and I avoid other kinds of descriptive qualifiers and adjec-tives—phrases like "excellent teachers" or "master teachers" or "bril-liant teachers" or even "good teachers"—when discussing pedagogical practices. I understand why other scholars and educational consultants use these terms, but I believe that such language may further an un-obtainable ideal of teaching as a superhuman undertaking. One of the main reasons I wrote this book is because I was tired of reading SoTL that undercut its own mission to improve readers' teaching and learn-ing by using terms like these. Some authors laud so many superlative award-winning teachers and detail such an overwhelming number of exemplar teaching techniques that instead of inspiring me as an educa-tor, I'm assailed by self-doubt, complete with a new hyperawareness of all my mistakes and shortcomings in the classroom. *Geeky Pedagogy*'s mission is the exact opposite: inspiring teaching self-efficacy.[45]

I hope to empower effective teaching—and learning. Effective teaching is inextricably coupled with student learning.[46] Educational reformer John Dewey pointed out back in 1901 that "the process of learning and that of teaching go together, just as do buying and selling. No one can buy unless someone sells, and no one can teach unless someone else is learning."[47] But what precisely does "effective teaching and learning" look like?[48] When I say "effective teacher" in this book, I mean a teacher who has found ways in their specific teaching context to increase skills and abilities among that specific population of students and to accurately measure and assess students' learning. Sound simple? Only if by "simple" you mean mind-bendingly complex, unceasingly contentious, and predictably difficult to do with real live people. But advancing students' knowledge and increasing students' skills is something we can *learn* how to do and keep doing more effectively, if we are willing to always keep expanding our own knowledge about teaching and learning and keep adapting what we've learned to our own unique teaching context.

There are numerous means and methods for expanding our knowledge about teaching and learning, starting with a plethora of books and articles. *Geeky Pedagogy* adds to this scholarship in three main ways. First, I emphasize that teaching and learning must be tailored to your unique teaching context, beginning by fully taking into account your GIN qualities, and extending to all the other specific and individual aspects of what and where you teach. The most cutting-edge pedagogical technique or the hottest new research on learning may or may not be applicable and useful for you, teaching your subject, at your college or university. Too often SoTL ignores or downplays the fact that effective teaching and learning can and does look drastically different from professor to professor, classroom to classroom, subject to subject, and college to college.

Second, I have made a concerted effort to avoid unnecessary jargon, obfuscatory terminology, elaborate diagrams, and convoluted datasets. If you're writing for your select group of colleagues on your select topic, go crazy with your specialized jargon and your insider lingo because that's how we in academia do things. But this book is meant for college teachers in a variety of disciplines, and trying to become a more effective teacher is hard enough without having to decipher the edu-babble prevalent in too much of the published scholarship of teaching and learning as well.[49] For definitions of the SoTL-specific terms I do use (including a couple I coined), please see the glossary. Similarly, there's no earnest sermonizing in this book about the hallowed halls of learning. Teaching is important work and can be personally and professionally meaningful, but we're not engaged in such sacrosanct toil that we can only talk about teaching in reverent, humorless tones. If there's anything worse than impenetrable SoTL argot, it's depictions of teaching as an unrelentingly solemn endeavor with no room for poking a little fun at all the ways teaching can be an exhausting, only intermittently fulfilling, and often downright weird roller coaster ride.[50]

Third, this book is an overview of the teaching and learning roller coaster, written with my own tribe of brainy, introverted academic nerds and scholars in mind. It is a critically reflective narrative précis of how we can approach the intellectual work of continually learning and relearning about effective teaching. This means it does not include long nitty-gritty lists of tips and tricks or detailed prescriptive step-by-step instructions. Those can be helpful and are readily available in SoTL but learning and relearning how to be an effective teacher is not a matter of simply trying out a new classroom activity, employing a new grading technique, or creating a new assignment. Rather, it requires continually renewed pedagogical practices, which grow and change over time over the course of a teaching career. It is an extended intellectual activity, a habit of mind, and *Geeky Pedagogy* is an introduction to that career-long endeavor. For additional materials that can help you continue to build your pedagogical expertise over time, such as bibliographic essays correlated to each of the book's chapters, please visit geekypedagogy.com.

In the following chapters, I've organized the many and varied things we have to learn about and have to do as effective teachers into five general tasks or approaches to learning about teaching: awareness, preparation, reflection, support, and practice. Because both multidisciplinary and discipline-specific SoTL are such broad fields, encompassing everything from scientific study to practical handbooks of specific teaching techniques to philosophical musings, learning about effective teaching can quickly become overwhelming.[51] My hope is that organizing your ongoing learning into five general categories will give you a way to navigate SoTL and empower you to engage in the intellectual work of effective teaching and learning. These five categories are not steps in a linear process but rather five overlapping and intersecting areas of widely defined activities.[52] Each can be tailored to your own unique teaching context and they emphasize how we GINs can productively approach our teaching as an intellectual endeavor, as a social interaction, and as fostering a geek culture of sharing.

It's not easy to learn how to teach effectively, and it's perhaps even harder to keep relearning how to do this, as our students, classes, and teaching contexts change. For some of us, the task is made even more difficult by working conditions such as contingent employment, racism, sexism, and other types of discrimination. And of course, it's really tough to *apply* what we've learned from the SoTL and from our reflections to our actual teaching practices—to progress from the study of teaching and learning to actually implementing the knowledge we've gained.[53] But with awareness, planning, reflection, support, and practice, we can move past our expert blind spots and be more than people who know a lot about something: we can teach other people how to know and do things, and we can share our knowledge in meaningful ways with our students. Because after all, as the Vulcans say about Starfleet, we're here to serve.

CHAPTER 1

AWARENESS

You see but you do not observe.
—Sherlock Holmes, "A Scandal in Bohemia"

———

A FEW years ago, I began taking yoga classes. The poses and stretches were a pleasant challenge but the silent meditation was torture. Be fully present, without judgment and without getting caught up in thoughts? That really doesn't work for me. As a highly cerebral person and as an introvert, I *love* my thoughts. Like many professional intellectuals, my brain is constantly teeming with ideas scurrying, burrowing, and rushing to and fro like brainy little hamsters. We scholarly geeks, introverts, and nerds—even those of us who fully understand the proven benefits of meditation and who are successfully cultivating mindfulness practices in other areas of our lives—frequently cope with college teaching stress by retreating into our minds and staying well *out* of the present moment. We may leave our most focused concentration back in our office or at our desk or in our lab or studio, and fail to pay full and deep attention to the disengaged students sitting in our classes who seem to hate the subject matter to which we've devoted our entire lives and are staring at us resentfully as we yak on and on about it.

That's why, as the first step in developing pedagogical effectiveness, it's especially important for GINs to cultivate our awareness skills as educators. Academia rewards its members for nonstop thinking. We love to retreat into our beautiful minds and roam the rich, glorious interior topographies of our intellects, but teaching and learning take place on the physical plane in the real world. So whether it's our first semester in the classroom or our thirtieth, when we are teaching we need to be paying close attention, to be as present and alert as we possibly can to what is actually really happening, as aware as we can be about what *is*—not what we wish or want, not thinking about what happened last semester or last week—because it is a prerequisite for being effective in the classroom.

If the term "mindfulness" or even "awareness" sounds too New Age, you can call it "being curious and inquisitive" or "seeing for yourself" or "paying attention."[1] Or just plain "studying," because awareness is an essential part of the intellectual work of learning and repeatedly relearning how to be an effective teacher: researching our specific teaching context by carefully studying exactly what constitutes our teaching context right now. Being fully aware of our present teaching reality, moment by moment, gives us the information we need to understand the situation, formulate it as a research problem, to think it through and consult the relevant scholarship, hypothesize, and then take effective action. We have to do this over and over, every term, every class, every office hour, and during every student interaction. In order to translate our geeky love for our topics into student learning and to interact effectively with students to the best of our introverted abilities, we need to be fully and consciously aware of and pay attention to our entire teaching context.

My husband often offers me a bit of timeless wisdom when my monkey-mind thinking on all aspects of a particularly knotty problem in my life, all its past possible causes and all its future probable outcomes, has gotten me worked up into a tizzy. "Jessamyn," he says sagely, "it is what it is." This is infuriating. A meaningless tautology! What's most aggravating is that he's right. We must actively observe *what is* if we want to be effective teachers, not what we want or fear or hope, not what happened before or may happen in the future. The intellectual activity of effective teaching and learning requires us, as Sherlock Holmes reminds us, to do more than simply see: we must *observe* what is happening in our classrooms and during our interactions with students. It's how we can figure what we must do in order to share the knowledge of our discipline with students effectively. But it all starts with first being aware of what is actually going on.

Specifically, we must bring a spirit of intellectual inquisitiveness to four key aspects of our reality in any teaching situation: first, how identity markers—race, gender, ethnicity, etc.—shape teaching and learning; second, the challenges inherent in learning itself; third, who our students are, as individuals and as a group, and finally who we are. We need to apply ourselves continually to understanding, learning, and repeatedly relearning as much as we can about these four ongoing realities, studying every unique teaching and learning context with fresh eyes. To be an effective teacher, the very first thing GINs must do is step outside our cherished Mind Palaces, apply our observation and research skills to our teaching contexts, and see them for what they *really are*.

Identity Is Important

Intellectuals are great at abstract thinking, at models and theories and conjecture. But we sometimes forget that like every other person on the planet we're embodied beings living in a society with its own expectations and stereotypes and consequences about those bodies. This is as true of daily life in academia as it is walking down a city street or buying a coffee at Starbucks. It's as true of teaching and learning as any other human interaction. Yet vast amounts of otherwise excellent SoTL fails to address how our body's identity markers and our students' identity markers come with all of us into the classroom. Furthermore, trained scholars and GINs may be particularly prone to ignoring this reality of our individual teaching contexts. Infatuated with our subjects, dreamily enthralled in the life of the mind, we may try to sidestep a fundamental reality of education that shapes all our interactions with all our students, even before any one of us has spoken a single word to one another: identity, as perceived via our physicality, is important.

Although graduate school crammed my head full of postmodern critical theory about culturally constructed subjectivity, not once did anyone mention: "And by the way, culturally constructed subjectivity will have a significant impact on your teaching work." As a white heterosexual able-bodied economically secure American, I just didn't stop and think about the real-life implications of identity in my future classroom. Certainly nothing in my academic training addressed in a practical way how race, economics, sexual identity, physical ability, gender expression, and so on shapes every teaching and learning context. This is true for many future college instructors. Even graduate students of color highly aware of the lived daily reality of racism, white privilege, and systematic white supremacy may sometimes envision academia as an escape from stereotypes and are deeply discouraged when they begin teaching and realize to what degree classrooms and universities are simply an extension of the world outside the Ivory Tower.[2]

Our race, gender expression, age, ethnicity, economic class, physical appearance and abilities, sexual orientation, and speaking voice all affect how students perceive us, how they accept our authority and our expertise, and how they respond to different pedagogical approaches we might implement. Women teach in a different context then men, and professors of color teach in a different context than white professors, and anything they do in their pedagogical approaches and interactions with students will have a different impact on learning and teaching than it does for white, cisgendered male professors. Sylvia Lazos summarizes this dynamic, explaining that women and faculty of color face certain student expectations that create obstacles which white male professors do not face, and so these professors "must ponder how their conduct will be perceived by students in the context of their gendered and raced role expectations."[3] As one study concluded, for black professors, "social constraints affect the negotiation of self and identity in the classroom, influencing the emotional demands of teaching and increasing the amount of work required to be effective."[4] Identity impacts how professors of color can approach their teaching as a scholarly activity and what they need to do in order to create a geek culture of sharing.

In addition to student expectations that intensify certain aspects of teaching labor for faculty of color and all female faculty, students are also more likely to question these professors' expertise. Just like geeks of color and women who engage in nerd culture challenge racialized and gendered assumptions about sci-fi fandom, technology, and gaming, so too do women and all faculty of color face racialized and gendered stereotypes about academicians.[5] Students are less likely to accept these professors' qualifications for university teaching automatically.[6] African American studies professor Kevin Everod Quashi explains that in his classrooms, "the professorial center does not hold. By this I mean that the normative centers or authorizing sites for an instructor, rather than being reliable, are instead conditional and sometimes contradictory."[7] Similarly, education professor Ana M. Martínez Alemán describes how the title of "professor" is a racialized one, and how this influences her teaching, noting that "to be a professor is to be Anglo; to be a Latina is not to be an Anglo. So how can I be both a Latina and a professor? To be a Latina professor, I conclude, means to be unlike and like me."[8] Not teacher, but "Other Teacher."[9]

As Lucila Vargas writes: "When students have never seen women of color in leadership positions or as sources of mainstream knowledge, our mere presence in the classroom is deeply disrupting."[10] Or as one professor succinctly summarizes this teaching and learning dilemma: "For a lot of them (non-minority students), when they enter your class-room, you're the first black person that they've ever encountered that has any sort of authority. And for some of them that's very difficult."[11] Unsurprisingly, this often leads to an increased possibility of conflict with students.[12] Yet it also opens up possible avenues for productive pedagogical strategies, as Jennifer Ho notes: "Teaching as a faculty member of color at a predominantly white institution, I have realized that it is not only my scholarship but my very body that students learn from in the classroom."[13] A diverse faculty not only fosters educational inclusivity and furthers social justice and equality on our campuses, but also increases student learning. Every time I model for students my professorial authority and expertise, I chip away at gender norms. My classroom presence alone calls into question stereotypes about power and knowledge. Those of us who don't match students' unconscious assumptions about what a professor looks like have the ability to expand student understanding and help better prepare them to live and work in the multicultural reality of the professional world today.

Still, the fact remains that people of color, women, LGBTQ, inter-national, and differently abled faculty teach college in what Roxanna

Harlow terms "disparate realities" than white men.[14] Regrettably, SoTL generally does a poor job of taking these disparate teaching realities into account, often assuming a teaching context not uniformly available to all instructors. Pointing to this common lacuna in the SoTL, one professor of color tells an interviewer: "I long for teaching situations like the ones that Stephen D. Brookfield [a preeminent pedagogical scholar] describes in which the teacher facilitates and the respect seems bidirectional."[15] Some of the "best practices" regularly lauded in SoTL have different implications for faculty of color, women, and others. For instance, SoTL discussions about establishing rapport and immediacy with students may suggest or imply that professors should be friendly and smile in class and during student interactions. But women, especially young women, routinely have the experience of a man who's a complete stranger casually assessing our demeanors and then feeling entitled to tell us that we should "smile more." At best, it's an impolite comment about someone's personal appearance. At worst, it's yet another daily manifestation of the patriarchal power structure that expects women to look and act in certain ways for the comfort and pleasure of the male gaze. When pedagogical research concludes that students want professors to be friendly and to smile, it's going to mean different things in our classrooms depending on our embodied identity.

I'm not suggesting that white male college instructors don't face teaching challenges or don't have to work hard in order to foster student learning, but there are important differences of which we need to be aware. I'm also not advocating that we accept this as an unchangeable truth we cannot combat. Of the four realities we must accept and pay attention to, the fact that identity is important because racism and sexism and the other isms are alive and thriving at our institutions like they are everywhere and will influence teaching and learning is obviously unjust. There are many things we can and should do to fight it and do our best to change it (see, for example, the Twitter thread #thisiswhat aprofessorlookslike, which deconstructs unconscious assumptions about professorial identity), including using whatever pedagogical tools we possess to advance student understanding of educational inclusion and diversity. But first things first: pay attention to how identity works and acknowledge this reality in the classroom. For scholarly GINs, this requires us to shift gears and move out of our customary hyper-intellectual view of the world and to pay more careful attention to our flesh and blood reality.

That includes understanding our own privileges and biases. As college instructors, we all to some extent enjoy a position of privilege with certain kinds of power and prestige, even criminally underpaid contingent faculty living in poverty and with extreme employment insecurity, and even faculty of color facing student doubts about expertise and authority. Furthermore, we all bring our own preconceptions and unconscious biases into our classes and make assumptions about students before we know a single thing about them beyond their physical appearance.[16] No matter how personally dedicated we may be to fostering educational inclusivity, implicit biases shape our interactions with students. To cite a personal example, one semester I had two exemplary students with two entirely different and unusual names in the same class. These young women look nothing alike but they are both African American students at my predominately white university, are friends, sat next to each other, and contributed to class discussion regularly. On several occasions I called one by the other's name for no reason whatsoever except that some buried and biased part of my old white lady's brain, shaped by my culture and society, saw them as somehow interchangeable.

GINs want to be judged and assessed on the basis on our disembodied thoughts and ideas. Most of our scholarly work is on paper or in a lab or online or on the canvas, in words, symbols, and abstractions, not the meat suits of our bodies. When we walk into a classroom, we want it to be our brain that really matters, not the shape or skin tone of the body housing it. We may incorrectly assume that we ourselves have moved past all forms of prejudice and preconceptions about others based on their appearances. But the flesh matters. It matters a lot. We don't have to accept it as a done deal that we're powerless to try to change, but before we undertake to build any aspect of our pedagogical expertise, we do have to accept that identity is important and it has an impact on how we teach and how students learn in our classes.

Learning Is Hard

Speaking of students learning, there's another teaching reality we need to understand as much as possible: learning anything new is extremely hard. I mean "literally forming new physical brain pathways" hard.[17] Not "requires some effort" hard. Not "study a little more" hard. More like "blood, sweat, tears, setbacks, failure, struggle, and pain" hard. The science of learning is complicated and always evolving but there's one simple, indisputable fact we need to understand: learning is *hard*. Paradoxically, GINs as a group are among the least well-equipped people around to grasp the implications of this for the classroom. We love learning and readily embrace the challenges it presents. Learning in an academic setting has come more painlessly to us than it does to others, so it's easy for us to forget how difficult learning is. Even more importantly, we forget how difficult it is to learn *our* topic—our beloved scholarly subject matter that we've studied, contemplated, researched, published, talked and argued about with other smart people for years. We all have an enormous expert blind spot smack dab in the middle of our teaching selves hampering our efficacy.

Picture a comic book nerd who knows every detail of an extremely detailed decades-long canon featuring their favorite obscure superhero. Picture that person trying to explain the character to someone who's never heard of the comic book and who isn't all that interested in the first place. As educational consultants Diane Cummings Persellin and Mary Blyth Daniels write, "Ironically, our expertise as instructors can pose pedagogical challenges when we assume our students have our level of fluency in organizing and interpreting information."[18] We often fail to see where students will struggle learning something in our field because to us, it's second nature. We mastered the habits of mind our discipline demands a long time ago. We "frequently use abstract language and advanced concepts when teaching novices" not because we want to purposefully baffle our students but because abstract language and advanced concepts are so much *fun!*[19]

Like a Batman fan laboriously tracing the Dark Knight's evolution from gritty pulp detective brawler with inner demons in 1930s comic books to gritty vigilante brawler with inner demons in the Nolan film trilogy of the early 2000s, we can and do automatically reference a vast network of previous knowledge on our chosen topics whenever we think or talk about them. In fact, we revel in that network. As one group of researchers states, "As experts in our fields, we create and maintain, often unconsciously, a complex network that connects the important facts, concepts, procedures, and other elements within our domain."[20] But, in marked contrast, most of our students have only a sparse and superficial basis for organizing their knowledge on the topics we know backwards and forwards, sideways, upside down, in and out.[21] We know a metric ton about our disciplines. We're the *experts*. So it's difficult for us to put ourselves in our students' shoes as newcomers to our subjects. Although we do constantly learn about our subjects, we're learning by building on and adding to previous and firmly established knowledge.

When we read and write new books and articles, conduct new research, and consider new theories, we're incorporating new ideas but we're not trying to do something we've never done before. We don't have to flounder and flail, gazing at a book or an experiment or an equation or a plant or whatever, thinking "I have absolutely no idea what is going on here." It's trying to do something you've never done before that makes learning hard. Indeed, research shows that learning how to do something actually requires you to fail at it first. You cannot fully understand how to do something without some struggle, and struggle always includes setbacks and failures.[22] Try to remember the last time you attempted to do something you'd never done before, something totally new and different. Run a 10K? Prezi? Ballroom dancing? Even if you ultimately did it well, you will also recall the ways you flubbed it at first.

Consider too the role of intrinsic motivation. Even if you can dredge up a memory of that long-ago day when a younger version of yourself first struggled and failed to grasp the subject about which you are now an expert, chances are that you were highly motivated to learn that subject. It intrigued and attracted you. It attracted you so much that you disregarded all rational arguments to pursue a more lucrative and viable career and set out to become a scholar. You were deeply motivated to learn it, so setbacks and failures were mere speed bumps, overcome and quickly forgotten. Now think about your students, especially general education students taking your course for the sole purpose of fulfilling a requirement. How intrinsically motivated are they to learn? How ready and willing are they are to fail before they succeed? How much tolerance do they have for confusion and ambiguity? How well did their high school education prepare them for struggling to create and utilize brand new knowledge, as opposed to parroting the right answers for a test? How ready are your students to be wrong and nonetheless plow through and continue working towards comprehension? In all likelihood, not very. Who is, really? It's unpleasant and uncomfortable and wreaks havoc with our individual insecurities and fears.

As a professor teaching classes on the history of popular culture, I often notice another way that learning is hard: learning something new about something you previously thought you understood is often even more difficult. You're not just forming new neural pathways—you're taking a jackhammer to comfortable, well-traveled roads in your head, reducing them to rubble, and building new ones.[23] Talk about struggle! Prior knowledge can greatly interfere with acquiring new knowledge. For instance, one day during my class on modern American culture, we were discussing what I thought was a convincing scholarly essay about the campy gay-ish qualities of Glinda in *The Wizard of Oz* and how to read the movie as a lesbian fantasy. My students scoffed and dismissed the article, illustrating the author's point that many people strongly resist any interpretation of mainstream popular culture that does not correspond to heterosexual norms; that a queer "interpretation of things [is] never 'just another way to see things' for most people, but something akin to delusion."[24]

I pressed the heterosexual student most vociferously objecting to the author's analysis, asking him why he was so convinced that *The Wizard of Oz* did not contain gay subtext. It just doesn't, he insisted. "Okay then," I said, "what do you see in the film?" He admitted that he had never watched the whole movie, although he had seen it playing on TV screens in gay bars when he went clubbing in New York City. With his very own eyes, he had repeatedly witnessed consumers queerly interpreting *The Wizard of Oz*! Yet he still couldn't accept the multiplicity of meanings in this pop culture text as discussed in the article. Why was this? Subconscious homophobia? Probably. But also because the essay asked him to not simply think about something but rather *rethink* something he thought he understood perfectly well (i.e., watching movies).

SoTL sometimes describes this learning struggle as a disciplinary "bottleneck" where students predictably get stuck.[25] Erik Myer and Ray Land term it a pedagogical threshold concept. More than just a key idea or theory, a threshold concept in any discipline is "transformative, irreversible, and reconstitutive" knowledge.[26] It usually facilitates a "shift in subjectivity" for the learner, who can linger for a long time in a liminal space of continued questioning and ambiguity, on the threshold of an understanding that will "engage existing certainties and render them problematic" and thus "troublesome."[27] When my history of pop culture students tell me jokingly (sort of but not really), "Professor Neuhaus, you've ruined [fill in favorite form of entertainment] for me!" they are articulating what it feels like to learn a threshold concept, and there's no going back.

The Wizard of Oz essay confronted my student with a threshold concept in the study of culture, that is, the meaning of any pop culture text cannot be fixed and will be used by different groups of consumers for different purposes. Really understanding this would have forced him to let go of what he thought he already knew about consuming popular culture. GINs often overlook just how difficult it can be for students to grapple with the threshold concepts of our fields and the transformative learning it can set in motion.[28] Our expert blind spots obscure the stumbling blocks we overcame a long time ago. These concepts no longer distress us. In fact, we delight in them, and it's easy to forget how uncomfortable it is to let go of what you thought you knew and step out into a new way of seeing something, realizing you can never go back.

There are entire libraries of research about learning, and if we want to be effective teachers, we should know some of the basics. A good starting place is the seven "learning principles" identified by pedagogical researchers in the influential book *How Learning Works*:

- Students' prior knowledge can help or hinder learning.
- How students organize knowledge influences how they learn and apply what they know.

- Students' motivation determines, directs, and sustains what they do learn.
- To develop mastery, students must acquire component skills, practice integrating them, and know when to apply what they've learned.
- Goal-directed practice coupled with targeted feedback enhances the quality of students' learning.
- Students' level of development interacts with course climate to impact learning.
- To become self-directed learners, students must learn to monitor and adjust their approaches to learning.[29]

GINs also need to understand some of the other well-documented facts about learning that impact our teaching, such as:

- Sitting still and listening is not an effective way to learn. Yes, fellow scholars, I know you can learn this way and so can I, but most people need a lot of movement, interaction, and actual application of ideas in order to learn.[30]
- Students do not learn content by merely listening to us talk about the content, because "telling students information does not translate to learning."[31] We're not the Matrix Operator uploading kung fu directly into Neo's cerebral cortex, so we need to plan for effective lecturing by interspersing it with small group activities or note review or other types of activities.
- Any type of learning must build on previous knowledge. For example, Stacy Bailey asks her literature students to think about their own first kiss to help them better understand *Romeo and Juliet*.[32]
- In addition to meaningful connections to previous knowledge, learning requires repeated practice over an extended period of time and frequent testing.[33]
- "Productive struggle" is an important part of learning because "trying to solve a problem *before being taught the solution* leads to better learning, even when errors are made in the attempt."[34]
- Learning is not a purely intellectual exercise. Emotions matter.[35] To learn anything, students must occasionally be frustrated and experience failure, but they can't get mired in that feeling. Students

with a growth mindset, that is, the ability to perceive themselves as advancing towards increased skills and understanding, are better able to cope with setbacks and failures and ultimately learn more (as opposed to a fixed mindset, believing that our abilities are inherent and can't be developed or improved).[36]

- When students are afraid of failing it will be physically harder for them to learn because it triggers their amygdala, the fear center of the brain.[37] It's almost impossible to learn anything when your lizard brain is flooding your body with the message to flee before the predator pounces.

- Your students' socioeconomic background, racial and sexual identity, ethnic heritage, and so on all matter because "culture impacts learning."[38]

Importantly, students are not usually familiar with these facts about learning. For example, we might know that in order to understand the material fully, students need to actively engage with and practice applying it but many of our new students don't. After years of high school classes reinforcing the idea that learning means listening quietly to a teacher talking, many students will inevitably respond with incredulity, confusion, and downright hostility when presented with more effective learning strategies. We can predictably expect this reaction—and not only from underprepared students but also from honors students who have achieved success in traditional academic settings.[39] Such a "dualistic way of thinking" means that most new students "believe that gaining knowledge is as simple as listening to and repeating the views of an authority figure."[40] Linda Hodges and Katherine Stanton point out that "students may have immature beliefs about how learning happens or how knowledge is created, not recognizing how tentative, iterative, and effortful a process it is," making it all the more pressing for us as effective teachers to be aware of how humans learn and to help our students understand it as well.[41]

However, authors on the science of learning tend to forget the importance of specifics. What does a new finding about how our brains work mean for *you* and *your* students, in *your* teaching context? Not to mention that even the best evidence-based learning technique will be a lot harder to implement if we've got a massive teaching load, no office in which to hold office hours, or are facing a particularly challenging, disparate teaching reality. In all cases, when we tackle the science of learning as part of our intellectual approach to teaching, we have to remember that there's never going to be one singular theory or technique that everyone can use in every teaching situation to enable every single student to learn everything they need to learn.

Learning is always ongoing, "a continuous and cumulative process. Prior learning becomes the fodder for further understanding and insight."[42] This means us too: effective college teachers are always learning how to teach effectively because everything we know about learning also applies to learning about effective teaching. Even when we approach teaching with the intellectual curiosity and skill we nerds bring to studying topics that interest us, we still face all the same obstacles and hurdles anyone faces learning anything. For example, faculty with a fixed mindset approach to teaching are not going to be able to advance their efficacy as well as those with a growth mindset about teaching.[43] Fear interferes with our ability to learn how to teach effectively, and it takes struggle and failure, testing and practice. Intrinsic motivation ("I want to learn how to be an effective teacher because I really want my students to be able to do this") is going to foster improvement better than external motivation ("I have to learn how to be an effective teacher because the dean said so").

All the important facts about learning that apply to students learning in our classes are just as important to the scholarly work of learning and relearning how to be an effective teacher. Learning is incredibly hard and it takes a long time, whether you're a first-year student learning how to write a research paper or a veteran teacher learning how to engage a new generation of students. We academic nerds have embraced a life of constant learning but when it comes to our students and to our own efforts to be effective teachers, we also have to keep remembering that learning is *hard*.

Know Our Students

I used to read a now defunct website called "College Misery" that published posts and comments about the numerous things students do that drive instructors right out of their ever-loving minds. At first, it seemed like a good outlet. After a bad class, I could go online and read other professors' humorous rants about how ill prepared, lazy, and irritating students are. But then all that internet snark began to color my lived reality, and I found myself obsessively cataloging and enumerating students' shortcomings like Professor Gollum, PhD, polishing The Precious. Everyone needs to vent sometimes, but we can't let occasional venting about reoccurring teaching frustrations evolve into nonstop complaining and overgeneralizing. Just as we must be aware of the reality that learning is hard, so too awareness—*it is what it is*—is the essential first step to knowing our students.

Emphasis here on *our* students. Unconscionably huge amounts of SoTL do not acknowledge how fundamentally different student bodies can be and how important it is to understand those specificities. I don't know why this isn't discussed more in SoTL, though I suspect it's because everyone's just searching for the one magic teaching technique that will work in every class everywhere for all time, amen. But some assignments, pedagogical methods, and teaching techniques that work well with most students at one type of institution just won't work with most students at another type of school. I slowly and painfully learned this during my first years of teaching. I assigned readings to a community college class that would have been challenging even for graduate students specializing in the field. I created elementary, step-by-step research assignments for high-achieving liberal arts college students who had previously completed more difficult work in their college-prep high school classes. I treated accomplished students like novice learners, and students in need of basic academic supports like Ivy League critical theorists and expert learners. I didn't know my students because I didn't approach teaching as an intellectual endeavor requiring curiosity and research into exactly who my students were—their previous academic experiences, their prior knowledge, their expectations, and their learning needs.

In her *Tenured Radical* blog, Claire B. Potter describes how early in her career she found out how essential it is to know your students and tailor your teaching accordingly. Working to make course content relevant to students, she would begin class with a short discussion "linking the day's topic to a political event that had happened that day." At a selective liberal arts college with young, high-achieving students, this proved effective: "They were very political, and had come to this college to have a 'relevant' education. My strategy made them feel valued and respected, and it did help them connect to the material." But when she used the exact same technique at a public commuter college, the returning adult students perceived it as a waste of time because they "were fully embedded in the world: they usually had families, carried a full course load at night, and worked full-time jobs during the day. They were sacrificing a lot for their educations and expected every minute to count."[44] The exact same exercise done the exact same way by the same instructor: for one group of students, it proved effective and advanced their learning, and for another, just the opposite.

Knowing our students means first making some generalizations when we are applying our scholar-teacher curiosity to learning about what kinds of activities and assignments will be most effective. While we want to avoid sweeping oversimplifications, if the majority of your students are about the same age, generational research that looks for shared student characteristics in demographics such as Generation Z and iGen can be helpful.[45] For instance, the newest generations of students will have grown up with ubiquitous cell phones and wireless technology. How does the incessant social media–driven universe in every pocket or on every wrist impact students' learning in our classrooms? The research is ongoing but as we build our awareness of who our students are, we should consider the possibility that being addicted to their phones is a defining characteristic of many young adults who will become college students in the next decade.[46]

Perhaps most predictably, we can assume that students of *all* backgrounds at all types of institutions are under tremendous pressure. College costs more than ever before (vastly disproportionate to standard increases in the cost of living), and the socioeconomic stakes for earning and successfully utilizing a college degree have never been higher.[47] In many ways, these pressures apply to virtually every single college student but, again, the specifics of our student population do matter. These proven and widely documented stressors on students today look different among community college students from those at elite universities. For students who are the first in their families to go to college the pressure to succeed includes certain burdens unlike those experienced by students from families where college is simply the expected next step after high school.

On a related point, the stress and fear of being wrong and of not succeeding appears to be increasing among all new college students.[48] Pedagogical scholar Rebecca Cox makes a convincing argument that fear of not succeeding academically and of not really "belonging" in college manifests in some of the student behavior that professors find most exasperating, such as not seeking faculty assistance, not reading the syllabus, and waiting until the last minute to begin assignments.[49] However, at elite institutions, among students with better academic preparation for college, the fear of failure may materialize quite differently. Students from privileged backgrounds are less likely to feel that they don't "belong" in college, and while their reactions to academic obstacles are rooted in fear of failure as well, it will take different (and, not incidentally, more confrontational) forms.

Fear is the basis for one of the most misunderstood and most challenging traits that seems to be growing among a wide range of students in the 2000s: academic entitlement. "Entitlement" conjures up an image of Brett, a Master of the Universe driving a Porsche (or whatever a cool car is) and demanding an "A" from the lowly professor because as a rich white man Brett believes he's entitled to everything he wants at every moment of his life. Fostered by the internet age of instant access and rooted in widespread educational and cultural changes in the late 1900s and early 2000s, academic entitlement is "a sense of being owed an assessment of performance inconsistent with students' actual effort or work" and the belief that "knowledge is a right that students should access with little effort and discomfort; teaching staff should provide all needed information and direction required for course success; the instructor is responsible for an individual student's performance in a class; all students should be recognized equivalently despite differences in individual effort; hostile confrontations with school faculty are acceptable whenever a student is unsatisfied."[50] Some commentators suggest that this attitude grows out of the consumerization of education—the belief that colleges more or less owe students a degree in return for tuition and that college is not an "opportunity for transformational intellectual experiences" but rather an "economic exchange."[51] At the very least, suggest some researchers, students will increasingly "expect their instructors to care about their individual desires and adapt the classroom around their personal needs and academic beliefs."[52] We can decry this changing view of higher education but that will not help us become more effective teachers. Awareness of the issue, minus handwringing and pearl clutching, will.

But academic entitlement can be hard to see for what it is, and "faculty may misinterpret academic entitlement as a form of student laziness."[53] Yet academic entitlement is actually more likely to grow out of *disempowerment* than privilege. Contrary to the popular discourse about snowflakes overly protected by helicopter parents and society's trophy-for-showing-up cult of self-esteem, academic entitlement most frequently manifests in students who are fearful, feel helpless, and who are "harboring doubt about their abilities."[54] Studies show that it is consistently associated with a student's belief in an external locus of control over academic achievement.[55] Many students believe that the power to do well in any one class depends not on their own individual effort or behavioral self-regulation or increasing their own skills but on factors outside their control. Namely, you, the instructor. Across many different teaching contexts, "students think classroom teachers are the most significant factor in student learning, and rank it *ahead* of their own study habits in importance."[56] They "see teachers as bearing all or a majority of the responsibility to educate and produce learning" and "students' perceived powerlessness in their own education translates into a lack of their taking responsibility for their own education."[57]

Students' academic entitlement and the consumerization of education can pose a particular problem for GINs who want to be effective teachers because so many of us resent, at the deepest level of our scholarly souls, any intimation that the pursuit of knowledge is not the foundation for a meaningful lifelong learning journey but rather a monetary transaction required for participation in the workforce. In addition, when contending with academic entitlement, we're trying to address at an individual level broad social and cultural issues. Effectively counteracting academic entitlement is more of a job for colleges and university systems, which should methodically educate all incoming students about "the concepts/expectations of good time management, the amount of time, the necessary sacrifices, the amount of effort and the production of high-quality assessment products so they may earn, not be given, a high quality educational experience."[58]

So we can't control many of the factors responsible for contributing to academic entitlement and, more generally speaking, students' lack of understanding about how higher education works. But as significant as they are, these and other factors outside our control don't eliminate the need for us to understand them, as well as the factors we *can* control. Our work begins with understanding who our students are. Be curious and take this on as part of the intellectual work of teaching: who are they? Do some research; form and test some hypotheses. The students themselves can be a great source of information. I've found that students working as resident assistants can often tell me what kinds of things my students are dealing with/doing. You might even approach administrators (cue Darth Vader theme). A short email to the International Students, Student Affairs, Equal Opportunity Program, or ESL offices could yield some good insights into the specificities of your students. Promotional material on the school website can also be a place to start. Have you taken one of the tours prospective students take? Met any parents of incoming students?

Learning about the student body generally is a great start but knowing our students also means knowing them as individuals. At the very barest minimum for any class of 50 or less, that means *knowing their names*. Don't try to weasel out of this by claiming, "I'm just bad at names." You know what you're really saying when you say that? You're saying, "I am Professor Important and all my students know my name but I don't have time in my busy schedule of being smart to learn theirs." Class size permitting, effective teachers learn and use their students' names because knowing our students is not an incidental or unnecessary frill for effective teaching. It is an essential step for establishing a productive and positive climate in our classes, promoting student development, and assessing their learning.[59] Effective teachers distribute "Prior Knowledge" surveys at the beginning of class or other types of questionnaires (and then read and reflect on the student responses); they ask students to meet with them individually at the beginning of the term; they create a variety of ways to learn as much as they can about students' preparation and expectations for the class.[60] So by whatever means necessary, we have to learn their names and learn a few things about each of our students.

Then, after you've done all that work trying to get a handle on who your students are both as a group and as individual learners, try to get your mind around the fact that in every class you've got a group of unique individuals embodying an infinite range of personal experience, previous knowledge, receptiveness, abilities, anxieties, problems, and hangovers.[61] At any one moment, in any one class, you might have a student who's at a critical point in their learning, someone who's ready and waiting to have their whole world outlook changed by the next question you ask them. And that student may be sitting side by side with another student who thinks that the entire class is a complete waste of time and who is determined to never, ever learn anything in your stupid pointless class. Students have this disconcerting habit of being individuals with individual issues and emotions. Like they're human people or something.

When we are fortunate enough to have some employment security, we're going to need to get to know our students again . . . and again . . . and again. Because new students keep coming and they bring all the issues and academic inadequacies they did last year, with some new ones thrown in. When we undertake learning how to be effective teachers, we are actually committing to learning, relearning, and repeatedly relearning. Weathered veteran or wet behind the ears newbie, every college teacher lucky enough to have continuing employment starts all over again every new term and every new class. Just when I started to get really good at explaining to students why they couldn't text in my classes *or* read messages, posts, etc. on their phones,[62] I started to notice students staring fixedly at their smart watches. Sure, we're becoming more effective teachers every semester, but our new students are starting from scratch every year. That could sound like an overwhelming task but perhaps less so if we see this through our academic nerd goggles and view it not as "rote repetition" but instead "new intellectual problems that need investigation and application of our brainy abilities." Not "oh god, another group of strangers" but rather "time to put on my thinking cap!"

One of the simplest ways to foster this approach and awareness is to make some changes to our internal dialogues regarding our students. For example:

Good: "My students struggle with time management and self-regulation."
Bad: "They're so lazy and they wait until the last minute to do everything! They're always asking me for extensions and extra credit, like they don't know how to be a student! Learn to manage your time, Junior! My class is important and I don't have to justify 'why you should learn this!' Time to grow up, Ace, and take some personal responsibility for yourself."

Good: "Many of my students are looking at their phones during class."
Bad: "I've told them repeatedly not to, it's on the first bleeping page of the syllabus, and they're still looking at their bleeping phones in class. They're social media–addicted, disrespectful, brain-dead morons who are driving me to an early grave. For this, I accrued six figures in graduate school loans? They don't care about their education? Then fine, *I don't care either*! Let them text. Or Snappychat. Or Instacrud. Whatever. I'm just going to ignore it."

Good: "Academic entitlement is a growing issue among college students."
Bad: "Oh, you think you 'deserve' a higher grade? Seriously? You've never come to office hours, you skipped half of the classes and when you are in class, you're barely sentient, let alone actually participating.

Why in the name of all that is good and holy do you think you deserve a higher grade? Because you are capable of writing and sending a semiliterate email complaining about your grade? This will shock you, your Royal Highness, but grades are earned, not given, and you earned yourself that garbage grade."

In each of these cases, the "Good" script is shorter because there's no editorializing, no commentary, no rage, and no struggle. What can we observe, without judgment but with intellectual curiosity, about what is actually happening? Working ourselves into a lather lamenting and resisting reality will actively hinder us from successfully enacting a plan based on what we've learned from the SoTL and hypothesized about our specific teaching context in order to address that reality. Awareness and acceptance doesn't mean doing nothing to improve or address these issues. We don't have to give up our high standards or dumb down our material or make allowances we don't want to make. But before we can challenge students to learn how to do new things, we have to understand where they're starting, and who they are.

Know Ourselves

When I was a teenager in the 1980s and going through an unfortunate "goth" phase, I longed for my outside appearance to better reflect what I believed to be my inner angst. But no amount of coal-colored clothing or corpselike makeup could transform my apple-cheeked, corn-fed Midwestern face into a death mask of existential ennui. Trying to contort my naturally happy, healthy features into the visage of an unholy ghoul was wildly unsuccessful. I looked like Rebecca of Sunnybrook Farm in zombie drag. A little self-awareness could have helped me avoid many bad fashion choices back then but I was young and had not yet grasped the essence of good personal style: be yourself. Yes, use clothing and adornments for personal expression. But don't try to be someone or something you're fundamentally not. Instead, *work with what you've got*.

Likewise, knowing and accepting who we are can save us a lot of futile struggle in the classroom. Understanding ourselves is the last of the four important realities of which we need to be aware. As educators, we have to learn and continually relearn how to work with what we've got, and that includes paying attention to who we are. In fact, the whole premise of *Geeky Pedagogy* is that we GINs in academia will become more effective teachers when we can clearly see ourselves as the nerdy, geeky intellectuals, brainiacs, wonks, eggheads, and introverts that so many of us are. Knowing ourselves can begin by proudly reclaiming the words that made us feel like dweebs in high school. Geek? You bet! Nerd? Totally, and that's *Professor* Nerd to you! "Geek" and "nerd" are the increasingly common twenty-first century shorthand for super-smart people who love school, and embracing these terms as a means for understanding ourselves can be a highly productive pedagogical practice.

Cultivating awareness of our geeky and nerdy qualities is helpful because after taking into account the specificities of ways embodied identity and employment status shape our teaching contexts, most of us teaching college classes have one thing in common: we've repeatedly experienced the rewards of academic success. We don't just have an expert blind spot about our own subjects but also about "school" generally. We know how school works. We know it so very well that it can be hard to remember that most people don't experience school as we have. Most of our students, even the ones who are earning good grades at elite universities, are not budding professional scholars. They may be highly intelligent and scholastically accomplished, and they may even be well on their way to gaining a real appreciation for the life of the mind. But unlike many of us, most of them do not dive joyfully and with relative ease into academics, swimming merrily along in a sea of books and data and long isolated hours of study like a fish who's finally found its watery home.

If we aren't consciously aware of this, it's all too easy to assume wrongly and potentially disastrously that our students are just like us in this regard. "They'll love this book because it offers an entirely new complicated take on this subject that's extremely hard to understand!" "Study guides are patronizing. My students will appreciate that I don't coddle them." And so on. All aspects of my pedagogical practices have improved since I've begun asking myself "Okay, this reading assignment/lecture/class activity seems totally cool to *me*, but how will my non-nerdy students respond to this?" I am constantly reminding myself that the thinking and writing that comes so easily to geeky me, in the academic setting that has brought me so much pleasure and satisfaction, is definitely *not* how many of my students are currently experiencing their schooling.

Equally important is to understand how being a confirmed introvert shapes my ability to teach effectively. For someone like me who loves being alone with her thoughts and gets tired just by being in the presence of other people, I have to continually, consciously prepare myself for the social aspects of teaching because the cold, hard reality is that the classroom is a social space. It's as much a social space as is the dreaded cocktail party, dinner party, any type of party. Social interaction in the classroom is specialized and serves a different function than other social spaces but, nonetheless, it's people dealing with other people. Chapter 2 details how we can best prepare to navigate the social aspects of teaching and learning effectively, but before preparation comes awareness: we have to know ourselves, and work with what we've got.

Happily, much like being a geek or a nerd, being an introvert is easier in today's world than in any previous era, as more and more people commonly use this term to describe themselves. Increasingly, people not only self-identify as introverts but also celebrate it with self-deprecating humor in blogs, memes, and Twitter threads like #confessionsofanintrovert that proudly proclaim our need to be alone in order to recharge our mental and physical batteries. ("First rule of introvert club is there is no introvert club. Thank goodness.")[63] Introverts can embody a range of personal qualities and abilities, including self-confidence, good public speaking, and adept social skills. What we all share is a need for more quiet solitude than extroverts do. There's nothing wrong or bad about this quality but it doesn't easily or readily lend itself to effective teaching and learning. In fact, it can be a real hindrance if we don't pay attention to and fully acknowledge this reality. News flash: you can't teach all by yourself. Students are part of the package and they're *always there*.

Don't waste time berating yourself for being an introvert. Just acknowledge it, accept it, and figure out how it might influence your efficacy as a teacher.[64] As Stephen Brookfield writes: "Acknowledge your personality. For someone as introverted as me it would be a major mistake to try and pass myself off as the pedagogic equivalent of Groucho Marx," adding "be wary of spending valuable, nonrenewable emotional energy on trying to be something that you're not."[65] Similarly, introvert Brian R. Little writes that after becoming fully aware of how important solitude is for him to be energetic enough to be "on" in the classroom, he incorporated scheduled breaks in his classes to be by himself for a few minutes. He discovered that the privacy one might expect in the bathroom can't be taken for granted when it comes to students seeking individual conversation, so now he hides in a stall with his legs tucked up.[66]

My first response to Little's essay was scornful. What a dork! Hiding from his students! But, *duh*, the whole point of this chapter is to accept *what is* without recrimination. Paying attention to and accepting important qualities about himself and implementing pedagogical strategies with those qualities in mind is exactly what Little did.[67] Well done, sir. As one group of researchers summarizes: "lower extraversion" like Little's is "related to higher levels of teaching anxiety," but "understanding the role of personality characteristics would allow the professor to adjust coping strategies that may be important to circumventing or minimizing anxiety-provoking situations that may arise."[68] In order to create such strategies, it's essential to "understand the role of personality characteristics," that is, *your* personality characteristics.

Knowing ourselves means being aware of our own individual and unique psychology and physiology and figuring out how these factors play out during the daily work of teaching and learning. For example, can you identify what kinds of things make you anxious in teaching situations? Because in order "to develop or prescribe techniques for coping with teaching anxiety," we "must identify the sources or triggering devices and times of occurrence."[69] Close awareness of and ongoing attention to our feelings and attendant physical reactions actually increases our ability to respond constructively: "Thinking 'Oh no! I'm so nervous!' causes the panic to spiral, whereas thinking 'Oh, I'm nervous again—but that's okay,' reduces the 'fight or flight' reaction."[70] Better understanding these physical components of teaching and learning as related to our introversion, and knowing the effort it might take us to interact positively with other people, leads to increased pedagogical effectiveness, from the first moment of a class to the very last interaction we have with a student.

Take, for instance, first impressions. What's the very first impression people get when they meet you? Not what you hope people think nor what your anxieties and neuroses are telling you about your first impression. For many scholarly GINs, the answer to this question might be some combination of "shy," "smart," "bookish," "stand-offish," "quiet," or "arrogant." If, like me, your natural, default first impression mode is "socially awkward smarty pants," that can be an impediment to reaching your students and you need to figure out how to work with it. That's not easy to do. Accepting ourselves, who we are, is challenging because we're all prone to extremes, falling into self-aggrandizing (among academics this usually takes the form of an inflated sense of our intellectual prowess) and thus ignoring our weaknesses or, at the other end of the spectrum, letting insecurities blind us to our strengths and abilities.

But being aware of who we are is well worth our effort because knowing ourselves is not some kind of inconsequential, pop psychology platitude when it comes to teaching and learning. In practical terms, it's an essential step to professional success in any college teaching situation and whatever our specific circumstances; it's a puzzle or a problem for us to examine as part of our intellectual teaching work. This applies equally as well to brand new teachers as to the old-timer finishing up his fourth decade in the classroom because every term, every college teacher meets a whole brand-new crop of students. Repeatedly relearning who we are may be even more important for the experienced teacher who's built up habits and is bringing way too many assumptions into class. With the exception of a desire to be an effective teacher, there is no one personality or personal quality that every single effective teacher must have.[71] But we do have to know and accept who we are and learn to work with what we have.

Conclusion

> Nothing that is is unimportant.
> —Spock, *Strangers from the Sky*

————

Mindfulness practices aren't for everyone, and some brainy scholars who prize mental acuity have no desire to be present only to the present moment without getting caught up in thoughts, judgments, or inner dialogue. But if we want to be effective teachers, we must accept Vulcan philosopher Kiri-kin-tha's first law of metaphysics: "Nothing unreal exists." Or as the Vulcan proverb goes, *kaiidth* (what is, is). Awareness of *what is*, learning and continually relearning it, is foundational to effective teaching. Nothing that *is* about our teaching context is unimportant but the four realities discussed in this chapter are essential: identity is important, learning is hard, who our students are, and who we are. Really observing what is happening right in front of us will allow us to understand, really understand, what is happening right in front of us. Resisting the four central realities of our teaching circumstances will cause us suffering. We will get stuck on what we *want* it to be, not what it *is*.

Awareness and acceptance—*kaiidth*. Now what are you going to actually do about these realities? On to preparation.

CHAPTER 2

PREPARATION

I'm ready! I'm ready! I'm ready! I'm ready!
—SpongeBob, "Help Wanted," *SpongeBob SquarePants*

———

A COLLEAGUE recently asked me how I keep my office so spic and span. "This?" I said, nonchalantly waving a hand around my tidy work area. "Oh, you know, just a little daily organizing." A more honest answer would have been "Because I'm secretly convinced that if I keep every book straight on my shelf and every paper correctly filed and my macramé Baby Groot, Wolverine bobblehead, and Hellboy figurine arranged just so on my shelf, I will keep fear, pain, and death away forever and ever." A part of me truly believes that with proper planning, nothing unexpected or untoward will disrupt the smooth progress of my life. Contrary to what my brain chemistry would have me believe, teachers can't plan for every contingency or keep uncomfortable things from happening. However, preparation does have an important place in effective teaching and learning, and lack of planning may be the most common teaching misstep made by college instructors.[1]

GINs aren't very different from any other group when it comes to personal and professional organization. Some of us are naturally inclined to detailed planning and lots of advance preparation while others let things pile up. Some of us need a pristine office in order to function while others require a fortress of papers, books, Post-Its, and clutter around us to be productive. Fortunately, like all aspects of effective teaching and learning, there's no single right way to plan for teaching and learning. We've got to plan, but when discussing teaching preparation SoTL often neglects to the address important specificities discussed in the last chapter. Planning looks different depending on your personality, your identity, the kinds of students you're teaching, and your employment status.

Preparation and Employment Status

Reverse course design, a trendy SoTL term once upon a time, simply means thinking carefully about all aspects of a class by beginning with your final goals. What do you foresee students being able to do at the end of the class that they couldn't do or couldn't do as well at the beginning? But scholarship on reverse course design often fails to mention that backwards planning actually begins with our employment status. Let's be real: the restrictions and requirements of our particular job context hugely influence the end game for any class we teach.[2] To take an obvious example, most tenured teachers are under less pressure to produce a batch of glowing student evaluations at the end of the term than nontenured faculty. Therefore, they have a lot more leeway to experiment with an innovative pedagogical approach that might be met with some student pushback. Too often, SoTL dictates about class planning presume a fantasy world where everyone is tenured and the sole consideration is the blossoming of young minds. That's a nice idea, but most of us can't afford to be so idealistic.

Before we can begin to think about what books to assign, what should be on the quizzes, or how exactly we're going to break up our lectures into digestible chunks interspersed with activity, review, and application, we need to think through the implications of our employment status.[3] Before you dot another "i" on your new syllabus, think long and hard and deliberately about what you *have* to do, professionally. Not what you *want* to do. Not what you would do if the only thing that mattered was reaching and growing each student's precious intellect. In addition, the reality of employment also depends largely on the specific department or program in which you're teaching. It can be a challenge navigating a workplace populated with a bunch of introverts and eggheads. The better you understand department dynamics and/or dysfunctions, including unstated assumptions, prejudices, and standing feuds, then the better you can prepare.

For instance, what is the university and department culture—both articulated and unspoken—around teaching and learning?[4] Is seeking assistance and/or ways to improve your teaching going to be perceived as a sign of weakness or of strength? If you're compiling a teaching portfolio, to what extent do your materials need to reflect specific pedagogical techniques such as learner-centered and active learning or the flipped classroom model?[5] If you're a TA, how will you document the work you do as a teacher and your efficacy in advancing student learning, in addition to student evaluations? Our employment status, our departments, our job search, and so on create boundaries around and requirements for teaching that we can't control. But understanding them before we even begin planning all the other things we're going to do this term? That'll help.

Preparing to Put on Your Professor Pants

P. H. Phelps writes, "I've come to realize that it is not so much about what students know but what they can do. Likewise, teaching is not about what I know but what I enable others to do."[6] Teaching requires us to translate stuff we know into stuff students know and can do. This requires social interaction, which can be daunting for intellectual introverts who entered academia naïvely expecting a tranquil Ivory Tower where we could read our books and think our thoughts while a harp plucks softly in the background. Religious studies professor Sid Brown speaks for many of us when she writes that some days "all I want to do is stay home and read a book."[7] But sociologist Cheryl Albers points out, "Every semester or quarter, we enter into a new *social situation*" (emphasis added).[8] Furthermore, as Liz Grauerholz and Eric Main note, SoTL often underplays this fact:

> The idea that the classroom is first and foremost a social space with unique dynamics seems to be missing in much SOTL research. That is, we often fail to recognize the classroom as a socially constructed

environment, which (though largely predictable in terms of roles and expectations) gives rise to unique dynamics, power structures, and experiences.[9]

For all our brainy ability to deeply and thoroughly understand our discipline, when it comes to teaching we need to better understand the classroom as a social space.

Content knowledge and even pedagogical content knowledge is not sufficient because "a teacher's success not only depends on effective methods of teaching and subject knowledge but above all it depends on the strong relationships teachers develop with their students."[10] Or as another group of researchers puts it: "Student-teacher interaction is at the core of students' classroom experience, even in online courses."[11] Moreover, we're hampered by the very knowledge we're attempting to share. It's all too easy for professor GINs to come off as know-it-alls purposefully trying to make other people (i.e., students) feel dumb. We can become ponderously bogged down in minutia that highlights our own grasp of every detail of our subject but leaves listeners (i.e., students) stupefied. We aren't just introverts trying to communicate ideas but introverted experts with big blind spots about how much prior knowledge and practice it takes to do the things our own brains do automatically.

Teaching and learning isn't just any old social action (which, let's face it, is hard enough for introverts). It's a complex interaction between individuals and between groups, unique to each teaching context, additionally shaped by realities outside of our control. But in all cases, it requires us to *communicate*: communicate clearly, communicate often, communicate ideas, and, yes, communicate certain kinds of emotions and personal qualities as well. So for GINs, one of the most important aspects of preparation for effective teaching is much broader and far more repetitive than creating a syllabus or a class plan. Every day before we teach, before every single class, before every office hour or student meeting, before we even walk over to the student center to get a cup of coffee, we have to put on our professor pants.

By "professor pants" I mean consciously and deliberately preparing to clearly communicate and to clearly convey, to the best of our unique ability in our unique teaching context, that we are ready, willing, and able to teach students how to successfully do things. Knowing our subjects isn't enough. Being published and acclaimed in our fields isn't enough. Waving our diplomas in their faces and wielding our scholarly credentials like a bludgeon won't work. Some of the most important hallmarks of effective teaching have almost nothing to do with what we know about our disciplines but everything to do with communication, including listening to and interacting with students. That's a challenging prospect for academics whose preferred method of human interaction is sitting alone and writing down what we know for other smart people to read and ponder in solitude. It's less formidable however when we frame this as part of our own learning, and approach communicating effectively with a growth mindset and as a subject for our ongoing intellectual investigation into professorial performance.

That word—"performance"—can really trip us up.[12] Damn it, Jim, I'm a scholar, not an actor! But the fact that we are GINs is exactly *why* we need to do a little performing. We're introspective people who enjoy quietly wrestling with ideas and concepts or test tubes and microscopes. We prefer to consider our words carefully and while some of us are great public speakers, many of us are hampered by self-consciousness or a tendency to mumble. In order to be effective, chances are that we have to do some things that do not come naturally to us. Some SoTL calls this your teaching persona, a conscious crafting of how you present yourself as an educator.[13] It doesn't mean lying about who we are or somehow completely transforming ourselves into a different person. But it does mean projecting and communicating certain essential things to our students, no matter what our personal qualities.

Sharp-eyed readers probably spotted the inexact phrasing in the previous sentence. Wait, *what* "essential things"? SoTL is packed with detailed descriptions of exactly what the best, award-winning, most outstanding teachers do. Frankly, it's kind of endless. This section is not a definitive list of what effective teachers do but rather a summary of what the SoTL shows are some of the most important things that effective teachers do that are *also* some of the biggest stumbling blocks for intellectuals and introverts who want to be effective teachers.[14] They require preparation because they will not come easily or naturally to many of us.

HALLMARKS OF EFFECTIVE TEACHING THAT CAN BE ESPECIALLY CHALLENGING FOR GINS

- Care for students and student learning
- Immediacy and rapport
- Authenticity and enthusiasm
- Clear communication of ideas and expectations

The first one on this list—caring—can sound jarring to scholars trained and skilled at habits of the mind. Isn't it our job as college teachers to expand students' thinking, not pamper them with hearts and flowers? We all have that motherly or fatherly colleague to whom students flock with their problems, and who seems to exude benevolent love and warmth at all times. I'm nothing like that, so does that mean I don't care? No, because in the context of effective teaching, we can convey caring in diverse ways. It does not require a lessening of academic standards or a warm fuzzy personality. Maryellen Weimer argues that "care for students can be expressed in different ways":

> There are even options for those with teaching styles not particularly nurturing or supportive. These can be things as simple as an occasional kind comment, a bowl of candy set beside the student chair in the office, or conscientious responses to email queries. Expressions of caring should be genuine, but they can be varied and should fit comfortably with your teaching persona.[15]

The possibilities are indeed "varied" and "can be expressed in different ways," but what caring about students really boils down to is being fair and treating students with basic courtesy and respect. Or as Ken Bain summarizes in *What the Best College Teachers Do*, effective teachers "tend to treat students with what can only be called simple decency."[16]

"Simple decency" in teaching and learning encompasses things GINs can incorporate easily into our pedagogical practices and that might not at first glance seem like expressions of "care" but absolutely convey caring to students. Things such as clearly communicating how you will assess their learning; starting and ending class on time; holding extra review sessions before a test; returning graded assignments in a timely way. Do you have a clear syllabus with transparent assessment requirements and equitable grading policies consistently implemented and do you regularly offer to help students? Then guess what? You are a caring professor! When I first started to get SET comments like "she cares a lot about students," I was surprised because I thought "caring" implied a lovey-dovey personality and lack of rigor that's just not me. But I was shortchanging students' understanding of effective teaching and learning. Many correctly interpreted my careful preparation for class meetings, my consistent use of clear grading rubrics, and my regular offers to assist anyone who needed help as evidence that I care about student learning. And never underestimate the power of transparency or simple statements about caring. Even the shyest introvert can say on the syllabus and aloud to students "I care about your success in this class."

The next items on the list—immediacy and rapport—require both verbal and nonverbal communication and are two of the biggest flies in the GIN professor's chardonnay. Our introverted personalities, our nerdy behaviors, and our geeky mannerisms really get in the way of developing these important qualities. Take "immediacy." Immediacy is "those verbal and nonverbal communications that outwardly manifest an instructor's care for students," such as "instructors' expression of interest in the lives of students, remembering students' names, and communicating availability. Examples of physical immediacy include eye contact, open body posture, smiling, and respectful listening."[17] Immediacy can be in the physical sense, such as arriving early to class, staying a few minutes after class ends, and keeping regular office hours. Immediacy is also in the social sense, such as listening to students when they talk, and being approachable.

Some researchers link immediacy to a quality they term teacher presence, a broad and somewhat esoteric quality of instruction that communicates to students desirable teaching abilities ranging from expertise to compassion to mindfulness.[18] Others cite "presence" as a kind of catchall term for a teacher's personal and pedagogical ability to create positive educational interactions with students, or "the sense that the instructor is actively and continuously involved in helping students learn."[19] Other definitions include "the design, facilitation, and the direction of cognitive and social processes for the purposes of realizing personally meaningful and educationally worthwhile learning outcomes" or "a state of awareness and readiness to respond compassionately to individuals in the group and to the group as a whole."[20] The ability to use silence to foster students' productive struggle working through problems for themselves is another trait of teacher presence.[21] SoTL regarding online teaching frequently references teacher presence as a component of a pedagogical framework called Community of Inquiry.[22]

None of these aspects of immediacy and teacher presence is effortless for introverts. For instance, "being approachable" is a teaching skill that all introverts must consciously cultivate and prepare to do every day.[23] Because we crave and need solitude, we sometimes project an aura of "Please, I'm begging you, just leave me alone!" Have you ever avoided saying hello to someone, not because you actively dislike the person but because it takes extra effort for you to do so? Then you are probably avoiding some simple social contact that demonstrates to students your approachability and immediacy. As Thomas Benton writes in his reflections on being both a shy person as well as an effective teacher, "partly because my shyness might make me seem unsmiling and withdrawn, I make an extra effort to be available for one-on-one meetings with students. I invite them to drop in for no particular reason, just so we can become more at ease with each other."[24] Here Benton hones in on a key reality for GIN teachers: he acknowledges that his personality might make him *seem* less available, interested, and caring than he actually is.

Moreover, in addition to our natural introversion, our expertise adds another layer of unapproachability and disconnectedness between us and our students, making it that much harder for us to build what SoTL calls "rapport." Think of building rapport as if we are physicians learning and using good bedside manners. The ability to relate to and communicate with patients is essential to a doctor's ability to facilitate healing.[25] Likewise, all your nerdy knowledge packed into that big brain of yours means exactly zip if you are unable to build rapport with students. Pedagogical scholars define rapport as being "available, friendly, accessible, approachable, interested, respectful, understanding, personable," and identify actions that increase rapport such as "making eye-contact, using humor," and "talking to your students before and after class."[26] In addition to whatever disparate teaching reality or employment status may be influencing our ability to achieve rapport, lots of GINs have at least a little trouble doing many of these things in any teaching context. Not because we're deliberately arrogant or antisocial but because we're introverted bookworms and those are socializing abilities that have less to do with our intellect and more to do with peopling skills. So we have to prepare for and consciously cultivate rapport.[27]

When broken down into specific tasks, preparing for and deliberately cultivating immediacy and rapport is something GINs can incorporate into their teaching and learning. We can use eye contact, greet our students, and learn and use our students' names. Yet introverted professors, whether brand new to teaching or with decades of teaching experience, often forgo one of the simplest ways to build rapport: arriving a few minutes early to class and conversing informally with students by asking them things like "How was your weekend?" "How are your other classes going?" "How did your team do?"[28] Such low-key neutral interactions are not a mere superfluity to effective teaching but rather a necessary component. They foster a sense of rapport, which in turn increases measurable student learning.[29] Extroverts may wonder why this kind of impromptu conversation would take any deliberate effort whatsoever but my fellow introverts understand when I say that I have to plan for and then very deliberately undertake friendly chitchat with students. I do it because it conveys to students that I recognize them as other human beings, not annoying interruptions of the many more important things I have to do.

Speaking of arrogance, it can be especially helpful for GINs to be aware of what *not* to do and to be mindful of behaviors that undermine rapport. Behaviors such as not knowing students' names or anything about them; being late to class and rushing out as soon as it's over; not keeping regular office hours; not making eye contact; and "being arrogant, condescending, and narcissistic."[30] A large survey of undergraduates found that one of their most common complaints about college instructors was professors' "intellectual arrogance—talking down to or showing lack of respect for students," and "being unhelpful and unapproachable."[31] In our work as teachers, we simply must not act as geek gatekeepers, humiliating and excluding anyone who does not know as much as we think they should know about our subjects.

"Lack of enthusiasm" is another behavior that we GINs may fall prey to, albeit unintentionally.[32] That's a real problem because enthusiasm is one of the few incontrovertible qualities of effective teaching and learning.[33] If the word "enthusiasm" makes you cringe, how about "intellectual excitement"?[34] Or "a strong inclination toward an activity that people like that they find important and in which they invest time and energy"?[35] Our nerdy obsessions with our academic subject are a strength for us here. As Weimer writes, our own "passion for the material can motivate students, and it, too, can be expressed in a multitude of ways. It doesn't have to be an opulent display of enthusiasm, dramatic evocation, or wild gesticulation."[36] Students may loathe the topic you're discussing, but they will be more willing to learn when you unashamedly geek out about the topic by saying how much you love it, showing how much you love it, and conveying that you really hope that students might learn to love it a little bit too.

Weimer describes a math professor's classroom behavior that illustrates what I mean by geeking out:

> He wiped his chalky hands on his pants and made a half-hearted attempt to tuck in more of his shirt as he walked to the side of the room. He stared at the problem for several seconds and then said to the class, "Do you see that symmetry? It's really beautiful and that's why I love math." I didn't see the symmetry, but I think some of the students did. And all of us got the message. With simple but genuine authenticity, this more disheveled than dynamic professor had shared something about his content that captured him.[37]

If you can geek out about your subject like this guy did about an equation, unashamedly showing students your passion, maybe even eliciting a bit of laughter from your students—that's a big win. They're laughing at you but in a good way. They're thinking "Jeez, what a nerd! I can't believe s/he actually likes this," but they're also thinking "Well, at least s/he cares. Maybe I can survive this class after all."

Weimer explains that enthusiasm for our content and communicating that enthusiasm to students can be an effective way to counteract pedagogical shortcomings:

> If a teacher loves the content and lets that love show, that commitment and energy can cover for a lack of organization and the occasional inability to explain something clearly. Enthusiasm allows teachers to show students how much they care, about the content, the learning, even about the students themselves, and that concern can cover a multitude of sins.[38]

It's that second part of enthusiasm we have to focus on: *showing* students "how much we care" and *communicating* our love of the subject. Some of the "sins" to which we GINs are unconsciously prone can really hamper student learning, so looking at what *not* to do can help illuminate what GINs need to do in order to prepare for effective teaching.

Some of the things that students perceive as "lack of passion for subject matter" and "indifference or hostility toward students" include:

- Monotonic voice
- Lack of clarity in explaining course content
- Failure to connect abstraction and theory to practice and life
- Inaccessibility, both figurative and literal
- Lack of interest in students as individuals
- Lack of encouragement
- Use of fear, embarrassment, belittlement as motivators
- Unclear, unreasonable arbitrary grading system[39]

Any one of the things on this list could easily be inadvertently conveyed to students due to a lack of social skills and communication ability rather than a lack of concern for student learning. Consider what one group of researchers concluded communicated nonimmediacy to students: when teachers "appear absent-minded, don't smile or make eye contact, don't move around the classroom, don't attend to students' questions, or blow off student requests without explanation."[40] All of which could be the result not of a professor who doesn't care about being an effective teacher but rather a GIN who did not adequately plan and prepare for the professor pants part of teaching—that is, consciously communicating care and enthusiasm, and building rapport and immediacy (always being aware, again, of how our identity markers may shape such aspects of teaching and learning).

Some SoTL terms this kind of communication between instructors and students as "authenticity," defined as "when teachers are viewed as approachable, passionate, attentive, capable, and knowledgeable." Conversely, students perceive inauthentic teachers as "unapproachable, lacking passion, inattentive, incapable, and disrespectful."[41] But the term "authenticity" can be confusing, since GINs often feel most "authentically" our professional selves when engaged in solitary pursuit of our scholarship or debating abstruse concepts in our field with likeminded intellectuals. However, like a teaching persona, authenticity doesn't require trying to pretend to be someone we're not. As one study concluded: "The process of teaching authentically need not be more complicated than making simple and direct statements regarding the level of concern and care that a teacher holds for students. However, teachers should enact such behaviors only so far as their personality and demeanor naturally allow."[42] As GINs we have to prepare for clearly communicating to students, taking into account what our "personalities and demeanors naturally allow."

For instance, authentic teachers, according to one student, are "happy when class begins and giving their all for it." Another said "I see teachers as authentic when I can tell they really care about what they're doing, when you can tell a teacher is doing this because it really is their passion, then they are being authentic."[43] GINs in academia are almost universally passionate about our subjects but to be effective teachers, we have to prepare for conveying that passion to students in ways they will readily perceive, such as appearing "happy when class begins." To communicate with students this way, we can't just map out an intellectual strategy. Our bodies are involved. It's a physical thing. For those of us who flunked gym class in high school (true story), this may sound awful. The whole reason I became an academic in the first place is because my head is my favorite place to be! Fortunately, the physicality of effective teaching is something we can learn, practice, and implement to whatever degree best works for us. As W. J. McKeachie states, "Movement, gesture, and vocal variation are trainable characteristics.

We are probably not going to transform a quiet, monotone into a maniac who rushes up and down the aisles shouting, but we can move them toward the middle of the expressiveness scale."[44] Importantly, expressiveness can take all kinds of forms, including those that come somewhat naturally to many GINs.

Introverts can't magically transform ourselves into peppy, bubbly cheerleaders but we can find ways to "convey the true zest for learning" that we feel.[45] It could be as simple as modeling our thinking aloud, which has the added bonus of demonstrating metacognition to students.[46] Communicating our enthusiasm to students does not require dramatically and effusively projecting something we do not truly feel.[47] But we can train ourselves to convey very clearly what we value most in our fields, like the math professor and his symmetrical equation.[48] It can be as easy as saying on the first day of class, "This semester we're going to read one of my favorite books of all time" or at the beginning of a class meeting, "I'm really looking forward to hearing your thoughts on this topic."

Geeking out effectively in a classroom does require some performing. One performance technique that's not too hard for an introvert to implement is to stand without speaking and "own the space"[49] until the class's attention is all on you.[50] In addition, introverts often need to more consciously project, clearly enunciate, deliberately and consciously use "vocal animation," and look at people when we talk.[51] But there's also value in talking less or even not talking at all. Philosopher Angelo Caranfa reminds us that "silence is the very foundation of learning" but almost every single college professor I've ever known (including me) talks too much.[52] I used to think that professors talk a lot because we're self-important gasbags but actually, many GINs talk a lot in class because we're a little nervous and a little on edge and having to interact with people is taxing. Talking—even didactic espousing—can be a coping mechanism.

Whether it's silence, vocal animation, or any other performative techniques, we don't have to become someone we're not. For instance, using humor is a proven way to increase student learning but that doesn't mean trying to do stand-up or becoming the class clown.[53] One example cited by Maggie Berg and Barbara Seeber is a professor illustrating an idea on the board with a badly drawn stick figure while acknowledging what a terrible artist she is.[54] That's some seriously low-key humor—don't wait for a big laugh if you try this one—but it's an easy way to demonstrate to students that you don't take yourself overly seriously. Using humor humanizes you and makes you appear more approachable, and for GINs, that's essential.

Although it differs from campus to campus and for each unique teaching context, student anxiety about approaching professors is an impendent to learning. In order to "be approachable," we have to "communicate approachability." *Those are not the same two things.* For students to perceive any particular teaching quality, including approachability, we have to consciously, systematically, and repeatedly prepare to communicate that quality.[55] One study found that "clarity" topped the list of characteristics college students cited as the most important trait in an instructor: professors should be "easy to understand," students asserted.[56] To be sure, learning is hard, so students might struggle, and moreover our subjects are often very much *not* "easy to understand." Therefore, it's imperative to communicate all our expectations regarding student behavior, learning, assessment, and grading as clearly as possible.[57] We must also plan for clearly communicating ideas and skills we're teaching students to use—things we know so much about that we can easily forget or skip over essential preliminary steps new learners must take. We must communicate that we *want* students to succeed and that we can assist them in their productive struggle towards learning achievement.[58]

It would be a lot easier if we could transpose our knowledge via Vulcan mind meld, "My mind to your mind, my thoughts to your thoughts." Instead, we have to use our words and our behaviors and communicate to students and prepare for effective communication. And our first communication with students is the syllabus.[59]

Preparing a Syllabus

Student procrastination is the bane of my existence. Even with all the things I do to encourage timely completion of work—regular reminders, scaffolding assignments, early formative assessment, and actionable feedback—approximately 99% of the obstacles that students encounter when they're trying to achieve success in my classes could be more easily overcome if they just started *sooner*. To be fair, some of what looks to me like procrastination is more accurately a combination of too many responsibilities and too little practice at good time management. Students may also simply try to avoid what seems daunting or challenging and then pretend to themselves that it can all be done and done well the night before it's due. Some research indicates that believing an academic task is irrelevant or pointless and/or overall disengagement with course material is the main predictor for student procrastination.[60]

Waiting to the last minute to do something is just as common among my peers, particularly when it comes to class planning generally and syllabi specifically. Just like our students, when we believe that something is going to be hard and/or not interesting, engaging, or important (or in our case, not our "real work," i.e., research and scholarship), it's easy to put it off. If we've been teaching for a while, we convince ourselves that our last syllabus was just fine, no review or revision needed, just change the dates and boom, done. But preparation requires our rigorous intellectual attention and we have to *do our syllabus and class prep in a timely way.*[61] Would you want students to cram for an important test in your class? Or would you prefer they space out their work and study at reasonable intervals? Do you want students to avoid doing the work you've assigned—avoid as a denial strategy rooted in fear of failure, inability to manage their time, because they can't see the relevance to their own lives, because their personal problems are overwhelming them, or whatever—and then try, unsuccessfully, to do it all in the space of a couple hours? Of course you wouldn't! So what are *you* waiting for, Chuckles?

This is the tough love part of chapter 2: we can't procrastinate on our syllabi and class prep. That's one rule of preparation that is inviolate. But now that you've turned off Netflix, put away the notes for your next book chapter, sent the kids to Grandma's or okayed a *Daniel Tiger* marathon and are finally preparing your syllabus, you actually have a lot of flexibility because the syllabi that effective teachers use can and do vary significantly.[62] One thing they have in common though is that they are the result of the teacher's intellectual activity. A syllabus is much more than a schedule of assignments: it reflects in a concrete way your understanding of the most important aspects of your field of expertise. Effective teachers view their syllabi as a "piece of scholarship" that reflects how we understand our topic and how we think it "*should* be organized for the purpose of communicating it."[63]

Our syllabus focuses on exactly what is worth students knowing and doing in our subject, beginning with a single crucial question: What do you want students in this class to learn how to do?[64] Everything starts here, with course learning objectives (or student learning objectives) and the student learning outcomes (SLO). The fact that these two different things can be so difficult to define and differentiate from each other indicates the complexity of the task before us when we're planning our syllabus. Learning objectives are the broad goals and intended purpose of a class, a program, a major, or even the university at large. They express, often but not always in some detail, what educators hope students will achieve during a course of study. Learning objectives may or may not be included on any one syllabus, but learning *outcomes* are an essential component of effective syllabi, stating as clearly and specifically as possible, the identifiable content knowledge, skill, ability, and end-product of a student's successful course of study. Learning outcomes are what students *do* (verbs matter) that we can then assess and measure in order to evaluate a student's learning.[65]

This brief summary of SLO only hints at how complicated, and often frustrating, it can be to formulate and then assess effective SLO for our classes. For starters, we're scholarly geeks and if we're lucky enough to be teaching in our field, we love the subject we're teaching, so we usually start with a very long list of what we think students should know about our topics. It's time to revise: What do you *really* want them to learn? The one or two or, at the most, three things? As Kevin Jack Hagopian explains: "Distinguish those features of your field that are actually marks of productive intellectual specificity from those discourses and habits that are merely professional conventions, and thus extraneous to true disciplinarity. This activity should hurt a little."[66] It *is* painful! We want students to experience the myriad joys of our wonderful subjects but our big throbbing expert blind spot can easily obscure the first necessary steps in our field; the things we take for granted that students need to *learn* how to do. To share our geeky love for Shakespeare or cellular biology or computer programming, to make students welcome at whatever nerd-con we're creating in our classroom, we have to plan for teaching novice learners.

As Linda Hodges and Katherine Stanton write, "Too often we provide students with the answers in our discipline before they even understand the questions."[67] In their discussion of how expert blind spots can hamper our ability to foresee what issues students will face, Hodges and Stanton describe the common occurrence of students complaining that "the exam problems were nothing like what we did in class":

> These remarks may lead us to assume that students are not paying attention, are not spending enough time on assignments, or simply are not studying hard enough. In some cases these assumptions may be true, but another interpretation is that these student comments reflect the differences in the way novices approach problem solving compared to experts.[68]

Experts know how to apply the larger concepts in our field to specific problems. We can see how different types of problems require application of a particular solution method. But novice learners believe problem solving should be quick and easy because they have simplistic beliefs about learning and about knowledge. They focus on the answer, not the process. Therefore, "our problem-solving exercises for students must explicitly require them to spend meaningful time analyzing principles involved and envisioning how these same principles might be 'disguised' in other settings."[69]

While experts can quickly see the underlying issues or concepts, new learners get distracted by surfaces, as another researcher writes:

> Even more irritating is the seeming inability of students to use what they have learned on any problem that is not an exact copy of the problem they used when they were learning it. This shows up frequently on tests, where students lament the use of tricky questions while the instructor thinks he or she is asking students to use information in a similar type of problem.[70]

This disconnect—students lamenting unfairness, professors thinking it's an obvious application—is directly attributable to our expertise interfering with our ability to identify a foundational skill and teaching students how to do it. As Stephen Brookfield notes, "Teachers in love with their subjects and caught up on the passion of communicating the elegant beauty of scientific reason, literary insight, or historical theorizing can easily overestimate how far students have progressed."[71] While we are off in la-la-land singing and dancing our way through sunny Subject World, our students are still trudging along Basic Knowledge Construction Avenue.

So we have to loosen up our fixed gaze on pure content transmission and instead pick out the few essential things students need to learn in our class.[72] We have to pare it down to the bare essentials. *What do we really want them to learn?* That is to say, what do we want them to learn how to do? Because we're not actually teaching a *subject*, we're teaching other people how to *do* things with and through knowledge about that subject. Contrary to what their high school education may have drilled into them, students are not passive receptacles of our recitation of facts and ideas. "Learning" is not students writing down what we say and then regurgitating it for the test. They have to *do* it.

That's just the beginning though. Now can you answer, in one clearly worded and jargon-free sentence, *why* they should learn this? Why your specific group of students should learn this? A concrete, real-world reason they should learn it? "Because knowledge is good" is not an answer. "Because critical thinking is important" is not a convincing answer either. Students may not even fully understand what "critical thinking" entails, let alone its possible benefits. Clarifying relevance of our course material will be increasingly essential for each new generation of students, and we must anticipate students repeatedly inquiring explicitly or implicitly "Why do we need to know this?"[73] It's so glaringly obvious to us why everyone in the world should know how to do the things we know how to do and that we think are important, but students often don't share our perspective.[74] When we undertake to demonstrate relevance to our students then, we have to try to see it from their point of view. Why do *your* students need to know how to do this? Making your course content relevant "requires that you understand your learners' world and the content in which they might apply their learning, now or in the future"; to plan "learning goals to be compatible with student needs, values, and abilities"; and to ask "what differences will this set of knowledge, skills, dispositions make in the lives of our students?"[75]

Relevance is linked to one of the notable proven facts about our brains and how we learn. "Establishing the value" of our course content by connecting it to students' other interests and providing "authentic real-world" tasks increase students' ability to learn.[76] Like anybody learning anything, "students need to perceive the material to be learned is of sufficient quality and relevant to matters that concern them now and into their future to warrant their time and effort."[77] We can't create intrinsic motivation out of thin air but making skills and content as relevant as possible can fan whatever tiny flame is already present by "teaching things worth knowing."[78] As Elizabeth Barkley writes about fostering student engagement, "teachers can increase student motivation by taking steps to increase the *value* of the learning to students."[79]

Once we have our short list of what students should learn how to do and why they should learn how to do it, we must figure out how students will demonstrate/prove they've learned it. And we must *be specific*. What assignments, tests, or projects, specifically, will document their learning? And how? How will you assess it? "I'll know it when I see it" is not fair to students. They deserve to know what we expect them to do and how they will show they can do it, and they deserve a clear and concise explanation. It boils down to telling students *why*. Why they're doing this, why you've assigned that, why, why, why. We're not the man behind the curtain trying to flim-flam students into learning. Tell them what they are learning how to do, and how they will learn to do it.

For example, why do we hold class discussions? Seminar-style classes are the highest ideal for the study of humanities and the natural habitat of nerdy intellectuals. Debating rarified ideas around a gleaming oaken seminar table is pretty much as good as it gets for people like us. But most students don't really understand *how* and *why* people use discussion to learn.[80] Although professors assume in-class discussions are obviously essential to learning, many students view discussion as "pointless" and a "waste of time."[81] Our syllabus is the first step in clearly communicating why things like class discussions are valuable to students. The same holds true for other things we might assume are obvious, such as regular attendance. The syllabus is the first place we communicate our expectations in all areas of learning, including behavior.[82]

However, there's another layer here to syllabus communication. A syllabus strongly reflects the tone we take throughout the class and our pedagogical approach.[83] Rules and penalties are part of an effective syllabus but so too do effective teachers use their syllabus to communicate those tricky qualities like rapport and immediacy. Some SoTL describes this a "welcoming" or "engaging" tone versus the classic "contractual" tone to your syllabus. It's not that a contractual type syllabus is ineffective per se but rather that GINs may especially benefit from communicating important instructor qualities such as enthusiasm and approachability via our syllabus.[84] Because I am a pretty reserved and not especially effusive teacher, I rely on my syllabus to do some of the cheerleading and encouraging that my students need to hear from me. On our syllabi we can intentionally set a tone of pedagogical caring by doing things like referring to "our," not "my" class; emphasizing how to contact us and ask us for assistance; framing the syllabus as a "promise" to students; and using wording that communicates our enthusiasm, the relevance of the material, and the rationale for important policies.[85]

Now that we've done all this planning, how can we ensure that students will actually read the syllabus and keep consulting it regularly? Reading it aloud on the first day won't work, but there are other techniques for getting students to read and understand the syllabus, such as a short syllabus quiz.[86] Constant reminders—in class and in person, via email, text, social media, Moodle or Blackboard, or painted with your arterial blood on the classroom wall—do work.[87]

And quite contrary to those snarky "it's on the syllabus" memes, it's possible that students *did* check the syllabus but are emailing you with a question that's fully answered on the first page of your carefully crafted syllabus simply because they're seeking a little reassurance and/or low-stakes interaction.[88] Immediate reactions like mocking derision and sarcastic impatience are not a good idea. No need to get all huffy about it. Instead, have a polite, formulaic answer ready: "Dear Student, Thank you for your email. I appreciate your attention to keeping up with assignments. The assignment for Tuesday is blah blah blah and noted on the syllabus. Please let me know if you have any further questions or if I can clarify anything else on the syllabus. See you in class!" Basically, we have to dial down our defensiveness, increase our awareness, and prepare accordingly.[89] Take this opportunity to put on your professor pants, because the syllabus can be a starting point for communicating one-on-one, building rapport, and demonstrating approachability.

Preparing to Assess and Grade Student Learning

Educators know that learning should be undertaken for the sake of learning and that knowledge and good grades don't automatically go hand in hand.[90] But most students measure their academic success almost exclusively by their grades.[91] When it comes to grading, "as with most teaching issues, advance planning is the key."[92] "How will you assess their learning?" is not the same question, exactly, as "How will you grade their work?" Assessing student learning means using a variety of tools as an instructor invested in student learning to ensure that our students are advancing their knowledge and gaining skills. This includes but is not limited to grading.

Consider, for instance, the utility of low-stakes assignments, required but not graded or accounting for only a small portion of grades. As a type of formative assessment, as opposed to summative assessment, we use such assignments to assess student progress and help students continue to improve.[93] Examples include:

- At end of class, each student summarizes in writing one thing they learned in class that day and one question they still have about the material.
- Students draw an (ungraded) concept map of the ideas discussed in the class thus far.
- In small groups, students identify a term or issue about which they are still confused and would like more instruction.

- Before beginning a research project, each student has to submit a proposal and students must have your approval before continuing the project.
- In any group of assignments, allowing students to drop the lowest grades for one or two assignments or to correct/revise one assignment and return for reassessment.

Low-stakes assignments can mitigate all varieties of student fear and anxiety, from "I don't belong in college" to "My highly successful parents will kill me if I don't get a 4.0 and anyway I can't imagine how I could go on living if I don't get into Stanford Law/Harvard Business School."[94] Such assignments give us the chance to offer actionable feedback. Instead of writing comments and consigning them into the abyss, students will be more likely to read and use our feedback if they can *apply* it to future graded assignments. These assignments lessen the stress of The Grade, opening up new possibilities for advancing knowledge because one of the things we know for sure about learning is that it improves with frequent checks and our ability to learn decreases when we're afraid.[95]

But eventually we have to assign grades. Assessment and grading of student learning is a massive, even overwhelming, SoTL subject. It's a complex undertaking, particularly in the humanities where quantifying and measuring knowledge and skills can be challenging.[96] Here are a few best principles about grading to keep in mind when you're planning your classes, which you can adapt to your topic, your group of students, and your specific teaching context:

- Be transparent. Our syllabi and other documents should state clearly and concisely how we're going to assess student work and we should stick to it, from the first day to the last. If we absolutely must make adjustments, never *add* required work because in students' eyes, this is an outright betrayal.
- Be transparent not just in terms of specific assignments but also the criteria we're using. What is "A" level work? What's the difference between an "A" and a "B"? Accept that we have to explain this.
- Give actionable feedback. Give them a reason to actually read, apply,

and use our feedback.[97] For instance, for research papers I give equal weight to the first and the final drafts, but the grade for the final draft is based solely on how well students have read and applied my feedback from the first draft.

- Nobody likes "constructive" criticism. It's always painful to see how we fall short in anything, so plan a way to give positive feedback as well.
- Try to space out assessment as much as possible. Students are stressed out at the end of the semester and so are we. Try to schedule some major chunks of grading sooner.
- Return graded work to students within seven to ten days. Timely grading is indispensable to effective teaching.[98]
- If you have any flexibility in what you can use to assess their learning, assign things you actually want to grade.

This last one is so obvious but so overlooked, perhaps because some academics possess a little streak of martyrdom. Climb down off your cross of professorial suffering ("Lo, see how I doth suffer and toil over grading these accursed papers that so stinketh!") and create assignments to grade that don't bore you to tears.[99] Of course, there are standards and conventions of your field to which you must adhere. But if there's any wiggle room to mix it up and to create assignments/tests that are more interesting to *you*, not surprisingly that's going to make you a more effective teacher, better able to facilitate student learning, and better able to assess and grade that learning.

Grading isn't easy but it's also very difficult to be on the receiving end—if you're a regular person, that is. Unlike the majority of our classmates back in college, we Lisa Simpsons of the world actively sought out a profession that in essence puts us in the position of being in school and being "graded" forever. What's the whole culture of academia if not having our intellectual work examined and assessed by others or, in layman's terms, being graded? In Professional Scholar World, critical feedback is how we advance. In Student World, grades are a necessary evil, the source of a great deal of emotional baggage, and the only lens through which most students see their academic progress, or lack thereof.[100] In short, they're a big honking deal. So think about and plan for them and tell students early and often exactly what's what when it comes to assignments and class grades. Repeat as needed. Repeat as needed. Repeat as needed.

Preparing for the First and Last Day

One of the most common planning deficiencies among faculty, especially experienced teachers, is for the first day of class. If your "plan" for the first day of your class starts and ends with "hand out syllabus," you need to do more planning.[101] We need to treat the first day as the most important class of the semester because, in many ways, it is. It's a cliché but also totally true that we only get one chance at a first impression, as a person and as a professor.[102] Unluckily for GINs, making a good first impression is often not our forte.[103] So we need to plan and plan carefully how to best use our single most significant opportunity to establish a positive classroom environment.[104] We need to deliberately plan for "orchestrating first impressions," "whetting students' appetites for course content," and even "reassuring students about their decision" to take this class, emphasizing that it will be a valuable investment of their time and money and will result in relevant knowledge and skills (if they apply appropriate effort, of course—no need to promise no work and all play).[105] It can be as simple as saying flat out: "I love teaching this class because it's going to be so useful to you in the following ways."[106]

First impressions and first contact with students is an essential component of establishing rapport. It doesn't have be unduly effusive or way outside our comfort zone. For instance, one group of researchers found that "a simple welcoming e-mail sent a week prior to the first day of class was sufficient to improve students' attitudes above a comparison group that did not receive an email."[107] We certainly can use a welcoming email to convey our enthusiasm and approachability but then we must actually *be* approachable. Namely, we have to be ready to answer questions cheerfully via reply emails that we already addressed in our first message but that the incoming student didn't read or didn't understand. "How do I get the book?" for example, when my first message very, very clearly explained how to get the book. Then there's this predicable response from at least one future student: "I'm going to miss the entire first week of class, maybe more. That's cool, right?" No. No, it's not, but

I'm ready with my respectful, caring, academically rigorous response, remembering that asking me any question at all is the beginning of an essential communication process.[108]

Whether or not you've contacted students via email before class starts, nothing is more important than the first class meeting. The SoTL on first class meetings is plentiful, practical, and applicable to many different types of teaching contexts.[109] Here are some of the basics:

- Plan as carefully for the first day as you would for any other professional presentation, bringing all your intellectual prowess to bear on conveying what you need to convey to this group of people.
- Plan to use the whole class time the first day because it shows students, right off the bat, that you highly value classroom meetings. Students will be used to instructors *not* doing this and may well be expecting to get out of class early, so be transparent and let them know that you are not going to waste a minute of class time.
- Don't go over the syllabus in detail. They'll lose interest and tune you out and then you'll just get snippy when they ask you questions later in the semester about precisely those things you went over in detail on the first day. But some syllabus review can be useful. I sometimes have students get into pairs to go over the syllabus together for a couple minutes and come up with questions for me about it.
- Consider using one or two icebreakers, depending on the class and on your students. First-year first-semester students may be more receptive to icebreaker activities than experienced students who as a rule are more likely to arrive with a higher level of academic and social skill.[110]
- Seriously consider foregoing PowerPoint or any screen-based teaching tool. As discussed later in this chapter, too many GINs become dependent on classroom technology without noticing its negative impact on student engagement. There is also a practical reason for skipping the tech: if for any reason there's a glitch in your technology on the first day, you will look inept and make an irrevocably poor first impression.
- Ask students "What do you want to learn in this class?" Not like a DJ taking requests, but rather as a way to encourage students to more

consciously reflect on their individual learning goals (in addition
to their usual external motivations such as earning a good grade or
fulfilling degree requirements). Bonus: this activity can offer us important insights into student expectations, abilities, and preparation.

- To wrap up, ask students to write a short (anonymous) reaction to
the first day. Or include a very short preview of the course content in
the first meeting—a short writing exercise or watching a film clip—
conveying to students that the subject is so interesting that you can't
wait to get started.[111]

In every way possible, foster student buy-in on the idea that it's not
"my" (the professor's) class, but rather "our" class, students and professors together.[112] For example, you might consider having students
create rules for class conduct and/or a positive classroom environment
themselves.[113]

All the things we are striving to do when we put on our professor
pants are majorly at play during the first day. The first day is foundational
to building rapport, creating a positive classroom environment, and
conveying our immediacy, enthusiasm, and care for student learning. It
sets the tone and paves the way, but it's only one day. Effective teaching
and learning means planning carefully for all class meetings, including
the last few weeks of the term and the very last class meeting. Everyone's
energy starts flagging as the term grinds to an end so it's incumbent
upon us to foresee this eventuality and plan for it. For instance, we might
devote a class session shortly before finals week to some in-class exercises, discussions, and pep talks designed to give everyone a little boost
towards the finish line.[114] Revisiting the learning outcomes, demonstrating how much students have achieved thus far, helping students plan out
how to successfully complete the final steps of the class—anything to
inject some necessary energy into the class.

Lastly, we need to mark the ending of the course as deliberately as we
marked the beginning. Possibilities include setting a truly celebratory
tone, like giving out awards and encouraging students to recognize
their own achievements. We can go more intellectual and talk future
resources or recommended readings. The specifics don't matter as much
as the fact that we consciously lead students in drawing our class to an

end.[115] Whatever is going to help us create a sense of accomplishment and closure is what we should do on the last day of class.

Preparing for Class Meetings

You've planned your course with all your intellectual tools, approaching it as an extension of your scholarship in your field, and based on your knowledge of effective pedagogy. You've crafted great assignments highlighting the relevance of the material and clearly explained how students will be graded. To kick it all off, you held an action-packed first day of class, conveying enthusiasm and building rapport. You get a gold star! But now it's easy to start skimping when it comes to planning how to foster student learning in every class meeting, particularly if we've been teaching for a long time and are getting complacent or if we're juggling multiple adjunct classes or struggling in any especially exhausting teaching context. Again, there is no one all-encompassing method, trick, or tool when it comes to classroom pedagogy and technique. Effective teaching's going to look, sound, and be different, depending on who we are and who our students are, but there are a few nontrendy, research-based pedagogical principles that GINs should implement.

First, we have to treat each class meeting "as a serious intellectual endeavor."[116] Being consistently well prepared for class ups the odds of our students arriving prepared.[117] If we treat class meetings like a waste of our time, so will our students. This one frequently trips up GINs in the classroom. As introverts, there will always be at least a little part of us that actually *does not* want to be there with all those people. And as scholars, it's so easy for us to get wrapped up in our subject studies and absorbed in our reading, our experiments, or our writing. Class meetings can feel like an interruption of our *real* life of the mind. But we can approach our class meetings as a different yet still intellectually engaging aspect of our scholarly work. Every class meeting is another opportunity for us to extend the circle of our geeky love for our subject.

So we have to be on time, always. "Absentminded professor who can't read a clock" is truly a bad look on everyone. Starting and ending class on time should not be difficult for us—it's basic adulting—and yields major benefits to teaching and learning. This simple action tells students all kinds of positive things about you as a teacher: "I know your time as a student is valuable and I respect it, so I won't waste it." "I am enthusiastic about what we are doing today and am happy to be here." "I effectively plan and utilize our class meetings to help you accomplish the learning goals." "I understand and accept my responsibilities as the one in charge of our class meetings." "I am consistent and trustworthy." As nerdy introverts, sometimes we can't convey what we want to convey with our awkward words, but our actions really can speak more loudly than our words.

Similarly, starting and ending every class is a key moment for us to convey the things we want to convey as effective teachers. Signaling to students "let's get started on the great things we're going to do today" in whatever way works for you lays the groundwork for a positive class meeting. Possible openings include greeting the class, stating outright "Let's begin, get out your notes," drawing attention to a prop, or relating an anecdote. Always tell students why you're doing whatever you're doing to help them learn. It's not a secret: what's the learning goal for that particular class? How does it build on the previous class? Get them to recall what they did in the last class and how it's going to keep building in today's class. Ending the class is just as important, with a clear recap of what we've covered, and reminders about upcoming assignments. Students might complete a short response to or reflection about the class meeting that day. We can even try some suspense building for the interesting things coming up in the next class: "I can't wait to hear what you think about this next chapter." The point is that "we must plan to end, not have it thrust upon us by the clock."[118] It's not so much what we do but more that we are consciously creating a starting and ending point for each class meeting because students need a sense of progress in each class, a feeling that we're all moving towards a goal.[119]

You might be tempted to do your talking with technology. Sorry tech-savvy geeks, but we have to be cautious and deliberate about the use of technology in the classroom. Visual aids are great. An endless PowerPoint presentation that turns students into passive viewers and sucks every ounce of energy out of the room is not a visual aid and is not great. A basic rule of thumb is that if our technology is becoming a crutch, it's becoming a problem. Check your use of technology with this AA-styled quiz:

- Are you using technology in every single class meeting?
- Do you need increasing amounts of technology in order to feel prepared to teach?
- Can you not imagine teaching without it?
- Do you tell yourself you're using it less than you're actually using it?
- Do you try to sneak it into class even if you really don't need it that day?
- Do you forget why you started using some particular technology in the first place?
- Do you ignore student or other kinds of feedback pointing out ways that you're over-relying on technology?

There is a place and time for pedagogically effective use of technology, if you're so inclined and if it works in your teaching context.[120] But if you're addicted to the tech, time to try something new.

However, although students are not learning if you're using the "Read PowerPoint Slides Aloud for Entire Class" method, and they're bored out of their minds if you're employing a "Drone on without Pause in Monotone-Lecture-Mode until Everyone's Comatose" class plan, they will nonetheless, against their own best interests, resist and resent it when you try something new and different. This is particularly true for professors trying to implement learning-centered pedagogy, an approach that upends common assumptions about schooling systems and demands a high level of student responsibility for their own learning. Why don't students automatically love professors who break the mold? Why don't they readily embrace innovative changes to what they've *always* experienced in the classroom, eagerly responding to class structures and activities that require them to take chances, risk failure and poor grades, to feel confused, unsure, and like they don't know what the heck is going on . . . Oh. Right.

"We're used to doing it this way and it's the way we've always done it" forms a mental/ emotional blockade that teachers must breach, and if we want to breach it successfully, we must plan for it. SoTL terms this highly predictable occurrence "student resistance" to learning.

Our unique contexts and disparate teaching realities shape student resistance, which can take multiple forms ranging from obvious rebellion to subtle avoidance behaviors. Effective teachers expect student resistance to learning, recognize it when it happens, and *prepare* for it.[121] Awareness and preparation go hand in hand when it comes to effectively contending with student resistance, writes one group of researchers: "Too often, instructors react to manifestations of resistance as though they are noise, background static that interrupts the 'communication' signal the faculty member is trying to get across, usually content."[122] In other words, we want to ignore resistance and get to the important stuff, but resistance is predictable and antithetical to learning, so we need to pay attention and prepare accordingly.

We have to especially consciously and thoroughly prepare for resistance if we intend to implement any pedagogical technique that is going to differ from the traditional classroom model because "active learning environments and courses using innovative teaching strategies tend to be 'hot spots' for student resistance because they violate student expectations and increase student anxiety about performance in a new environments."[123] Sid Brown describes this kind of resistance to outside-the-box pedagogy, writing that many students expect "a lecture from an authority: 'Why don't you just *teach* me if you know so much?' (After all, most students have been trained to *receive information* from teachers, not grapple with their teachers and fellows to *create knowledge*.)"[124] Rebecca Cox also identifies this dynamic, in which students are "wholly comfortable as passive recipients of professors' expert knowledge," adding that "students associate the traditional models of teaching with faculty competence and respond to alternative models with skepticism or disrespect."[125]

Such skepticism can be so powerful that, as one study documented, even when students objectively learn more from a nontraditional teaching model, they may express more dissatisfaction at the end of the class.[126] Let me repeat that: even when students *learned more*, they *liked* the nontraditional model less. That's shocking when viewed through our GIN goggles. We see the world of learning as a fun-filled playground where gaining knowledge is just a giddy spin on the academic tilt-a-whirl. We love taking responsibility for our own learning but most students don't—at least initially—and will respond to such pedagogy by saying things like "I didn't learn in this class because the teacher didn't teach" or "I don't want to teach myself. *You* should be doing it, you pencil-necked geek" (okay, maybe not the "pencil-necked geek" part). The authors of the study conclude:

> Many students' expectations of or prior experience with college classes entail teachers standing in front of the room and "telling." Anything that deviates from this appears out of place and discomforts students for at least two reasons. First, all their experience says that our job is to do the talking, leaving them the choice of engaging with the subject or not. A second reason for their discomfort, however, is how they view the process of learning. Dualistic thinkers believe that gaining knowledge is as simple as listening to and repeating the views of an authority figure. . . . [Doing anything else seems like a] gross dereliction of our duty."[127]

Similarly, as pedagogical researcher Kathleen Gabriel summarizes, students faced with active learning will argue that it's a "'professor's job' to tell them what they need to know and to deliver a well-prepared lecture. Some students will even suggest that they have paid with their tuition dollars for their teachers to teach them. . . . They believe somehow that teaching is something that can be done only by the professor."[128]

Richard M. Felder and Rebecca Brent describe this same common student reaction to learner-centered pedagogy, which is a radical change from teachers "telling them everything they needed to know from the first grade on. . . . When confronted with the need to take more responsibility for their own learning, students may grouse that they are paying tuition—to be taught, not to teach themselves."[129] If we want to be effective in our class meetings, we have to prepare for student reactions like these because in point of fact, the only way to learn *is* to "teach yourself." One of the dictums of learning is that "the one who does the work does the learning" because "as much as we (and often our students) would like to think that we as teachers can simply transfer knowledge into learners' brains, it is just not possible. Students need to do the work required to learn."[130] As Ambrose et al. summarize, "learning is not something done *to* students, but rather something students themselves do."[131] Most students don't understand that learning works like this, so we have to prepare and plan for it.

However, even the most aware instructor proactively planning for some resistance to learning cannot force learning down the throat of a student who for—whatever reason—is fundamentally unwilling to learn. Brookfield reminds us that

> I cannot motivate anyone to learn if at a very basic level they don't wish to. All I can do is try to remove whatever organizational, psychological, or pedagogic barriers are getting in the way of their learning, provide whatever modeling I can, build the best possible case for learning, and then cross my fingers and hope for the best.[132]

Keeping this reality in mind, what can you do about it, given all the specifics of your teaching context such as job status, student population, identity dynamics, and department expectations? What are, in Brookfield's words, "the pedagogic barriers" your students face and in what ways can you "build the best possible case for learning" in every class meeting? Once again, it all starts with your preparation.

Preparing for Conflicts and Confrontations

There's one more type of preparation we need for effective teaching and learning: planning how to reduce the likelihood of conflicts with students, proactively, while at the same time acknowledging their inevitability, and preparing for occasional confrontational interactions with unhappy, angry, and emotional students. Making an effort to be fully aware of our teaching reality and to prepare for it entails acceptance of the fact that students act out when their emotions get the better of them. We can't wave a magic wand and remove every potential conflict from teaching and learning, but we can mitigate conflict with good preparation.

A lot of SoTL handles even the most egregious student misbehavior with a pair of dainty rhetorical tongs, terming it student incivility. That's an awfully polite term for a wide range of problematic behaviors, from mildly disruptive to overtly disrespectful (especially to instructors who don't conform to stereotypes about what professors look like) to downright threatening, harassing, or even violent.[133] Students may be having diagnosable mental problems manifesting in unsettling remarks or odd behaviors.[134] Online classes create a whole new arena for student misbehavior.[135] All possible avenues for effectively navigating student incivility begin with awareness of what is *really happening*, who we are, who our students are, and proactively minimizing with strategic planning potential problems and paying attention to classroom management.[136] If you think classroom management has a kindergarten-ish ring to it, get over yourself. Our students' understanding of "rudeness" is starting to differ in significant ways from previous generations, increasing the need for us to foster student learning in professional standards of behavior.[137]

What really trips GINs up is not that disruptive things happen in class or that students experience strong emotions. Rather, it's that disruptive things and unhappy or angry students require us to interact with other emotional human beings full of messy, contradictory feelings, impulses, and histories.[138] We have to look them right in the eye and *have a difficult conversation*. Obviously, it isn't easy for people in any type of workplace to respond to conflict and other tense situations in a calm and professional way. However, for introverts who seek out and thrive in the often-isolated life of the mind, getting up close and personal with students in real life can be particularly arduous and can markedly undermine our teaching self-efficacy. So we need to prepare deliberately and carefully for difficult interactions with students, whether an entire class is falling apart due to students' misbehavior or whether a single student is standing in front of us and is upset, angry, needy, or afraid.[139]

In these instances, many academics can easily forget that college is an emotionally fraught undertaking. Our active and agile brains are used to taking center stage. We forget how often Mr. and Ms. Emotional Responses circumvent Boss Brain and take over the human host. As Brookfield eloquently describes it: "For those of us trained to believe that college classrooms are rational sites of intellectual analysis, the shock of crossing the border between reason and chaos is intensely disorienting."[140] Attending college, let alone succeeding there, is a developmentally, financially, psychologically, and personally taxing endeavor, eliciting a wide range of possible emotional responses and expressions, some of which may seem irrational and disproportional. Recognizing this and planning for it makes us more effective as educators.

Students can be teary, angry, baffled, manipulative, hostile, or groveling and may perceive you as having a great deal of authority and power, which means they'll bring a whole passel of issues to their interactions with you—issues that have little if anything to do with *you* as an individual. Students are accompanied by an invisible army of all the other adult authority figures in their lives, from parents (and *that's* never a complicated relationship, right?) to the tutor they had a crush on in high school to the social studies teacher who made their life a living hell in seventh grade.[141] On the other hand, you may be facing the opposite problem of not being able to teach from a place of authority and expertise in the classroom, depending on your individual teaching context. If you're a professor of color and a student has never before had any one-on-one contact with a nonwhite authority figure, that's a potential minefield. In all cases, students "relate to you as a stereotype" and some of their baffling behaviors make more sense when we are aware of how such stereotypes may be shaping their actions.[142]

In addition to individual and unique life experiences students bring to their one-on-one interactions with you, certain commonalities are also at play. For instance, we have to recognize that virtually all people in their late teens and early twenties, even the most privileged students, are going through a life stage of major development, transitioning into full adulthood and everything that entails.[143] That's *hard to do* and it will make them tired, cranky, and hormonal, and cause them to sometimes overreact, misinterpret, or melt down. Also, because learning is hard, there *will* be an emotional component. Brookfield points out that we need to plan for this: "Being aware of the emotionality of learning helps prepare teachers for the inevitable outpouring of anger and resentment that some students express as they explore new intellectual arenas and new skill sets."[144]

Nobody likes feeling lost and confused yet that feeling is endemic among students, who may well "experience the college classroom as a foreign place," where "they have to take exams [but] they don't know the subject or the rules."[145] On top of that, college is a pressure cooker for most students because it's obscenely costly, with no reassurance that a great job will be waiting after graduation. What might at first glance appear to be just dumb and irresponsible behavior—procrastination, repeated absences, being tardy, missing assignments, making under-their-breath side comments in class, unwarranted complaining—may well be rooted in real obstacles such as food insecurity or homelessness, and/or fear.[146] Without discounting personal responsibility or jetti-soning appropriate academic consequences for their actions, we can better foster student learning when we take into account how individual circumstances and fear, not necessarily disrespect nor laziness, may be at the root of certain behaviors.

What can we do in those uncomfortable, irritating, and frustrat-ing moments? One thing that really helps during negative or highly emotional interactions with students is to be fully present and aware of what it is actually happening. It makes it easier to spot the things that our students are doing that have little to do with us personally. For example, don't you just hate it when a student falls asleep during class? After all that effort you're putting into teaching and learning, they have the unmitigated gall to doze off! But here's a mind-blowing idea: what if the student falling asleep in our class doesn't really have much to do with us? As Angela Proviteria McGlynn writes about this predictable occurrence: "We see it as a reflection of our performance when it just may not be related to us at all."[147] If a student's deeply sleep deprived, as most college students are, falling asleep isn't something they're choosing to do in order to be disrespectful to us yet we feel as offended as if it were. Clearly, students *should not* be sleeping in class. It's unprofessional, distracts other students, and interferes with their learning. But if (when!) it happens, we need to see what is actually occurring, without our damaged pride and touchy ego getting in the way. If we can take it less personally by being fully present to what's actually happening, we will be better situated to take productive action rather than just angrily reacting.

During particularly intense interactions, like when a student is disputing a grade, being as absolutely attentive as we can will enable us to assess more accurately what's happening and will ensure that students feel we are taking the concern seriously, which doesn't mean that we have to agree to the premise of their complaint or acquiesce to their request.[148] One study about student-faculty conflict of particular relevance for GINs found that when conflicts arise, the most important predictor of successful resolution isn't what the professor actually decides or does but *how* the professor does it: "The actual action seemed to mean less than the manner in which it was done" and "interpersonal style may be as important as the specific remedies faculty employ to resolve conflict."[149] Once again those aspects of effective teaching that have little to do with our intellect and everything do with our ability to engage in positive social interactions are front and center.

These researchers found that the most productive way for faculty to handle conflicts with students depended first and foremost on the faculty member's ability to *communicate* with students: being able to clearly demonstrate to students that we are not dismissing their concerns, that we're listening to what they're saying without defensiveness or hostility (introverts may have an edge here because we're often good listeners), and that we are responding to student concerns thoughtfully and respectfully.[150] For instance, offering students the opportunity to do make-up work could be viewed by students as *either* a positive *or* negative resolution to the conflict, depending on how the professor responded to the concern in terms of the professor's verbal and nonverbal behavior. Therefore, "strategies to appease students with leniency may be misguided. Enhancing the quality of their interpersonal relationships in the classroom may be a more effective strategy for creating and maintaining positive perceptions of their teaching."[151] Maintaining awareness of the "quality of interpersonal relationships in the classroom" is central to effectively handling all conflicts with students.

For GINs, it's doubly important that we remember to communicate effectively and to engage in positive social interactions with students because it's easy for us to let those things slide in our rush to get to the good stuff, that is, subject-based content. Some conflict is unavoidable but we can make any conflict with a student worse by "acting defensively, retaliating, humiliating the student, or denying the problem," and to resolve disputes effectively, no matter what specific course of action we take, we need to "involve students in discussions that convey respect and empathy."[152] "Convey" is the all-important verb. As introverts and intellectuals, we can't neglect essential social interactions and personal communications that effective teaching requires.[153] Knowing that we have to prepare for this just as we prepare for all other aspects of teaching can help.

But there's another kind of preparation we can do that will reduce such conflicts. As the same study pointed out, "carefully explaining policies early in the course, maximizing the objectivity of grading and exams, and instituting policies that minimize the need to evaluate the legitimacy of students' excuses are likely to be helpful" in reducing conflict with our students.[154] That means clearly communicating *all* our course policies, everything we need students to know and understand in order to succeed in our classes, keeping in mind who our students are and what they know. For instance, Darren Fullerton suggests that when teaching the newest generations of students "it may not be enough to have policies on attendance and cell phone usage. Instead, professors must help students understand the rationales for those polices. Can attendance requirements be connected directly to students developing necessary knowledge and skills that they might find meaningful?"[155] Even fully taking into account disparate teaching realities, clearly communicating how we're assessing and grading student work, and our expectations and the consequences if expectations are not met, is the single specific strategy most likely to cut down on negative encounters with students.[156]

No matter how well we plan, prepare, communicate expectations in order to minimize conflicts, and accept the reality of conflict, it can still be hard to deal with students, their emotions, and their actions that are unrelated to us as individuals (though we nonetheless take them extremely personally). So be ready to recognize those interactions you can expect to arise every term and identify the ones you find most personally challenging.[157] Try to figure out what types of student interactions make your heart pound, your hands tremble, your stomach clench, and your blood pressure shoot up. You're a Jedi Master and you never have these physical reactions to stress? Bless your heart, how *nice* for you. For the rest of us ordinary Muggles (to mix my nerd metaphors), we can identify what types of student interactions particularly irritate, annoy, or confuse us if we pay a little bit more attention to what our animal body is telling us with physical symptoms like flushed face, rapid breathing, and increased heart rate.

As an introvert I need to prepare myself very consciously for all types of peopling but especially for effectively dealing with student conflicts and confrontations, and for this, I am a big believer in scripts. Not endlessly and laboriously rehearsing what you're going to say to So-and-So about Such-and-Such but having ready standard responses and answers when you get standard questions and complaints.[158] First, identify when and how tense situations will predictably arise. For example, how do your students tend to cope with poor grades? What issues and factors are shaping what manifests as emotional reactions around grades? What common issues do they latch onto and what language and phrasing do they use? "I did everything you wanted." "I *have* to get an A in this class." "I am an A student."[159] Do you know that after midterms you're going to get a flood of panicked emails and office visitations? Is finals week guaranteed to bring at least one weeping student to your office? Then plan it into your schedule, anticipate it, and prepare for it.

For instance, Sid Brown offers this example of a script she uses during one-on-one meetings with students who have begun to exhibit problematic class behaviors:

> "I'd like to have a frank conversation about your performance in class. First I'm going to tell you some things I see in your behavior, then I'm going to tell you what those things seem to communicate to me. Then I'm going to ask you to offer your reflections on the situation. Don't worry: you will get your say."

After some discussion, and to move the interaction to a productive end, she suggests a statement like this: "So what's the solution? It sounds like there are some things I need to do as the professor and some things you need to do as the student."[160] This kind of script could work for you—or it might not. As always, it depends on you, your student population, your job status, your identity, and your personality.

I have some standard responses ready for reoccurring issues around grades and attendance that I encounter, and it helps me keep my cool. For example, there's an email we all occasionally receive from students and we universally detest: "I couldn't come to class today. Did I miss anything?" I've worked to get over my initial reaction to this, which is indignant, sarcastic, and goes something like "Why no! Of course you didn't 'miss anything'! Our class meetings are always devoid of any meaningful activity. Also, because you are the center of the universe, when you didn't show up I just canceled class and we all went home and played video games." Instead, I reply, "I hope everything is okay. I'd like to meet with you to go over what you missed today." Then, face-to-face in the privacy of my office, I can offer the student a little bit of advice about the best way to approach professors: "I know you didn't intend it this way, but when you say 'did I miss anything?' it sounds like you don't think our class meetings are important."

The realities of your job may not make this kind of response possible but the bigger point is that I'm ready for this remark and I have a strategy for coping with it that helps me act, not react. Importantly, I do this in person. The best practice for all conflicts is, when at all possible, do it in person.[161] As intellectual introverts, we may be tempted to use email to avoid difficult interactions with students, but these can easily trigger an unproductive and emotionally escalating back-and-forth. If I must use email, I always begin with "Thank you for your email." It's a signal I use for myself to take a deep breath and answer calmly, without sarcasm or irritation. Even when I write it through gritted teeth, "Thank you for your email" keeps my own emotional response in check.

I have another script for one of the most common difficult student-professor interactions: academic dishonesty.[162] Over the years, I've developed assignments that thwart plagiarism and I take time to discuss it frequently with students, but it still happens so I have some set responses. I apply all previously stated policies, including my university's academic honesty policy, consistently and transparently, and I clearly convey that I hate the sin but not the sinner. I have a box of tissues handy and some pithy life coach–type maxims to ease the pain: "Everyone makes mistakes but it's what we do after a mistake that shows our real character." You can't imagine ever saying that? That's fine because like every other teaching situation, you have to tailor this to your teaching context. But what you absolutely must do is prepare, prepare, and then prepare some more.

Preparation boils down to this: never, ever assume that you and your students are on the same page unless you have made absolutely sure you're on the same page.[163] We have assumptions and expectations that they don't have, and vice versa. Just like we tend to generalize and lump all students together, students do the same darn thing with professors. For example, for years I wondered why students always asked me on the first day of class "Are these books required?" when the syllabus stated, "These books are required." Finally, I asked a student about it, and he pointed out that some instructors assign expensive textbooks and say the book is "required" but then don't test the students on it or in some other way assess their reading of the book. Students perceive this as disrespectful to their time and a waste of their money. For them, "required" means "linked to grading somehow."[164] A colleague of mine, a caring and rigorous teacher, routinely "requires" students to purchase a book because it is such a thought-provoking collection of essays on his beloved topic that he truly believes students should read it in order to learn about that topic. But he doesn't test them on it or discuss it directly in class so students see it as pointless. He's making a classic academic nerd mistake. We *love* our subjects and we truly, wholeheartedly believe they're worthwhile to study, above and beyond grades, but most of our students don't. If this happens to a student, they're always going to wonder from then on, do I really need to buy this book? Then they'll ask me, do I really need to buy this book?

The biggest sources of resentment and misunderstanding in teaching and learning are not intellectual and academic but rather emotional and social. Communicating and social interactions aren't going to come easily or naturally to many of us, so we must plan and prepare for the interactions we know are coming our way. And give yourself a break. If you're an introvert and talking with people is tiring for you, then let yourself be tired. Schedule it, plan for it, and assume it's going to happen. Anger directed or misdirected at you from students is a sure-fire way to ruin your day? Try to accept anger as a reality—*kaiidth*. Knowing that it will definitely happen from time to time, we will be able to figure out what to do and how to move on. Like SpongeBob ProfessorPants, we'll be ready, ready, ready.

Conclusion

> Don't panic.
> —*The Hitchhiker's Guide to the Galaxy*

———

Even when we anticipate the emotions associated with learning, even when we prepare as best we can for predictable conflicts, it's easy to become overwhelmed. Putting on our professor pants isn't easy, as Jay Parini writes:

> I always feel a little frightened as I leave my office and begin the long march to the classroom, my arms loaded with notes and text, my head crammed with ideas I have not quite properly formulated. I wonder what the hell will happen when the class begins. Will I make sense? Will the students respond in a sympathetic way? Will I look and sound like an idiot? Is my face well shaved? Is my fly unzipped? Will I make it through 50 or 60 minutes without feeling like a complete fool?[165]

Whether we're new to teaching or have been around the block many times, we introverts and academics often "feel a little frightened" when it's time for us to leave our lovely Mind Palace and venture out into the rough and tumble world of teaching and learning. Social interaction and communication skills demand things that may not come easily to us, and then there's always the chance that we're going to end up "feeling like a complete fool"—every intellectual's worst nightmare.

I believe that a lot of professorial defensiveness, our outraged reactions to student complaints and our arrogance or dismissiveness in the face of student confusion and concern, is rooted in our fear of feeling foolish—or worse, of failing. Failing to effectively communicate with our students and draw them into our geeky love for our subject. Preparation isn't a magic talisman that will keep all miscommunication, failure, and conflict out of teaching and learning. There will always be new twists and turns in the roller coaster ride that we weren't anticipating. But thoughtfully preparing for social interaction and clear communication will go a long way toward preventing and mitigating conflicts, misbehavior, and confrontations. It will help us heed the advice of that well-known guide to galaxy hitchhiking: don't panic.

In the process, maybe you can cut yourself and your students a little slack. Practicing compassion as a teacher can be tricky because assessing learning sometimes means being the bearer of bad news. However, there is a time and a place for compassion in college teaching.[166] Empathy and compassion don't mean letting students avoid responsibility or not rigorously assessing their work—things some *students* might define as professorial "compassion." Rather, it means recognizing that we're all humans together in an existential stew pot of anxiety, failures, pride, hope, ego, illness, delusion, and struggles ranging from mundane to life threatening. For our own sanity and efficacy as teachers, it can help to remember this, and it can help us feel less personally attacked or frustrated by students. We're not going to let them off the hook when they mess up but we might be able to see it more in a big-picture context than a myopic it's-an-insult-to-me context. "Well, it's finals week and they're stressed out, sleep deprived, and afraid of failing" versus "Again with the complaining, whining, begging, and bargaining! Why, oh why, are they so intent on making me miserable?"

Whether it's changing our inner dialogue, giving students clearly stated grading criteria to mitigate potential conflict, or making a conscious effort to build rapport and immediacy, we can better foster student learning when we are fully *prepared* to foster student learning. However, we are also always learning and repeatedly relearning how to prepare for class meetings and for all other student interactions. We cannot do that without careful reflection, as we see in the next chapter.

CHAPTER 3

REFLECTION

There is nothing like looking if you want to find something. You certainly usually find something, if you look, but it is not always quite the something you were after.

—Thorin Oakenshield, *The Hobbit*

———

I ONCE attended a teaching workshop that should have been facilitated by a bereavement counselor rather than an educational consultant. All the participants exhibited to some degree the five states of grief—denial, anger, bargaining, depression, and acceptance. Some seemed to be reliving traumatic teaching experiences from years ago, while others spoke about current students with a bitterness that I've never seen before or since in any teaching-related forum, because usually if you've bothered to attend a teaching workshop you retain at least a shred of optimism about your students. We comprised a professoriate rainbow, embodying a variety of racial and other identity markers: newbie and oldster; male, female, gay, straight, married, and single; tenured, tenure-track, and contingent; humanities, sciences, education, and business. Yet for all our differences, we spoke with a single anguished voice. The topic of the workshop and the cause of this pedagogical wailing wall? Student evaluations of teaching (SET).

Scratch almost any professor and you'll find beneath their shellacked surface of intellectual prowess and academic confidence a soul scarred by the anonymous SET process, one of the most potentially damaging aspects of the byzantine world of college teaching. And don't look to SoTL for clarity. No other single topic elicits so much analysis with so very few agreed-upon conclusions.[1] You can easily find a convincing, carefully conducted study, citing numerous other convincing, carefully conducted studies, all published by established and knowledgeable scholars using professional research methods, to support virtually *any* assertion about student course evaluations. Evaluations can't measure student learning or teaching efficacy and/or are irrevocably flawed by racial, gender, or other bias? We've got the studies to prove it. Evaluations are an accurate assessment of student learning and teaching ability, reflecting little or no gender or racial bias? Studies show that as well. Somewhere in between? Both? Sort of? You better believe we've got studies showing that. How exactly do individual personalities, psychologies, and values shape SET? What about grading policies and practices? It's hard to say.[2] As one group of researchers writes:

> Given its near universal usage and the accumulation of thousands of articles resulting from more than 40 years of research, one would expect a converging consensus rather than divisive controversy on the topic of student evaluations of teaching (SET). However, equally strong research exists to support as to counter the validity, reliability, and usefulness of SET.[3]

The questions regarding "validity, reliability, and usefulness of SET" encompass wide-ranging debates on virtually all aspects of the system.[4] Scholars don't even agree on what to call them. Are they student ratings of instruction (SRI), opinions, evaluations, or what?[5]

For GINs who want to be effective teachers, there are two main reasons that student evaluations of teaching cause so much pain and suffering. First, they are often the only way we receive any type of feedback about teaching, therefore taking on disproportionate weight and influence, both on our own perceptions of our teaching as well as the assessment of our teaching by others. Most institutions use SET to some degree when making personnel decisions, which gives them significant power over instructors' careers. They can impact all aspects of our teaching from the most specific course details (Should I keep using this textbook?) to the most profoundly life altering (Will my contract be renewed?). These forms play an enormous role in administrative assessment of our teaching, with little real understanding on anyone's part—students, professors, or administrators—of the complexities, difficulties, usefulness, and limitations of SET.

The second reason SET can inflict so much pain is because if there's one thing geeks and nerds know how to do it's get good grades. It's why we continued on for our advanced degrees. Unlike most people, *we* liked school so much we wanted it to go on and on. No matter how long it's been since our last official report card, we expect nothing less than an "A" in all academic activities. If we didn't literally get straight As in the subject we're teaching (though a lot of us did), we nonetheless succeeded far beyond most people's interactions with our subject. So if we care about being effective teachers and have put time and effort into facilitating student learning, when our students "grade" us with their evaluations, even one negative remark from a single student can burn itself into our memory.

This chapter offers ways to effectively handle and respond to student evaluations because they are an important reality and they can help us reflect on our teaching. However, I also argue for adopting a much broader pedagogical practice of regular reflection on our own individual teaching in our own unique context.[6] Reflection doesn't have to be unduly time consuming or "spiritual," and it can be undertaken in a variety of ways, tailored to our personality, job status, and other specificities of our teaching context. In fact, GINs bring a lot of skills and training to the practice of reflection on teaching since we're good at amassing and reviewing data and evidence and thinking through big issues methodically and clearly.

Reflection is not the same thing as assessment of either teaching or learning, though there's overlap. Rather, building on awareness and preparation, reflection is a recurring, proactive, self-directed strategy with effective teaching as its goal.[7] In *Becoming a Critically Reflective Teacher*, Stephen Brookfield describes reflective teaching as "the sustained and intentional process of identifying and checking the validity of our teaching assumptions" and "the habit of constantly trying to identify, and check, the assumptions that form our actions as teachers . . . [in order] to help us take more informed actions so that when we do something that's intended to help students learn it actually has that effect."[8] An increasing number of studies demonstrate that reflection is an essential component of effective teaching at every stage in our teaching careers, from our very first class to our very last.[9] The scholarship on reflective teaching includes online teaching and, in at least one study, directly links increased faculty reflection with improved SET.[10]

As Gerald Hess and Sophie Sparrow summarize, "Reflecting upon, observing, and writing about one's own teaching may well be the most effective activities [all] professors can do to improve their teaching."[11] For GINs, reflection can fuel a scholarly approach to teaching, bringing all our geeky curiosity, nerdy investigative interest, and sharp researcher minds to our teaching work.[12] Some educators include this activity in what they term contemplative pedagogy.[13] Just as we need to utilize SoTL and other types of support for our teaching (see chapter 4), we have to use reflection on our own teaching and learning experiences in order to become "experts on our own teaching."[14] As one scholar summarizes the work of reflective teaching: "Reflective teachers continually examine their efforts in the classroom as a way to identify what approaches work best for students while understanding that there is no single best way to teach."[15]

Critically reflective teaching presupposes a teaching context that allows room for making corrections, adjustments, and informed responses to teaching problems and issues. It's one of the most vicious ironies of academic job insecurity that teaching efficacy is crucial to being rehired every term, yet the best way to learn how to be an effective teacher requires the opportunity to reflect on and learn from experience. Moreover, in any teaching context, using reflection to create and implement actual classroom practices is by no means a simple task.[16] It won't happen automatically: "I reflected on this so Shazam! I am now immediately imbued with all power and skill necessary to address it effectively!" But by not limiting the important work of reflecting on our teaching to one thing and one thing only (i.e., end of the semester SET), we can significantly improve our ability to foster a geek culture of sharing in our classrooms.

Student Evaluations of Teaching

When I was listening to the other participants in that workshop lament the SET process, I couldn't help but see a parallel between "us," the noble suffering instructors, and "them," the cruel unthinking students. The fundamental, defining feature of being a student is having your academic work assessed and graded—day in and day out, for work you love doing as well as work you don't want to do, by many instructors, each with their own systems and idiosyncrasies. As Spurgeon Thompson describes it, "Over and over they are told whether they are good enough to continue being told whether they are good enough. Even the most rigorous professions don't require the kind of extensive, multifaceted performance-review structure that five graded courses a semester constitute."[17] It's natural that students react emotionally and negatively to poor grades, even if they've indisputably earned that poor grade. No matter how transparent we've been about assessing their learning, or how clearly we've communicated our expectations and consistently implemented fair grading mechanisms, it's no wonder that they feel personally attacked by our negative comments. And yet many of the workshop participants seemed unaware that, similarly, we *feel personally attacked* by negative SET.

Virtually every one of us in that room could quote verbatim negative comments from our student evaluations, even the most demonstrably effective teachers among us. A few years after the workshop, I read one of these other teacher's personnel files during a promotion review, and found it literally overflowing with glowing testimonies from students over the past twenty years. He is clearly one of the most beloved and effective teachers on campus, but the only thing he talked about in that workshop was the very occasional negative SET comment. He remembered every wounding word.[18] Before we do any other reflecting on our teaching, we need to acknowledge how painful negative feedback—whether totally credible or completely unfounded—is for us as geeks and nerds teaching subjects in which we are deeply invested. The gap between instructors' intentions to teach effectively and the reality of a negative student evaluation creates real problems for us, and derails the utility of SET for critically reflective teaching, as Joseph Mick La

Lopa writes: "In the face of negative ratings and a lack of instructional support, those who have prepared long and hard to cover the content only to get lackluster feedback may develop negative attitudes towards students and SET."[19]

If anything, La Lopa understates widespread faculty attitudes towards SET. Linda C. Hodges and Katherine Stanton find that "student evaluations are the bane of many a faculty member's existence and an identified source of real faculty anxiety." Because we are so successful in other aspects of our scholarly endeavors, negative student evaluations of our teaching are not only painful but also contribute to our discounting of feedback and shutting down reflection on teaching:

> We naturally expect our students to appreciate how we have taught them and reward our "performance" with good marks. When these expectations fail to materialize, we are disappointed, confused, and angry. Our reaction can lead us to discount these sources of information and may even contribute to our disillusionment with the value of our work.[20]

We can become "disappointed, confused, and angry," and increasingly unmotivated to engage in any type of reflective activity about student feedback. We will perhaps even develop "professorial melancholia" as one study ominously posited.[21] Another warned that "a pathological pattern of behavior can develop . . . including increasing hostility toward students, administrators, and eventually, arrogance, alienation, and even possible substance abuse and verbal or grade abuse of students."[22]

The anonymity of SET compounds its emotional component because sometimes a student course evaluation *is* a personal attack: name-calling, use of profanity, and inappropriate comments about our personality or physical appearance can regularly appear.[23] Young female professors should fully expect ratings on their sexual attractiveness, for instance. In fact, one of the essential realities of teaching and learning discussed in chapter 1—"Identity is important"—is probably the most contentious and unresolved aspect of SET. In what ways and to what extent do stereotypes about faculty's embodied identity impact SET? Do such biases and preconceptions fundamentally undermine the usefulness of SET? According to reams of research, the answer is a resounding, "it's complicated."[24]

For GINs who want and need to be effective teachers, the most important issue is not whether or not our identity is a factor in SET but rather how the proven fact of disparate realities in our unique teaching contexts includes SET. Those of us who are not white or male or who in some other way fail to fulfill the narrowly defined stereotyped ideals of what a professor looks and acts like can and do regularly achieve positive SET. But, crucially, what we have to do in the classroom and in our interactions with students is not the same as those who look the part of "professor." Sylvia Lazos summarizes this aspect of SET for women teaching college classes: "Although in overall ratings, women appear to be, or are close to being, on a par with male professors, a more careful examination shows that women have to labor harder to satisfy student expectations." She continues:

> Women function under a different scaling system than men. Stereo-
> types can influence the evaluators' understanding of a trait. Stereo-
> types shift not only their balance in expecting things from teachers
> but also their perceptions about what it entails to achieve those quali-
> ties. Students expect women to engage in a different set of behaviors
> to satisfy a particular trait. To be considered caring, women had to
> spend more time meeting students outside of class and being accessi-
> ble during office hours. Students were more harshly critical if their
> women instructors were not available.[25]

Lazos is far from being the only scholar who's reached this conclusion about a "different scaling system." Numerous studies show that "female professors [are] expected to offer greater interpersonal support and [are] judged more strictly than male professors in providing it."[26]

To put it another way, SoTL shows that all effective college teachers in all disciplines need to establish rapport with students and demonstrate caring for student learning in order to receive positive student evaluations, but women and faculty of color need to do it *better* and be *more* "warm, friendly, and supportive inside and outside the classroom" and we must use better "interpersonal skills" than white men.[27] GINs who already have to very consciously put on their professor pants to manifest such qualities in teaching and learning may have to even more deliberately work to do so because of disparate teaching realities. While a number of studies indicate that race, gender, and other identity issues don't overly influence student evaluations of teaching, plenty of other studies conclude that social biases are at least a factor in evaluations.[28] However, what I want to emphasize is not that bias makes useful SET impossible but rather that the teaching labor required to achieve positive SET is influenced by our teaching context, including the reality that identity is important.

Students will view our teaching at least partially through their assumptions and culturally learned knowledge about us and this will shape how they respond to certain questions about our teaching, on certain kinds of SET forms, regarding certain types of courses and instruction. For instance, women and faculty of color have to much more consciously "manage our authority" in the college classroom and in our interactions with students than white male professors must do.[29] Moreover, women and faculty of color are more likely to experience the extremes of anonymous SET comments, which can and do include comments that are flat-out abusive.[30] Even if it does not fundamentally undermine their potential utility, one of the complexities of SET is that it can include inappropriate and hurtful comments intended to debase the professor with racist, sexist, or homophobic remarks or other hateful language.

In this way, students are just bringing to SET what they've learned online. We live in a Yelptastic world of social media and online ratings and reviews, the sole purpose of which seems to be making other people feel like garbage. In virtually any online forum, users rarely prize positivity. Vicious invective is the norm. It's a new fact of life that today people feel free to type things that they'd never have the nerve to say face to face. Trolling is not just a minor side effect of the internet age. It's a full-blown worldwide epidemic.[31] Universities mostly administer their course evaluations online, further blurring the line in some students' minds between "constructive, appropriate, thoughtful feedback" and "crude attacks meant to demean, intimidate, and humiliate." Thompson concludes that "as evaluations move online, and in an age when students feel less constrained by social conventions, student evaluations have become [blunter], sharp-edged, and consequently more meaningless. They have become either as bland as a cheerful status update or as cruel as online bullying."[32]

The problems and complexities of student evaluations don't end there. The format of evaluations matters greatly. Instructors usually have to use a standardized form created by a long-defunct committee, maybe with some clear assessment goals in mind and informed by a nuanced understanding of how students actually learn, but probably not. For example, many SET forms employ vague "ratings scales" that are, in the words of Ronald Berk, so "poorly constructed" that "if they were bridges, they would probably collapse."[33] What does a "5" really mean on a 1–5 scale? Perfection? Or just satisfactory? Similarly, the wording of some SET questions is so imprecise and so unclearly related to learning that the questions rarely yield substantive replies. For instance, "What did you like about the course?" As Maryellen Weimer asks, "Since when did 'like' become a relevant criteria for the assessment of an educational experience?"[34] Weimer isn't suggesting that students' active *dislike* is a marker of effective teaching and learning. Rather, she's pointing out the problem with the question's wording.[35] "Likeability" is not the same thing as "advancing academic abilities."[36] Because learning has an emotional component and because learning is hard, rating or evaluating teaching and learning by a vague "enjoyment" or "satisfaction" scale will always be an ineffective measure.

Or take another common SET question: "Does the instructor respect students?" We want to check this because students can't feel disrespected and also be able to achieve their best learning. But what exactly constitutes "respect"? If students and instructors define this word differently, as they may well do, the question will not yield helpful feedback. Also, students can only answer this question based on their own interactions with the instructor and what they witnessed in class. Better questions on the SET form would assess specific respectful instructional actions in the class. Questions such as "Did I start and end this class on time?" "Did I listen to student comments and respond to student questions in this class?"[37] We have to figure out exactly what students are able to accurately evaluate, and then plan accordingly.

While students may be able to identify an effect of a poor teaching technique, they don't have the vocabulary or training to explain exactly what the technique was that led to the effect.[38] Claire B. Potter summarizes, "While students can have good insights into why a class worked or didn't work, insights that need to be listened to, they are not master teachers, nor has anyone ever taught them how to evaluate a classroom experience."[39] It's up to us to be able to sift through SET comments with the eye of the skilled educators that we are. For instance, if students write "boring PowerPoint slides," they are telling us something we need to know. It is clear feedback and worthy of us taking some time to reflect on our use of slides in the classroom. But if a student writes "Boring class," that's not so clear. They may be referring to a problem we had effectively conveying our enthusiasm for the material or some other aspect of our class organization such as overreliance on PowerPoint slides, which would be valid points worthy of our careful reflection. However, they could also be referring to their own deep disengagement with their education, a much more complex issue over which we have some, but not a lot, of control. Students are often unable to sort out these nuanced issues in their own classroom experience.

Moreover, Stephen Brookfield points out that skilled teachers who facilitate learning can expect some hostility from at least some students.[40] It's essential that SET forms do not set us up for failure by ignoring this aspect of learning. Stanley Fish argues that sometimes "effective teaching involves the deliberate inducing of confusion, the withholding of clarity, the refusal to provide answers," but "that kind of teaching is unlikely to receive high marks on a questionnaire that rewards the linear delivery of information and penalizes a pedagogy that probes, discomforts, and fails to provide closure."[41] Fish is not arguing that student feedback is irrelevant but he's pointing out potential problems with evaluation formatting, specifically with forms that "reward linear delivery" and penalize more innovative pedagogy.

As Fish suggests and many others demonstrate, student-centered or active learning classrooms will discomfort students and force them to reconsider their assumptions about how teaching and learning works. Resistance to active learning techniques expressed in negative SET is an entirely predictable response based on the students' previous under-standing of how school works. In order for SET to offer productive feed-back, the SET forms we use have to take this reality into account because students themselves are often "satisfied with passive learning and don't appreciate faculty who make them work for their grade beyond taking a multiple-choice test, especially not assignments requiring critical thinking and problem solving."[42]

Last but definitely not least, students complete their course evalua-tions at the end of the term. What's the final week of classes like at your school? I'm guessing that like at my university, everyone—students, teachers, support staff—has just about *had it* with everyone else and everything to do with school and is counting the minutes until it's over. The last weeks are a grueling slog of completing high-stakes final exams and papers (students), grading high-stakes final exams and papers (professors), and ratcheted-up stress about everything you should have done better all semester and are paying the price for now (students and professors). The final week of classes is not only a terrible time to ask students to reflect on their learning and on a teacher's performance over the course of the class—it's just about the *worst* time, when emotions are running hottest, resiliency is at its lowest, and resentment, panic, and blame are closest to the surface.[43] Given this fact, and also the fact that learning is a long, slow, cumulative process over the course of years, a better gauge of teaching efficacy would be student evaluations administered a year after the class ended, or even longer.[44]

We must ask for student feedback, and evaluations can give us in-formation—*some* information—on the effectiveness of our teaching. We must accept that SET can tell us some things but also that they can't tell us some other things—and exactly what those things are is a source of rancorous debate among scholars. In addition, we must be aware of the complexities of SET in our particular teaching contexts. Fortunately for GINS, although we need to be aware of the emotional component of reading student feedback, effectively interpreting SET is an *intellectual endeavor*. SET is a prime opportunity for putting into action a systematic, scholarly approach to our work of teaching, rather than engaging in haphazard emotionally charged torture sessions obsessively rereading the worst comments, then stuffing them away, and doing our best to forget the whole thing until student evaluation time rolls around again at the end of the next term (hypothetically speaking because of course I've *never* done anything like this).[45]

Hodges and Stanton argue that when we approach SET "as part of a scholarly approach to teaching, making meaningful adjustments to future classes and informing curricular choices in productive ways," we can bring our "scholar's eye to these 'data' as a source of insight into student learning challenges."[46] They explain how using SET as part of a scholarly approach to teaching can reduce anxiety and hostility about the process and foster productive reflection:

> This perspective may lessen our stress as we read our evaluations and may encourage us to move more readily into the scholar's question: "What is this student a case of?" As such . . . we may see our evaluations less as judgments of our performance and more as insight into our students' intellectual growth—insight that may engage *us* in intellectual growth as teachers and scholars.[47]

By approaching SET as another area where we can use our research skills and our "scholar's eye" to view SET as a source for learning and relearning how to be effective teachers, we can help mitigate the negativity and emotional toll of the anonymous SET system.

In what ways can SET provide us with valuable and actionable "data" for our critical reflection on our teaching? Although the SoTL on student course evaluations is plagued by a lack of definitive conclusions, it does offer some good guidance about how instructors who want to be effective teachers should approach SET. Overall, it shows that the more we can help students value and understand the role of their feedback, the more likely it is that our SET will yield actionable feedback. If students know we value their feedback, and if we foster student buy-in on the process itself, student evaluations tend to be not only more thoughtful but also overall more positive.[48] *The more we can demonstrate to students that we value SET and see it as important, the more likely it is that students will offer thoughtful feedback.*

In practical terms, the research agrees upon three specific, actionable steps to fostering constructive SET in most teaching contexts:

- Solicit SET using a *variety* of methods *frequently* throughout the term.
- Read and reflect on end-of-the-semester summative SET with another person, preferably someone with some expertise in how to interpret SET.
- Collect feedback on teaching from as many sources as possible in addition to student feedback.

SOLICIT STUDENT EVALUATIONS OF TEACHING USING A VARIETY OF METHODS FREQUENTLY THROUGHOUT THE TERM

Virtually every college teacher in virtually every teaching context should solicit student feedback in a *variety* of ways *throughout* the semester, particularly midterm SET.[49] We all need positive reinforcement, so don't forget to include questions about what's going right in the course and what's working well.[50] Midway through the term is also a good time to remind students about their own self-regulation as learners, including time management and effective study habits. A simple "stop, start, continue" form (what can I/you/we stop doing, what can I/you/we start doing, what can I/you/we continue doing to foster learning in this class?) works well at the midpoint in the semester, for instance.[51] Then we need to address any issue that arises out of our midterm evaluations, transparently and directly.[52] Depending on our teaching context, we can probably make small adjustments to the class without undermining our authority. In fact, doing so demonstrates confidence in our own abilities and a willingness to respond to student concerns. If the SET is way off, we must clearly, calmly, and noncondescendingly explain why we can't change that aspect of the course. Exactly how to do both these things depends very much on our individual teaching contexts. Some student populations, for some professors, may (incorrectly) see this as a sign of weakness, and therefore we would need to be more discreet in addressing student feedback.

Requesting student feedback at midterm is the bare minimum. Many scholars argue that offering students numerous opportunities to give feedback is foundational to critically reflective teaching and improved teaching and learning. Possible times to solicit student feedback include at the end of the first class, the end of the third week of classes, right after students turn in the first major exam or assignment, and a few weeks before the end of the class.[53] Just as our students need formative assessment on their academic progress to improve their work and to apply our feedback and thus demonstrate progress, so too do we as instructors need formative assessments of teaching in order to make progress. Long before we get to the final SET form at the end of the semester, we need abundant lower-stakes formative assessment before we're hit with high-stakes summative assessment.

Numerous experts assert that repeatedly checking students' point of view is necessary for effective teaching and learning: "The key to being a good college teacher is regularly collecting data from your students concerning how they are learning, week in week out, and then using that information to guide your decisions."[54] "The most important knowledge that skillful teachers need to do good work is a constant awareness of how students are experiencing their learning and perceiving teachers' actions."[55] Effective teachers "continue to mold their courses by accepting student input and respecting student ideas."[56] A "great teacher" is someone who "strives to be a better teacher" by continually "requesting feedback on his/her teaching ability from students."[57]

Our expert blind spot is one of the most important reasons we need to get frequent student feedback.[58] Brookfield calls this the "unacknowledged problem of college teaching: we teach what we love," so "in our soul it is completely incomprehensible that anyone would resist learning something that produces such joy in our own life."[59] Because the novice learner's view of our subject is so different from ours and because we make various assumptions about how students are interacting with course content, we have to make sure continually that they are keeping up with the material. Dorothy Wallace emphasizes that unless you ask students directly, "you don't know what they are thinking. The students look happy and intelligent, but they actually didn't understand anything you just said. . . . [Conversely] they look confused, but actually they just realized what you really meant."[60] Soliciting student feedback early and often is one of the most proactive, productive ways we can ensure that we are actually sharing an exploration of our subject with our students and translating it for them in ways they can learn, thus fostering a geek culture of sharing rather than exclusion. We can create our own types of forms or draw on the SoTL for forms such as the "Classroom Survey of Student Engagement" or the "Classroom Critical Incident Questionnaire."[61] From content learning to incivility (particularly microaggressions between students), checking in with students throughout the semester can significantly decrease the shock and hurt we may experience if we've limited student feedback to summative SET.[62]

READ AND REFLECT ON SUMMATIVE STUDENT EVALUATIONS OF TEACHING WITH ANOTHER PERSON

Once we've received summative SET at the end of the semester, we should try to read, evaluate, and discuss student course evaluations with another educator we like and trust, or in confidence with an educational consultant.[63] This person can help us maintain perspective and increase our ability to disregard deliberately hurtful comments and to recognize reactions to class factors over which we have no control (the class is required for General Education, classroom was too hot, met too early in the morning, and so on). Our co-reader can also help us keep in mind the Murphy's Law effect when it comes to disgruntled students: the one and only time you canceled your office hours because your kid got sick is the one and only time Student So-and-So showed up for office hours and sure enough, they wrote "Never there for office hours." In addition, if our co-reader has some understanding of the broader context of teaching at your institution, they can point out ways that this individual student comment may be less about you specifically and instead a response to a more widespread problem, such as many faculty on campus routinely skipping their posted office hours.[64]

COLLECT FEEDBACK ON TEACHING FROM AS MANY SOURCES AS POSSIBLE

Finally, SET should never be the sole source of any summative assessment of teaching. Instructors in almost all teaching contexts can improve upon their reflective teaching by seeking feedback and assessment from as many sources as possible. The contentious SoTL regarding SET is notably consistent on this point: "Student ratings proponents and researchers unanimously recommend personnel decisions be based on more than just the faculty member's student ratings."[65] As Berk argues, "Given the complexity of measuring the act of teaching in a real-time classroom environment, it is reasonable to expect that *multiple sources can provide a more accurate, reliable, and comprehensive picture of teaching effectiveness than just one source*" (original emphasis).[66] Some of those "multiple sources" include exit or alumni surveys, peer observations of teaching, teaching and learning scholarship, course materials, learning outcome measures, videos, evidence of supportive interactions with students, participation in professional development, and written narratives, including explanations of particular class circumstances.[67] There are many possible avenues to additional feedback and assessment, all of which will enable you to put SET in a broader context, and see it as just one piece in a much bigger picture of your teaching. Organizing such materials into specific course portfolios and general teaching portfolios constitute what many consider the gold standard of reflective teaching practices.[68]

As reflective teachers, we need to incorporate SET as one important but only one of many types of evidence into our documented efforts to approach teaching as an intellectual endeavor. We need to reflect very consciously on what SET can and can't tell us, bringing all our awareness skills to this aspect of teaching and learning. In addition, we also need to be aware of and prepare for how being GINs may impact and influence our SET.

GINs, SET, and Student Perceptions of Teaching

I wish I could carry a big blinking neon sign reading "Nerd Alert" over my head every time I walk into the classroom. When I'm trying my hardest to convey care for student learning and to communicate my expectations, I wish there was some kind of geek-translator feed I could pipe directly into every student's brain. Because I'm an expert and I love my course content, and can get sidetracked into far too many details about it, and also because I'm an introvert who gets tired easily in social interactions, there can be a big gap between what I intend to convey and achieve in the classroom and how students perceive my work in the classroom.

GINs usually have this disadvantage to some degree when it comes to teaching and learning generally and to SET specifically. When grappling with negative SET, sometimes we don't have a teaching problem precisely but rather a communication and perception problem, which *becomes* a teaching problem and hampers student learning. Social awkwardness is social awkwardness and the classroom is a social space requiring positive personal interactions between professors and students.[69] At some point then "perception" becomes "reality." As one study of faculty-student interactions concluded, "For students, perception of faculty often trumps reality."[70] This matters to teaching and learning and it matters very much to SET. Greg Reihman describes this issue:

> If you think you have clear goals but the students think you don't, then the pedagogical benefit of having clear goals is effectively lost and, for all practical purposes, you don't have clear goals. If you are regularly available in your office, have extra office hours during tests, and meet students whenever asked, but still get low numbers [on "Availability" ratings], then the problem may be that students don't know that you are as available as you really are, or they may find it difficult to approach you, in either case, student perception matters and has an impact on how students learn.[71]

If students "don't know you're available" or "find it difficult to approach you," it could easily be about their perception, not what you intend to convey. But if students *perceive* us as unapproachable then we are unapproachable, no matter how much we *feel* like students should be able to approach us.[72]

Student perception comes down to our social and communication skills—not usually our strong suit, considering our big expert blind spots, our need for solitude, and all the other things that go with being a GIN. For all their potential shortcomings as a measure of learning, student evaluations of instructor communication and clarity are a relatively reliable measure of instructor communication skills and clarity.[73] If students perceive you as unclear, then you are not being clear. If they don't understand your expectations, no matter how clearly to your own mind you've explained your expectations, you've communicated ineffectively. Viewing student comments as *perceptions* of our teaching or a *miscommunication* enables us to locate areas where we have been less effective as teachers but not because we didn't try or because there was some deep flaw in our pedagogy or because we can't do it more effectively in the future (employment status permitting). It lessens the sting of negative evaluations by looking to them not necessarily for final and complete assessment of our actual teaching abilities but rather as broad indicators of student perceptions of teaching or reactions to teaching.

GINs often face an uphill battle when it comes to student perceptions. We are extremely smart, a quality highly rewarded in other parts of our profession but sometimes a liability in the classroom. We are used to wielding our brain like a weapon in the face of others' judgments, but that unconscious habit undermines things we have to do when we put on our professor pants and prepare for the social interaction of teaching. And as introverts, sometimes we truly don't want to interact with most other people but more problematically for SET, even when we do, we can *seem* like we don't. We may mumble, avoid eye contact, or blurt out slightly weird comments. We look down at our papers, books, or screens as if we're so absorbed it's impossible for us to tear our eyes away. Student perceptions of and subsequent SET regarding our authenticity and approachability can be a real stumbling block for us. Not because we aren't aware of the need to be authentic or because we haven't prepared for it or because we haven't tried to be effective but rather because what students perceive as "authentic"—being personable, interacting easily with students, expressing concern for their learning, being attentive and available and approachable—can feel unnatural for us and requires a lot of planning and effort.

We therefore have to practice *awareness* and *preparation* for SET assiduously. For example, across many types of classes, student populations, disciplines, and instructors, when professors provide their student with clear, consistently implemented information about assignments and grading, their evaluations improve.[74] Communicating ideas and expectations is one of the few things SoTL agrees upon that teachers can do to help students learn and to improve SET.[75] Even the geekiest nerd who has trouble reading social cues can take the time to provide students with clear assessment criteria and plan for deliberately communicating expectations to students.

Nobody loves reflecting on ways they've fallen short and need to improve, but we can't ignore student feedback or pretend that students never have anything constructive to say about our teaching. Student evaluations of teaching are a flawed mechanism for assessing teaching efficacy, particularly in light of disparate teaching realities, and those flaws are significantly exacerbated by the ways most colleges and universities create, implement, and utilize them. Additionally, we face GIN-specific challenges when it comes to student perceptions and how they impact SET. But we can productively address these issues by cultivating our awareness of the challenges, preparing for them, and then using SET to consciously reflect on our teaching, being sure to draw on other evaluations of our teaching and putting SET in context and looking for patterns, not outlying comments. Most importantly, our reflection practice shouldn't begin and end with SET.

Reflective Pedagogical Practices

"Reflection" is a broad term and can take many different forms, but what all good reflection practices for GINs in academia have in common is that we undertake them deliberately and regularly, and with a specific goal—to increase our efficacy as teachers by increasing student learning.[76] Fortunately, for we who love thinking through problems and analyzing complex issues, incorporating reflection into the work of teaching and learning is closely related to metacognition. Discussing reflective practices for college instructors, Merylann J. Schuttloffel defines reflection as "the process of examining one's own thinking and decision-making prior to taking action."[77] Jennifer A. Moon defines reflection similarly in her work on learning journals: "a form of mental processing with a purpose and/or anticipated outcome that is applied to relatively complex or unstructured ideas for which there is not an obvious solution."[78] When it comes to our scholarly work and research, GINs are irresistibly drawn to "complex or unstructured ideas for which there is not an obvious solution." A reflective pedagogical practice just means viewing teaching and learning as a complex situation without an obvious solution as well.

John Dewey, forefather of modern education, advocated reflective practices in 1933, asserting that "a demand for a solution of a perplexity is the steadying, guiding factor in the entire process of reflection," and that reflection can "transform a situation in which there is experienced obscurity, doubt, conflict, disturbance of some sort into a situation that is clear, coherent, settled, harmonious."[79] When we're honest with ourselves, all teachers face "perplexity, obscurity, doubt, conflict, and disturbance." Hey, if reflection can make teaching and learning a little more "clear" and "harmonious," then sign me up! Reflection, Dewey argued, "gives an individual an increased sense of power" and "emancipates us from merely impulsive and merely routine activity. . . . It converts action that is merely appetitive, blind, and impulsive into intelligent action."[80] Anyone who's been teaching for more than a semester or two has fallen at least occasionally into "merely impulsive and merely routine" activity, and who among us would not enjoy "an increased sense of power" when it comes to teaching and learning?

Reflection is the missing step for many college instructors between encountering teaching and learning problems and dealing effectively with them, because "reflection is the engine that moves the learning cycle along its path to further learning, action, and more reflection. Without it, the learner is 'stuck' in the experience without gaining any new understanding."[81] Evelyn Boyd and Ann Fales identify "reflection" as the "core difference between whether a person repeats the same experience several times, becoming highly proficient at one behavior, or learns from experience in such a way that he or she is cognitively or effectively changed."[82] As Dannelle D. Stevens and Joanne E. Cooper argue, "Reflection is more than merely thinking or musing. Reflection is a complex and intentional intellectual activity that generates learning from experience."[83] Pedagogical reflection enable us to learn and repeatedly relearn how we can best foster student learning—reflection leads to learning which leads to action.

Similarly, in *The Reflective Practitioner*, Donald Schön defines reflection as the key attribute of skillful practice. He argues that "a vital attribute of all effective practitioners, no matter in what area they operate, is that they are able to reflect on their ongoing experience and learn from it," terming this process "reflection in action," distinct from "considered reflection that takes place away from the press of immediate action when we pause and take stock of what we are doing."[84] Schön's distinction between "reflection-in-action" and "reflection-on-action" is useful for building pedagogical reflective practices, suggesting that when we want to be effective teachers, reflection will occur both during our teaching and interactions with students and also when we are not actually teaching but "taking the unprocessed, raw material of experience and engaging with it as a way to make sense of what has occurred . . . exploring often messy and confused events and focusing on the thoughts and emotions that accompany them."[85]

For GINs who want to be effective teachers, reflective practices serve a vital function by enabling and empowering us to approach our time in the classroom and our interactions with students as an opportunity to *think*. Which we love to do. Our GIN-ness can also be an asset when we "pause and take stock" in a systematic way and try to "make sense" of the more amorphous, "often messy and confused," events of our unique teaching context and the "thoughts and emotions"—ours and our students'—arising out of educational experiences. We're good at probing ideas and considering different avenues. We readily do it in our scholarly fields. When we engage in pedagogical reflection, we apply our thinking superpowers to reflecting on our own teaching efficacy, applying the high metacognition skills we regularly use in other aspects of our work to our teaching and learning.[86] One group of pedagogical scholars describes this process as being a teacher-researcher "wrestling with the hard questions about our classrooms," striving to "habituate weaving the analytical and theoretical with the practical so that these remain integrated in our practice and we continue to learn and grow as teachers."[87] As teacher-researchers of our unique teaching context, we can more productively "wrestle with the hard questions" and combine "the analytical and theoretical with the practical" if we view our teaching and learning experiences as another opportunity for us to apply our intellectual curiosity to understanding what we and our students experience day to day.

As we'll see in chapter 4, SoTL is one of the best ways to engage in critically reflective teaching by joining the larger conversation about teaching and learning, both from a multidisciplinary perspective as well as in your own specific discipline.[88] But in addition to SoTL, we need to be able to locate opportunities for reflection in our daily teaching context. For instance, one such reflective practice is to make notes and comments on a copy of our syllabus after class meetings, while grading assignments, and after student interactions. As Marilyn Roberts writes about this reflective process, thinking of our "syllabus as a document in process rather than a finished text" fosters a sense of researching our own individual teaching context.[89] A reflective pedagogical process need not be unduly laborious or time consuming. It can be as simple as making notes on a syllabus or keeping a running list of what's going well and what's not based on summaries of class meetings and student work. It doesn't have to be a major chore or take up big chunks of our time, especially if we use an app or other tech incorporated easily into our daily routine.[90]

Written reflection can be particularly useful for introverts and academics who like to use writing for thinking. For this reason, some find that writing a statement of one's teaching philosophy can be a reflective practice.[91] Others keep a teaching journal.[92] Forget the "Dear Diary, today Tommy said hi to me in study hall!" stereotype about journaling. A journal can be part of an intellectual approach to teaching—a "device for working with events and experiences in order to extract meaning from them," and then translating reflection into action.[93] Written reflection need not add hours of work to what we're already doing to prepare for class, lead class, and assess student work. For example, it's easy to switch into autopilot when grading exams and papers. But consider incorporating reflection into this process by selecting and keeping copies of the best exams or the best papers, using these samples to reflect on what exactly students learned how to do in your class and as evidence for research into your own teaching context. Less pleasantly, but also usefully, if a particular assignment didn't work well, keeping a sample will allow you to reflect more clearly on what went wrong and hopefully what adjustments you can make in the future.

There are also additions we can make to students' classroom activities that provide opportunities for reflection—activities that don't make a lot more work for us or for our students and might actually foster some reflection on the students' part as well. For instance, the end of the semester activities discussed in the last chapter can advance students' understanding of their own learning and may also give you an idea of what students are taking away from your class, thus creating an opportunity to reflect on your teaching. Sometimes if my teaching load allows for it, I require students to meet with me one-on-one at the end of the semester and reflect on what they've learned how to do over the course of the class. We might administer some type of brief learning evaluation at the beginning of class and then the same one at the end and compare them. We may be assessing student content or skill learning but we're *also* using these assignments and feedback from students to add to our knowledge about effective teaching in our specific context.

Building our pedagogical knowledge through reflection keeps us focused on continuing to improve and to reframe our mistakes as learning opportunities. We anticipate that our students will make mistakes, knowing that getting it wrong and then struggling to correct mistakes is an essential part of learning. We know how to do the things we're teaching students to do but we are also still learning—*because everyone is always still learning*—how to teach our subject effectively. So we *will* make mistakes. Reflective practices empower us to be able to learn from our missteps. You flubbed a lecture, miscalculated students' previous knowledge, or repelled students during your office hours instead of welcoming the chance to communicate one-on-one? Stop berating yourself or your students and instead give yourself an "A+" for learning something new about how to increase your efficacy. (This is with the caveat that mistakes obviously have consequences, and without job security, reframing teaching "mistakes" as "learning opportunities" will be far more difficult.) The messy, emotional parts of teaching and learning are never more evident than when the learner has to grapple with failures and mistakes, and "learner" means all of us. Nobody likes to think about the things they could have done better. Reflective practices offer us a way to mitigate our own defensiveness, hurt feelings, embarrassment, or arrogance and view our teaching as an interesting opportunity for examining problems and making improvements.

More than any specific technique or "trick," and more than any single personality quality, reflection separates the effective from the ineffective college teacher. Instead of trying to find a shortcut or a magic pedagogical formula, argues K. D. Tanner, we should instead "refocus on what has been shown again and again to be the path to effective teaching and learning: the development of reflective instructors who are analytical about their practice and who make iterative instructional decisions based on evidence from students sitting right in front of them."[94] Similarly, Daniel D. Pratt asserts that the ability to "thoughtfully revisit assumptions and beliefs [we] hold regarding learning, knowledge, and teaching" is "what faculty development should be rather than the mastery of technique."[95] This holds as true for brand new teachers as for experienced practitioners who may be operating on years of assumptions that should be reexamined. Our teaching context is always changing because students change, curriculum changes, and we change. Reflection allows us to keep approaching teaching and learning as interesting sites of investigation for us as teacher-researchers.

Bringing awareness and then reflection to teaching, you will probably begin to notice—if you are paying close attention—that a lot of other factors besides your actual work as a teacher go into the overall success of a class. Careful reflection may show you that what you thought was an awful *class* is in fact just *one* troubled student making it unpleasant for everyone. Your attention is being sucked up by the difficult and demanding and is being drained away from the good and the rewarding. Which brings us to a reflection practice that I believe you should consider doing, no matter how much your analytical intellectual self resists its Oprah-esque overtones: gratitude.

GINs and Gratitude

During my first year of full-time teaching on the tenure track, I was so worried about negative student encounters that I kept a grim journal summarizing every even slightly uncomfortable interaction with a student, just in case I would need documentation for my review file.

Paranoid? Yes, a little. On the other hand, a tenure track job is very possibly a once-in-a-lifetime opportunity. I wasn't wrong to be on the lookout for the many ways that the teaching-learning process can be a fraught one and could negatively affect my career. But there was a big problem with my logbook of teaching woes. At the end of the year, I had a detailed list of everything that went wrong or was discomforting and unpleasant. What was missing was every single thing that went *right*: when students learned how to do something, when I received a compliment, and when I enjoyed a particular discussion and saw that many of the students got something out of it.[96] Which, by the way, happened a lot more often than the bad stuff. But what did I put down in writing so I could read it over and over again and *feel* it all over again, chipping away at my confidence, optimism, and desire to be an effective teacher? To color how I saw all my future classes and future students? All the worst stuff. Every distressing, demoralizing moment.

An especially important and useful reflection practice we can bring to our teaching is gratitude.[97] I know that may sound like hooey to many intellectuals—a "count your blessings" inanity in the face of injustice and inequity.[98] But a plethora of studies in psychology, medicine, counseling, and education demonstrate that some type of gratitude practice has a proven positive impact on people's quality of life.[99] Gratitude can be incorporated into scholarly, reflective pedagogy, and instructors who do it regularly see practical, concrete results such as improving our teaching efficacy, increasing student learning, and decreasing teaching-related stress and burnout. I use the phrase "do it" deliberately because simply *feeling* gratitude is not especially effective and being forced or obligated to "feel grateful" really doesn't work. Rather, gratitude begins as an inner attitude and leads to an expression of thanks—taking an action—towards someone or something.[100] It means recognizing what you received from another person or from the circumstances in which you're living. For some people this may involve a deity, but even the most ardent atheist can include gratitude as part of reflective teaching and learning because cultivating gratitude—like all other aspects of teaching and learning—is unique to every individual teaching context.

As convincingly elucidated in Kerry Howells's innovative *Gratitude in Education*, in the context of teaching the most effective gratitude practice is the recognition of the gifts we receive as teachers and acknowledgment of those gifts, without expecting anything in return, no strings attached. Howells offers this new paradigm, the "gift paradigm," to replace the highly problematic "exchange paradigm" (or consumerist model) of education.[101] In the gift paradigm of education, teaching and learning advance knowledge through a series of gifts given and received by students and educators in community. Being the cerebral GIN you are, maybe this sounds antithetical to critical thinking and infeasible in any case. After all, many aspects of academia and teaching actively foster conditions that create *ingratitude*. Even the most accomplished and evolved student is not necessarily going to shower you with thanks. Being fully appreciated by all your students for all the work you do to help them learn is just never going to happen. "Gee willikers, Professor, thanks so much for providing me with the opportunity to earn a failing grade! I've really learned a lot about self-regulation and personal responsibility from this 'F' and I'm going to take my academic endeavors much more seriously from now on! You're the best!"

Negative student emotion is only one way that academia fosters the exact opposite of gratitude in its participants. Think about your learned colleagues. By and large, are they happy-go-lucky people, with a spring in their step and an affirmation on their lips? Or are they cranky, hypercritical eggheads with years of training and experience in picking apart arguments, ideas, and other people? Do they regularly express gratitude towards their students or complain frequently about how dumb, ill prepared, and a total waste of space students are? Do the crotchety tenured silverbacks in your department routinely express gratitude for the enormous privilege of earning a living with their mind or do they continually lament how overworked they are and how underappreciated? Don't even get me started on administrators. When was the last time a dean or VP at your university expressed gratitude, with no strings attached, for those of us laboring in the learning mines? Then there's the public at large. Do you often see commentary from Joe Citizen or Senator Big Shot about the great job we're doing in higher education? Do a lot of people talk about how much time, energy, and care we college teachers pour into helping students learn? No, no, and *hell* no.

How, in this seething caldron of negativity, resentment, and complaint, are we supposed to practice gratitude? Why would we even want to if it's going to turn us into brainless Pollyannas who can't see the reality of the caldron in which we're being boiled alive? The biggest misconception about a gratitude practice is that it's just "positive thinking," or blinding oneself to the unpleasant or the negative, creating passivity and acceptance of the status quo, including inequality or injustice. But remember chapter 1? Gratitude, like awareness, isn't the end of your actions, a final gesture that shuts down all agency or accountability. Looking for the good or "gift" in any situation never means ignoring or dismissing the negative or trying to put "a positive veneer over a negative situation."[102] In fact, it means seeing all aspects of every situation fully. It's easy to get trapped in futile complaining (as opposed to thoughtful critiques spurring subsequent change and action) when we're facing the same student issues year after year, or employment insecurity, or disparate teaching realities. Gratitude practices shift us out of that trap by expanding our view of our situation. Far from encouraging passivity, awareness and gratitude can force us to move out of Resentmentville and into Reality Town.[103]

Where is the gift in teaching and learning? I'm not talking about being showered with manna from heaven. I mean little daily things. For example, Howells discusses a teacher working in an especially toxic environment who was experiencing major stress and burnout. When pressed, this teacher could think of only one thing every day that felt like a gift: the beautiful tree growing outside her office, a pleasure to look at every morning.[104] Trees or nature may not be your thing (I'm more of an indoor cat myself), but for this person, the tree was a gift bestowed with no strings attached, just there for her to enjoy. By recognizing a gift, and the action of acknowledging and marking the gift with some type of action—even just saying to oneself "I'm grateful for that tree, thanks tree!"—this person adds something positive to her teaching context.

I know that sounds sort of dopey, but extensive research on our brains, psyches, and emotions proves that regularly acknowledging and expressing gratitude for the tree outside her office can only benefit this teacher. The teacher didn't do anything to "deserve" that tree. There's no pressure to feel indebted to the tree. It's just there, and the teacher can be grateful for it and express her gratitude with no expectations of anything further. It won't make her toxic work environment less toxic. The toxicity is real. But then again, so is the tree. That tiny moment of gratitude is not a magic *replacement* but rather a real and important *addition* to her working reality. When teaching it's easy to spot the negative. It takes conscious effort to pay attention to the positive, and an even more concerted effort to perceive these positive things as a gift. But by making that reflective effort, we force ourselves to pay attention to what's working well. It's a fact of the human psyche, perhaps an evolutionary tic, that our attention is much more readily drawn by the negative than the positive.[105] Quick, name the student last semester who gave you the biggest headache. You knew it immediately, without even trying, right? Now, name a solid "B" student who did fine, was kind of quiet but now that you think back, seemed to have actually learned something. That one is harder to recall. Your lizard brain paid a lot more attention to the student who elicited negative emotions and your attendant physical responses.

Donald G. Schoffstall describes how he has learned to reflect more consciously on positive aspects of teaching by keeping an easily accessed folder labeled "Good Stuff." It contains email messages, feedback forms, and other examples of ways he has facilitated student learning that help counteract the impact of a "frustrating day or troubled class."[106] Similarly, Pat Whitfield recommends creating a "Be Kind Portfolio" for ourselves, organizing and making readily accessible the thank you notes, certificates, "all the material culture" encompassing "the little but tangible things that demonstrate our success—and those of our students." Whitfield calls this a "magic bag to dip into" on particularly discouraging days.[107] Paying more attention to what is going *right*, what we're doing right, doesn't mean ignoring the things that go wrong. On the teaching and learning roller coaster over the course of a term or even in a single class meeting there will be gifts and there will be problems. One doesn't cancel out the other, but most of us have a lot more practice at noticing and paying attention to the problems. Acknowledging the gifts that we receive as teachers balances this tendency and alerts us to what is working well.

For instance, let's say a student asks you a great question or makes a great point during class. Because you want to be an effective teacher, you praise the student, giving positive reinforcement for good academic work, helping them to continue it and demonstrating to other students how to keep learning and improving. That's effective pedagogy! But take another look at that moment. There's also a gift here. That good question is positive reinforcement for you as well. It shows you that the student is listening, participating, and responding. It helps you to teach effectively and to better facilitate learning for all the students. There's the gift. You could say, "Well, that's just what they're *supposed* to be doing as students. It's not a gift to me!" That's true, but limiting ourselves to this kind of thinking just builds up resentment about everything students don't do and how hard and thankless our jobs are, and so on. If we plan on becoming embittered and disempowered as teachers, that's a good start. Instead, try to remember that we have big brains and we can effortlessly hold onto two contradictory ideas at once: Idea #1: student is doing their job. Idea #2: student just gave us a gift.

Adding "gift" to the mix is not fooling ourselves into seeing something that's not there. Just the opposite. It makes us more aware of the entire situation. Acknowledging the gifts we receive as teachers helps to clear our minds of habitual complaining and resentment, giving us a more complete picture of the reality.[108] If this still sounds too woo-woo, look at it through the science of physics. A black hole grows the more objects it absorbs.[109] The physics of teaching is the same. Feed your teaching with negativity and bitterness, and negativity and bitterness grow. For example, although it has increased in recent years, the plague of academic entitlement manifests in only a small minority of students. Yet as one group of researchers rightly points out, these students "require a far greater portion of our time and energy."[110] A minority of students, even a single problem student, can easily suck up all our time and energy if we allow it, and pretty soon that's all we're thinking about when we're thinking about teaching.

Will there be treacherous forces, evil intentions, and recurring issues such as academic entitlement, student apathy, department feuds, and budget cuts? Of course. But can we counteract the power of the Dark Side with the light saber of gratitude? Yes, Padawan, we can. The key is to start small and easy. One of the biggest misunderstandings about gratitude practices is that if we don't feel grateful at all times and all situations, we're not doing it right. Give me a break! We're not aiming for sainthood, and we for sure don't need to struggle with yet another standard or protocol imposed on our already heavy workload. Gratitude shouldn't be a top-down imposition. Also, if you've got perfectionist tendencies, fight your natural inclination to view gratitude as a mystical state of grace that you can only do if you do it wonderfully well every single moment of your life. Some days you'll find a gift with ease and other days you won't, and that's okay.

Here are three examples of simple ways most instructors in most teaching contexts—don't limit yourself to your classes—can recognize one small moment of gratitude and then build on it toward a more general gratitude practice:

EXAMPLE #1

A student arrives to your 8:00 a.m. class on time, awake, and ready to participate productively. That's the gift and you act on it by greeting the student with eye contact, saying their name, and expressing gratitude for their preparedness. You can build this into a gratitude practice by greeting all students at the beginning of class, consciously and deliberately.[111] Try saying something like "Thanks for being here" or "It's good to see you here today." If in your heart of hearts, you truly wish they had all stayed home, don't force yourself to pretend that you're grateful they're in class, but also don't discount the power of practice. Sometimes I start my greeting without really "feeling" grateful but just by taking one second to say it, I shift my outlook: "Today's class is going to be pretty interesting. I guess I am kind of looking forward to it after all."

EXAMPLE #2

When one of your favorite students asks you for a recommendation letter, send an unofficial copy to the student along with your thanks for the rewarding experience of being their teacher. You know the kind of student I'm talking about here: the one you were always happy to see in class because they had a genuine interest in your arcane field or they exhibited the kind of intellect and leadership that could elevate a whole class or they overcame truly daunting odds to succeed. In whatever way they gifted you with moments of teaching happiness, saying thank you to that student could be the start of a gratitude practice recognizing and personally thanking students who make teaching fun. Your first reaction might be that such students are rare, but once we get into a habit of looking for and recognizing them, we will almost certainly find them. In the words of Thorin Oakenshield, to find something, you have to look for it.

EXAMPLE #3

Your department's administrative assistant helps you sort out a bureaucratic tangle regarding conference travel or classroom assignment. Send them a thank you note or email. Some professors are oblivious to the work of administrative and nonteaching staff, yet all students and faculty depend on them for effective teaching and learning.[112] It's not difficult to express gratitude to those who maintain facilities, schedule classes, assist in administrative tasks, and the like. It's especially important if you've fallen into the bad habit of avoiding contact with nonteaching staff unless something has gone wrong or you need something. Try instead to build a gratitude practice that includes expressing appreciation for things going well. This is useful for when every single student has gotten on your last nerve and teaching seems like torture. Where's the gift? Maybe a clean office, the well-organized mailroom, quick turnaround on a printing or copying job, and so on.

Gratitude can benefit our mental health but it can also improve our teaching efficacy. Here's a common scenario: A student who has been doing poorly all semester comes to our office to complain about their grade.[113] If we consciously look for the gift in the situation, what could we find? How could we act on and express our gratitude, and also foster student learning? Well, to start with, the student is expressing a desire—however inarticulately, misguided, or mistaken—to learn and succeed in your class. Try saying to the student: "Thank you for taking the time to come here and talk to me and showing me that you want to succeed in this class." Does this sound insincere? Maybe, but the more we say it, the more easily and naturally it will come. Saying it makes it truer, or at least true-ish. No matter how whiney and irresponsible they are being, it is *also* a fact that the student made the time to come to your office. In a world where teenagers communicate mostly through texting and social media, this student actually looked up from their phone and is now speaking words to you. Take the gift.

Here's another possible gift: the student is giving us an opportunity to do meaningful work. It can feel degrading to be forced to wrangle with a student about a grade, especially for scholarly geeks who are most comfortable in the lofty world of ideas rather than the grubby reality of grades. But in the broader context of labor and capitalism, and even in exploitative contingent positions, this is work that really means something, and that's a gift. Teaching and learning is always an important endeavor. We can't express our gratitude for this directly to the student. An upset student doesn't want to hear that their personal turmoil and academic failure is giving existential meaning to our paycheck. But we can express it, either by saying so explicitly to ourselves or writing it down in a gratitude journal. I must emphasize that a gratitude journal doesn't have to be filled with platitudes or saccharine affirmations. It's simply a record of what's going *right*. Stuff going right always occurs, even if only in limited ways, in every single teaching and learning context. It doesn't cancel out the problems, but stuff does go right and keeping a written record of it expands our powers of observation and our ability to reflect productively on teaching and learning.

Yet another possible gift: the student is giving us the opportunity to reflect on our assessment mechanisms. We may conclude that our assignments, rubrics, and grading process are working just fine but we've taken the opportunity to reflect, using evidence from this interaction as part of our ongoing research into our own teaching context. Or maybe the student's reaction is evidence not of a flaw in our grading criterion but rather a need for better communication. In either case, reviewing our assessment mechanisms after a grading dispute with a student can be undertaken as a gratitude practice if we can lose the hyper-defensiveness and instead try to see this as an opportunity for continuing to gather data and information about our teaching context. In all cases, a gratitude practice can fuel our ability to foster student learning in this situation. Recognizing the gift in their concern about their grade and thus increasing our ability to act rather than react results in our increased ability to help students learn. Building confidence in our teaching by seeing what's going well results in greater teaching self-efficacy.

For GINs, a reflective gratitude practice can contribute to student learning because it helps to balance out the other taxing things we do in order to be effective teachers.[114] For us, just making sure we are approachable can be a huge depletion of our vitality. Meeting a bunch of new people every single time we begin a new class is a major drain on our energy supplies. Communicating clearly with students is no simple task for us, yet we have to do it over and over again. Putting on our professor pants, getting out of our geek-exclusion mode of thinking about our subjects, pushing through our blind spots: all these things take a toll on us, even when we enjoy many aspects of teaching. A gratitude practice helps us see that in addition to the many things we have to *give* to our work as teachers and which deplete our personal resources, we also *receive*. Gratitude practices as part of our reflective pedagogy can refill our mental and physical teaching tanks.

Moreover, incorporating gratitude into our teaching reflections can improve our ability to convey to students our enthusiasm for our topic and for student learning. For example, as previously mentioned, one way students recognize an instructor's enthusiasm is perceiving a professor is "happy when class begins."[115] Gratitude is one of the best ways to get us to a place where we can show that we are indeed happy when class begins. If for no other reason, the fact that gratitude increases our ability to demonstrate enthusiasm for teaching is a compelling and practical impetus for incorporating gratitude into reflective pedagogy. When we are deliberately keeping track of what's going right, it's much easier to approach a class meeting positively. When we are practicing feeling grateful for what we receive from students (again, without glossing over or ignoring reality), we are empowered as introverts who have a hard time peopling in any context to get out of our heads and do the necessary social interacting effective teaching requires.

The most successful conference presentation I ever gave at a teaching conference was about gratitude practices. The GINs in the standing-room-only audience radiated an almost palpable desire for cultivating gratitude as part of teaching. The pressures at most universities these days—budget cuts, declining enrollments, racial and political tensions, administrative bloat, disparate teaching realities, ad nauseam—contribute to this hunger. But so too does just being a GIN who wants to be an effective teacher. We love our topics so much, yet often struggle to translate them to students and to engage students in what to us is so meaningful and important. We really want our students to learn, but sometimes we don't clearly communicate that desire. We think they're learning, then discover that they're not, or at least not as much as we'd hoped. We thought we were being approachable and friendly only to discover that some students didn't perceive us that way at all. We're isolated in our echo chamber of a classroom and in academia, which often frames teaching as a strictly solo endeavor. Gratitude practices aren't a magic trick for eliminating such challenges, but they are a powerful tool. When the Shelobs of teaching and learning loom above us, threatening to poison all our pedagogical endeavors, gratitude can be our Light of Eärendil.

Conclusion

One simply siphons the excess thoughts from one's mind, pours them into the basin, and examines them at one's leisure.
—Albus Dumbledore, *Harry Potter and the Goblet of Fire*

————

Of all the wonderful magical objects in the Potterverse (Floo powder! Room of Requirement! Invisibility Cloak!) the one I would use most frequently as a teacher is the Pensieve. If only there were a way to take all the fast-moving events of every class and student interaction, and all my thoughts and emotions about those events, and pour them into a basin to examine at my leisure. Pedagogical reflection for Muggles is more complicated. We have to undertake it deliberately and to create and maintain ways and means for reflection—before, during, and after teaching—in our pedagogical practices. We face not just individual (lack of time, for example) but also institutional (limited support for any reflective pedagogy beyond SET, for instance) roadblocks to creating and maintaining a reflective pedagogical practice.[116] In addition, without establishing clear goals for our reflective practices as practitioners of our discipline, our reflection will stall. On the other hand, if reflection narrows down to solely focusing on purely pragmatic techniques, we lose out on the many ways reflection can lead to deeper meaning in teaching and learning.[117] And then of course there's the *really* hard part: we have put any insights we've gained by undertaking pedagogical reflection into action.

Only by repeatedly reflecting and acting can we keep improving both aspects of effective teaching, as Steven and Cooper state: "Learning from experience requires shuttling back and forth from observations, to examination and reflection on those observations, and then acting on those conclusions. The more people reflect on action, the better they get at reflecting and the more they can learn about themselves."[118] The only way to get better at putting reflection into action is to keep *putting reflection into action.* We have to keep getting feedback, gathering our own observations, and reflecting on our experiences of teaching and learning in order to act on our conclusions—before, during, and after every teaching experience.

This applies as equally to new teachers as to experienced teachers. Without ongoing reflection, our expert blind spots and our assumptions—our previous knowledge—keep us from acquiring new information, understanding, and knowledge.[119] The realities of teaching and learning are always changing and no matter how aware we are, or how much we prepare, if we fail to reflect on what we're experiencing, we will miss problems and issues we need to address. Resentment flourishes when we fail to reflect on our teaching experiences, especially if we never make an effort to foster gratitude. Resentment toward our colleagues, administrators, and most of all, students. Like my colleagues at the teaching workshop wounded by student comments on their SET, when we feel powerless in the face of teaching and learning challenges and fail to approach it with our researcher's curiosity and a desire to productively reflect on our teaching experiences, it's all too easy to become mired in resentment or anger, obscuring the reality of the problem and forestalling any productive action, and then we're well on our way to case of full-blown burnout.[120]

Preventing burnout with reflection and action is a process we have to create for ourselves because in most day-to-day ways, college teaching can be an isolating experience. We get a lot of peer review on our scholarly research, but actionable feedback on teaching is all too rare. So rare that SET takes on disproportionate importance, which can be a real pitfall for GINs. That's why it's essential to incorporate numerous other types of reflection into our own assessment and outside assessment of our teaching. To empower us to *act* as a teacher rather than *react*, I believe this should include some type of gratitude practice, in whatever form best complements your individual teaching context. College teaching may be a "closed door" job in numerous ways but we are not trapped in a Fortress of Solitude, alone in a howling pedagogical wilderness. Indeed, all of the things effective teachers do that we've discussed so far—awareness, preparation, and reflection—require support from our colleagues and peers.

What does this support look like? Onward to chapter 4.

CHAPTER 4

SUPPORT

I don't think I can survive this place on my own.

—Science Specialist Michael Burnham,
"The Wolf Inside," *Star Trek: Discovery*

———

WHEN the Center for Teaching Excellence opened on my campus, I was the first in line for a consultation. I found a teaching mentor in the center's director, Dr. Becky Kasper. Becky gave me a lot of good advice about teaching, but she said one thing that didn't make sense: "You have a confidence problem. You question and doubt yourself. Try telling yourself right before you go into class, 'I am a great teacher.'" Huh? I didn't need some sappy self-affirmation! I felt completely confident. I liked my students, felt supported by my department, and earned solidly positive SET. Sure, I wanted to keep improving my teaching, that's why I went to the CTE in the first place. But a "confidence problem"? No way. Not me.

I never credited Becky's comment about my confidence level in the classroom. When I won the SUNY Chancellor's Award for Teaching Excellence a decade later, I was honored but not shocked. "I've earned this," I said to myself, complacently. When the university president announced the honorees at commencement, I calmly stood to acknowledge the recognition. At that moment, five words scrolled across my mind's eye, and I heard them as clearly as if they'd been spoken aloud: "*I don't deserve this award.*" Rising up from my subconscious where it had been festering all along, my deep-seated confidence problem emerged in full force to mar a crowning moment of teaching achievement. Yet nothing in my own perceptions and evaluations of my teaching or my feelings about teaching suggested to me that a lack of confidence might be undermining my efforts to help students learn. That insight had to come from someone else.

Having self-determination in our classroom work is one of the greatest privileges college teachers enjoy. It's also one of the biggest impediments to effective teaching and learning because everyone at one time or another needs the perspective, expertise, and insights of other people in order to keep improving. Or rather, we need these things without a sharpened sword of employment decision hanging over our necks. If the only conversation we ever have with anyone about our teaching is part of the hiring, rehiring, or tenure process, that's a very limited conversation. If it's part of an employment decision, we can't bounce ideas around, debate pedagogical approaches, freely admit mistakes or areas we could improve, or simply brainstorm with another teacher. And yet this is the very thing most likely to promote effective teaching and learning: giving teachers time and opportunity to observe other teachers, to discuss teaching with other teachers, and to reflect carefully and honestly on their teaching. But the strictures of academia at most colleges and universities do little or nothing to create such opportunities and the activity of teaching itself takes place in a bubble of sacrosanct academic independence.

Academic freedom is one thing, and floundering around trying singlehandedly to navigate and succeed at the incredibly complicated assortment of activities, emotions, and intellectual processes lumped together as "teaching and learning" is another. Our teaching context will very much shape how we seek out support, information, and opportunities to engage with other educators, to learn from them and maybe pass on our own hard-earned wisdom as well, but seek it out we must. This is an essential pedagogical practice for anyone teaching college classes and it takes some psychological effort to get started because we first have to break out of the academic mindset that prizes *individual* brilliance and achievement above all. Competition in the Ivory Tower is merciless. We apply for jobs in a Hunger Games hellscape where individuals must mercilessly fight for an infinitesimal number of tenure track jobs. We apply for funding and publish books and pursue research by and large as individuals, and reap the awards or suffer the setbacks as individuals. We're not supposed to need help to be excellent scholars. We often make the same assumption about teaching.

This chapter does not address personal and professional support for work-life balance, underrepresented faculty, or legal support via campus offices such as Affirmative Action or employee unions.[1] Rather, it focuses on how anyone seeking to continue improving teaching and learning can and should draw on the available resources on campus, at conferences, and in the scholarship of teaching and learning. We can tailor such support to our personalities, disciplinary fields of study, student population, available time, and employment status, but as GINs, no matter what our teaching context, we often struggle with that first essential step in seeking support for teaching and learning. As introverts, we have to gear ourselves up for interaction. As nerds and geeks, we have to admit that even with our supersized brains and intellectual prowess, we can't do it all on our own. The practices I discussed in the previous chapters—awareness, preparation, and reflection—can be improved significantly if we undertake them while simultaneously actively garnering support for those practices. Learning and relearning how to be effective teachers cannot take place in a vacuum: we need support to do it well.

Teaching Centers, Peers, and Mentors

My positive experience with a campus center for teaching and learning (CTL) is not unusual. These increasingly common centers range in size, professionalism, and staff but are almost always our most valuable resource for teaching and learning support. Staff can provide services ranging from individual syllabus consultations and class visitations to department consultations and campus workshops.[2] Staff are also indispensable to productive usage and management of SET, including administering midterm evaluations and discussing possible course adjustments, eliciting other types of feedback from students, and helping us respond effectively to and providing dispassionate outside perspective on summative SET.

In this way, CTLs can contribute to all three of the effective teaching practices discussed in the previous chapters. Staff members will understand the realities of our student populations and campus culture, helping us to become fully *aware* of our teaching context. They will be up to date on SoTL and can provide resources for all aspects of our *preparation*, from basic essentials like effective learning assessment mechanisms or utilizing technology in the classroom to putting on our professor pants—building rapport, demonstrating approachability, and preparing for positive student interactions. Finally, a CTL can be our best immediate help for *reflection,* particularly but not limited to interpreting SET.

Importantly, in virtually all cases we can access their services confidentially. This feature is crucial to the utility of teaching centers because unfortunately in many departments at many colleges, openly stating, "I could use support and assistance in improving my teaching and my students' learning" is tantamount to saying "I'm not a good teacher," even though the exact opposite is true. Fortunately, in twenty-first-century academia we are slowly but increasingly able to acknowledge that accessing support for teaching and learning is not an admission of weakness or lack of skill. Even highly experienced and effective college teachers with tenure have a lot to gain from CTL services, since we all have to keep learning and relearning how to remain effective in the classroom.[3] For those in more precarious employment situations, the teaching center is still the best bet for confidential assistance in improving teaching and learning, not least because a CTL helps us identify what we are already doing well. They will find something, I promise.

And when they find areas where we could improve student learning? Ideally, we know we need support for good teaching, have dialed down our defensiveness, and are ready for thoughtful, well-informed feedback about our teaching. The CTL will help us articulate our questions and continue to advance our knowledge and our individual awareness, preparation, and reflective practices. It may sting a bit to hear that your cherished decade-old lecture about imperialism and racism in late nineteenth-century American political cartoons is too long. (Yes, I'm talking about myself and yes, unnamed CTL consultant, this is me admitting you were right.) But if given in the context of a good consultation, in the spirit of improving teaching and reflection on teaching, and alongside identifying all the things we're doing effectively, the constructive criticism we risk by seeking support from a CTL will not be overwhelming. Even if they have significantly bad news to deliver, a good CTL will offer suggestions and strategies for improving and moving forward.

It can be useful to think of seeking support from CTL as an activity undertaken with what Buddhists call Beginner's Mind: approaching our experiences with an open-minded curiosity and in the spirit of discovery. Instead of assuming we always have all the answers (a common symptom of Professoritis), we assume that there's always more to learn and relearn. When we're in a beginner's frame of mind, we ask, in any situation, what's happening here? We approach it with open-minded curiosity. As scholars of our own teaching, we can utilize the resources of a CTL to help delve into the problems and puzzles we encounter in the classroom and during our interactions with students.

One of the most essential functions of a CTL can be organizing and facilitating both systematic as well as casual conversations among faculty about teaching. Awareness, preparation, and some kinds of reflection can be effectively fostered on our own. But these are always evolving practices that need regular infusions of knowledge and information, not just from our own research and intellectual work but also from the research and intellectual work of others, especially those teaching and learning in the same campus culture as we are. Reflection on our own is important, but reflection with other teachers is also essential.[4] Simply getting together with other teachers and talking about teaching bolsters our self-efficacy in the classroom and improves our teaching.[5] This will look different depending on employment status and other aspects of our individual teaching context, but for almost all of us, just talking about teaching and watching someone else teach makes us more effective teachers.[6] Whatever the mechanism, whether informal conversations or peer review or teaching portfolios or organized communities of inquiry, support for improving teaching is, at its heart, teachers talking to other teachers about teaching.[7]

Such conversations can take a wide variety of forms, from faculty learning communities to teaching squares to peer observations and

review.[8] Again and again, professors report that "communities of practice" and networks of support for teaching, tailored to address their
specific teaching context, improve their own individual teaching efficacy.[9] Peer review is the standard for all our other scholarly work and
it should be the standard for effective teaching as well, in both informal
and formal structures.[10] Traditional modes of scholarship—presentations and publications—can provide peer review about teaching, as
discussed in the next section. But we can also create avenues for peer
review in our specific teaching contexts. One participant in a teaching
circle described this process:

> I will always remember a colleague's comment in one teaching circle
> that we need to uphold standards of teaching in the same way we up-
> hold standards of scholarship, which means being willing to point out
> when certain practices are not good enough. The purpose is not to
> rate other teachers or pedagogical theories, but to help instructors
> improve and teach more effectively.[11]

This participant rightly notes that the purpose of any type of teaching
peer review is not to "rate" other teaching faculty. We have to tap ever
so gently on the closed-door part of college teaching because GINs are
sensitive flowers when it comes to their teaching. Supportive networks
like teaching circles need to emphasize continually that their goal is improving teaching and learning, not sitting in judgment of one another.[12]
As the same participant noted: "At their best, TCs served as a kind of
peer review of teaching practices. It took considerable self-conscious
humility—not any academic's strong suit—to submit one's practices to
peers and listen to their feedback."[13] Indeed, one of the biggest roadblocks to productive conversations about teaching and learning is how
difficult it can be to get teaching faculty to accept the premise that
we ourselves are all always learning and relearning how to best foster
student learning.

Additionally, clarity regarding disparate teaching realities must be
part of any campus teaching peer review process and support structures.
Systematic support for improved teaching must include a thorough
understanding of what kinds of teaching and learning (and subsequent
SET) challenges face female faculty and all faculty of color.[14] In this

sense, support may be even more crucial for faculty of color in order to navigate college teaching successfully and to develop pedagogical awareness, preparation, and reflection:

> The current sink or swim approach to learning the craft of teaching in the academy may contribute to low retention rates for scholars of color in graduate education and among academicians. That is, the preparation of future and current faculty of color should address all dimensions of their training as teacher/scholars, including the possibility of teaching and conducting research at PWCUs with resistant students or colleagues.[15]

The "preparation of future and current faculty of color" for effective teaching and learning at primarily white institutions would be significantly improved by campus support and published SoTL that clearly addresses the "special classroom challenges" and the lived experiences of faculty of color.[16]

For all of us, participating in a group like a learning community or teaching circle can help identify the individuals on our campus who are most interested in supporting good teaching and learning. As introverts, it takes effort to reach out to the other GINs around us, introduce ourselves, and network. But if we can break out of our self-imposed isolation, we may be able to work with colleagues to create systems of feedback and support for teaching and learning. It's a hard pill for brainiac introverts to swallow, but you just can't do this on your own. It may help to think about this in terms of "collaboration," whether working through a teaching center or locating support for teaching on campus in other ways. Coteaching or team teaching with a trusted colleague can be one of the best ways to keep learning how to be an effective teacher. One study on coteaching summarizes this process:

> The very possibility of the presence of another nonstudent observer makes a teacher more conscious of his process, more aware of his assumptions, and thus more likely to consider his performance from the point of view of the student; the effort to assess student learning in

this systematic way shifts the teacher's attention away from content and toward the students.[17]

"Shifting attention away from content" is challenging for those of us who love our subjects. But as this study suggests, one of the great benefits of seeking support is how it prods us to build our pedagogic content knowledge and to engage in the three types of activities necessary for effective teaching discussed in the previous chapters.

So too does mentoring have a demonstrated positive impact on teaching and learning, and some colleges are forward thinking enough to have formal mentoring programs. This person should be open to discussing teaching challenges and helping identify our strengths and areas where we can continue improving.[18] If you have an official mentor but this person isn't particularly helpful in regard to teaching, or if there is no such program in your teaching context, find yourself your own teaching mentor.[19] Maybe ask your students about the teachers they respect or classes in which they learned the most. Chances are if you can identify a great teacher on your campus and this person isn't too handicapped by GIN-related social awkwardness or inflicted with a bad case of Professoritis, and if you can nerve yourself up to take this person out for a cup of coffee and talk about teaching, they will be highly flattered and you will get some excellent insights into effective teaching on your campus with your student population. If you can arrange informal class visits or review assignments and syllabi with this person, maybe you've got a mentor in the making. Maybe you're mentor material yourself, and mentoring will keep improving your own teaching and learning.[20]

Just asking a colleague out to lunch to talk about teaching can be helpful. But that's only if we completely trust that colleague. In fact, some scholars suggest finding mentors in our field but who are *not* employed at our same institution.[21] We don't have to be best friends with this person but we have to trust that there's a basic level of friendliness, good will, and understanding that effective teachers are always learning and relearning how to be effective teachers. We have to trust them to know that seeking out advice and feedback about teaching is a sign of strength, not weakness. We have to trust that they are working on being reflective and effective teachers themselves and will not succumb or encourage us to succumb to the temptation to indulge in endless griping and complaining about students. Expressing some frustration about some specific aspect of our teaching context is okay and maybe even necessary. Nonstop railing about dumb annoying students who do dumb annoying things every dumb annoying day of every dumb annoying year is not okay.

Let's say, for the sake of argument, that there's not a single person anywhere on your campus that you can trust in this way. (That would be hard to believe, but then again, this is academia we're talking about.) You're still not in this all alone. To take an often-overlooked example, all teaching and learning centers have a website. Even though they're aimed primarily at their own campus members, many also contain excellent resources online for people interested in being effective teachers.[22] We also have abundant published scholarship of teaching and learning. SoTL is a relatively new field but gaining credence and proliferating fast.[23] There's a lot to navigate and discern and some things to discard when we enter through the gates of SoTL, and a lot to gain. Importantly, we can very easily modify and adapt it to our unique and specific teaching context. No matter who you are, no matter what your field or employment status or where you teach, there's some SoTL that can support your teaching and your students' learning.

SoTL Publications and Conferences

For many GINs, our deepest most true self, even when we are achieving highly effective teaching and our students are learning copious amounts, may not manifest itself in the classroom. Instead, it may emerge most readily while engaging in our fields of study—the passionate composing or quantifying or writing or reading or examining or experimenting that drove us to become experts in the first place. Our academic nerdiness helps us study our subjects and advance knowledge in our fields, but many of us are less likely to apply our geeky researching skills to teaching and learning. The best thing about scholarship on teaching and learning is that by its very existence, it helps us adjust this mind frame, to move from thinking about teaching as "something I'm supposed to automatically be able to do" to "something I will always keep learning about, no matter how much teaching experience I accrue or whatever the specifics of my teaching context."

There's always something new to think about—a technique, a theory about learning, a new technology tool—and perhaps incorporate into our teaching, particularly if we cultivate a Beginner's Mind. When engaging in SoTL, we are embodying and acting on the growth mindset we hope to see in our students: instead of seeing our teaching efficacy as a finite quality, we view it as something we can always keep expanding and improving.[24] In the words of one study, doing scholarship of teaching and learning means "viewing the work of the classroom as a site for inquiry, asking and answering one's own questions about students' learning in ways that can improve one's own classroom and also advance the larger profession of teaching."[25] The impetus for all our scholarly work—inquiry—is at the root of SoTL as well.[26]

As David Arnold writes, SoTL "connects us to a larger community of scholar-teachers who are grappling with similar problems and concerns" and "can revitalize our teaching by getting us to see our classroom (and our grading chambers) as places of scholarly investigation and problem-solving rather than drudgery."[27] GINs are energized by approaching issues as inquiry and investigation, and SoTL encourages us to view teaching and learning precisely this way. Arnold argues:

> For those of us who are teaching the survey to hundreds of students year after year with no TAs or research support, teaching can feel like all output without any return, emptying our emotional, physical, and intellectual reserves without an opportunity to refuel. Teaching in this sense becomes a "problem"—too many underprepared students, too many exams, not enough time. But what if—as Randy Bass asks— we think about teaching problems as scholarly problems, which generate questions, rather than misery, and frame an investigative process rather than student complaints?[28]

SoTL reframes teaching problems in this way—not as employment-ending deficiencies but instead as an investigative process that generates questions.

SoTL thusly redefines our teaching tasks by speaking to the person-alities and professional inclinations of us GINs. We build on the same processes we use to make our mark in our scholarly fields—our restless probing of a very narrowly defined and specialized topic—and apply them to teaching and learning. In the 1999 article cited by Arnold in the above quote, Randy Bass contrasts the idea of a problem in teaching with a problem in our research:

> In scholarship and research, having a "problem" is at the heart of the investigative process; it is the compound of the generative questions around which all creative and productive activity revolves. But in one's teaching, a "problem" is something you don't want to have, and if you have one, you probably want to fix it. Asking a colleague about a problem in his or her research is an invitation; asking about a prob-lem in one's teaching would probably seem like an accusation.[29]

What SoTL can achieve, Bass argues, is "changing the status of the problem in teaching from terminal remediation to ongoing investiga-tion," making the "problematization of teaching" a "matter of regular communal discourse" and "teaching practice, and the evidence of stu-dent learning, as problems to be investigated, analyzed, represented, and debated."[30] It's manna from academic nerd heaven! A problem or issue "to be investigated, analyzed, represented, and debated" is our home turf. A discourse about those problems, shared among ourselves instead of shut behind the individual classroom door—that's SoTL to which we intellectuals and scholars can fully commit.

As Mary Taylor Huber and Pat Hutchings write, "Scholars of teaching and learning understand classroom difficulties as problems and puzzles to be systematically explored and addressed in ways that contribute to a growing teaching commons" and SoTL "recognizes teaching as substantive, intellectual work."[31] The existence of a "teach-ing commons" where teaching is upheld as intellectual work helps us introverted academic loners who prize intellectual work to reframe our own view and the commonly held assumption that college teaching is a solo endeavor. When we practice teaching as serious intellectual work, we redefine teaching and learning as an essential part of our cherished life of the mind and our engagement in a broader field of intellectual exploration: "Teaching, in this view, takes into account theory, inquiry, and evidence about learning, and, like other intellectual pursuits, is enriched by participation in a wider community of people similarly engaged."[32] Just the fact that there's a body of research and scholarship out there—journals, books, and conferences—dedicated to teaching and learning legitimizes this better way of approaching college teaching.[33] SoTL chips away at the persistent fiction that good teachers are born not made. Instead, just like we do in our geeky pursuit of whatever nerdy topic it is we love, when it comes to teaching we can learn from the scholarship and keep expanding our knowledge and, hence, our abilities to foster student learning.[34]

What is more, and what might be especially appealing for many introverts, a wide variety of SoTL publications are immediately available to us with no human interaction required. If, for example, the idea of finding a teaching mentor fills you with dread, start with something easier: read a journal article about a teaching issue that is of particular interest to you. Even a little bit of reading on a single teaching topic can have a positive impact on teaching. For many GINs, we People of the Book, sitting alone and reading is as natural as breathing. So here's some fantastic news: reading about what worked for other teachers will help you improve your own teaching. Many excellent SoTL books aim their advice directly at brand new teachers who may be most urgently in need of a lot of practical advice right away. But other books and articles are also useful for mid-career or even late-career college teachers engaged in relearning how to be effective teachers. Sometimes SoTL is an even more necessary support for teachers who've had a fair amount of experience, because it's all too easy to accumulate assumptions, get stuck in routines, and become complacent instead of continually improving awareness, preparation, and reflection.

That being said, SoTL has its share of problems. It contains a fair amount of what Maryellen Weimer describes as "soft food," that is, "books and articles that don't require teeth, not the substantive nourishment out of which new insights and understandings are grown," instead offering lists of simple teaching tips or tricks—useful, but only to a point.[35] SoTL also attracts its share of hardliners convinced they've found the one way to be a good teacher for all time, oblivious to disparate teaching realities. And like any academic field, SoTL contains some bitter schisms. Some scholars believe that the *only* convincing SoTL builds on quantifiable information and data-driven studies measuring student learning in highly objective ways.[36] I couldn't disagree more with delineating some SoTL research methods more inherently valid than others. There's room under the enormous SoTL umbrella for rigorously defined scientific experiments that seek to measure student learning methodically, especially in those fields with a clearly quantifiable knowledge basis.[37] There's also room for philosophizing about teaching and for offering more esoteric reflections on the complexities of teaching and learning, for personal narratives, and other wisdom-of-practice scholarship.[38] There's also ample room for student voices and for quality writing from the student point of view in the classroom, yet student voices and perspectives too rarely appear in published SoTL or at teaching conferences.[39]

SoTL is also short on detailed descriptions of the mistakes people make when teaching.[40] We know how important failure is to learning; that the opportunity to make mistakes and then try again, correcting those mistakes and moving forward, builds self-efficacy and self-regulation in students and advances learning. Yet SoTL infrequently discusses our own teaching mistakes, even though effective teachers need to learn from their pedagogical missteps. Ken Bain points out in his landmark study of highly effective college teachers that such instructors continually embrace the learning opportunity in teaching failures. Effective teachers have a "willingness to confront their own weaknesses and failures. When we asked one of our earliest subjects . . . to give a public talk about his teaching, he tellingly chose as his title 'When my teaching fails.'"[41] Although being aware of, recognizing, and learning from teaching mistakes and a "willingness to confront" failures—to acknowledge them and to learn from the times "when teaching fails"—are foundational to effectively fostering student learning, only occasionally do I see a SoTL presentation or read an article that describes in detail, carefully reflects on, and positions in the scholarship real-life teaching mistakes.

One reason for this lack of open discussion is the employment advancement and tenure process, which at most institutions does not encourage honest self-criticism and reflection on *any* aspect of our work. But another reason is the culture of academia and academic publishing in general, which generates a lot of petty, unconstructive criticism. Anyone who's received an unnecessarily vicious or belittling anonymous peer review for a scholarly article or manuscript (which is probably anyone who's ever submitted anything for peer review) will be leery of publicly revealing a major mistake that hampered their efficacy in the classroom. Yet such mistakes provide some of our most essential learning and relearning about teaching.

SoTL is about helping each other be more effective teachers and facilitating better student learning, so surely that begins with all of us admitting that we had to learn how to teach, and that we made mistakes along the way. In one of the few published SoTL essays to explore the author's own mistakes, Graham Broad writes that failing to approach teaching as an aspect of his scholarly work was his biggest error:

> As a graduate student in history, I was trained to maintain the highest evidentiary standards in my scholarship, to situate my research in a body of existing literature, and to scrutinize every claim I made for any possible error. And yet, when it came to teaching, I went entirely on instinct, teaching the way I was taught, assuming it was good enough. It wasn't. . . . My teaching has improved by leaps and bounds whenever I have applied the same standards and critical scrutiny to my pedagogy that I have always applied to my research.[42]

In part, applying "the same standards and critical scrutiny" to our pedagogy that we do to our other types of research depends on individual initiative, as described here. But there's a cultural problem too. Academia fosters closed-door teaching, so it's difficult to even define the standards for teaching and learning and undertake peer review: if we don't know what our peers are doing or thinking or trying when it comes to teaching and learning, how can we productively engage in assessing our own work as teachers by peer standards?[43]

Even when we are actively seeking out published SoTL and working to find ways to engage in peer-reviewed scholarship and research on teaching and learning, we may not understand what exactly our learned colleague is trying to say, since jargon plagues even some of the best-researched SoTL. Of course, every scholarly field revels in its own Members Only dialect, and complicated ideas often require complicated language. Give me an episode of *Buffy the Vampire Slayer* and I can happily deconstruct it all day long using impenetrable cultural studies pomo-speak.[44] The problem with excessive jargon in SoTL is that unlike a lofty discussion about female subjectivity and intersectional feminist theories of the body in popular vampirism texts, teaching and learning takes place in real life, with real people and real consequences. Faced with the complex and recurring challenges of teaching and learning, and seeking to build our knowledge and skill by reading books and articles on teaching, we should not have to wade through endless and pointlessly obscure insider and trendy jargon. Time and time again, the specter of Comic Book Guy haunts the pages and presentations of SoTL, lording some specialized insider knowledge over everyone else instead of working to make new information or reflections about teaching accessible for the rest of us.

Also, as I've already suggested, far too much SoTL ignores how different teaching contexts and identities shape teaching and learning.[45] Learning how to engage our students effectively in our discipline is going to look very different in a large survey-level lecture class at a state university from a small honors seminar at a liberal arts college. Identity markers and disparate teaching realities matter too: if I'm a woman or any faculty member of color, other factors will be at play. SoTL needs to delineate more carefully different challenges and institutionally influenced factors in effective teaching and learning. The reality that "identity is important" escapes even some otherwise insightful and well-informed SoTL, both published work as well as conference presentations. So when you're reading, keep your individual and unique teaching context foremost in your mind. Don't be fooled by bells and whistles, unless those bells and whistles are going to help *you* advance *your students'* learning.[46]

Just like published SoTL, conferences and professional presentations about teaching and learning can be resources for improving our teaching. The best thing about teaching conferences is the feeling of returning to the Mothership because everyone is a lot like you—namely, they're GINs who want to be effective teachers. Unlike most scholarly conferences, attendees at SoTL conferences are not there to play the "I'm Smarter Than (You Think) You Are" game. There may be some heated Q&A—the best SoTL presentations often provoke debate—but the questions are usually real questions about the material instead of comments calculated to show off one's big brain or slamming the presenter with denigration thinly veiled as a question ("I was surprised you didn't mention Obscure Scholar X and Little Known Publication Y since your argument clearly restates that work. Why didn't you address it?" Bonus points if Obscure Scholar X is also the person asking the question.) At SoTL conferences, you can find a spirit of generosity and learning together sadly lacking in other kinds of professional scholarly conversations. Just by being there, the mere fact of your attendance, you've already admitted, "I'm not perfect and I could stand to learn something about this topic." In my experience, that's a rarity at the Modern Language Association or American Historical Association annual conferences, but pretty standard at SoTL conferences.

In this way, much like reading SoTL publications, simply attending a teaching conference shifts our mindsets, possibilities present themselves, and teaching becomes less of a solitary vigil and more of a shared endeavor. Teaching conferences can play an important role in helping us to feel supported in our quest for improving and learning and relearning how to be an effective teacher, particularly if we're working in an especially dysfunctional or stressful teaching context where we do not feel supported on a day-to-day basis. The practices of awareness, preparation, and reflection are demanding, and without a sense of belonging to some bigger community of other teacher-scholars, it's easy to become overwhelmed and isolated. Teaching conferences specifically and SoTL more generally can counteract that effect. At the very least, at a SoTL conference we can advance our knowledge about teaching and learning because we have the opportunity to watch other people teach.[47] The most effective SoTL conference presentations I have seen have sparked a lively dialogue among an interdisciplinary group of teachers; they fostered a conversation that, like any great classroom discussion, inspired us as *learners* seeking new ideas about teaching.

Of course, all the engaging, thought-provoking conversation about teaching and learning in the world doesn't amount to much if we don't apply what we've learned. Just like awareness, preparation, and reflection, the practice of regularly seeking support for our teaching must be translated to actual teaching—stuff we *do* in real life. Scholarship of teaching and learning can contribute to a community of practice, and in the words of one study, "catalyze change" in our teaching, but only when we take the insights of SoTL into our individual and unique teaching contexts and put them into practice.[48] The "scholarly" part of "scholarly teaching"—reading, listening, taking notes—is the part that may come most naturally to GINs. Taking the insights from a book or article into our classroom, or the new understanding we gained from a presentation, out of our brains and into our teaching actions will take more effort. And most of all, it takes experience and practice, as discussed in the next chapter.

Conclusion

> We must find a way to look after each other, as if we were
> one single tribe.
> —King T'Challa, *The Black Panther*

———

Most of us see ourselves as an academic lone wolf, chasing down our prey—publications, grants, tenure—with the strength and cunning of our own unassailable intellect. The systems and structures of academia encourage precisely this approach to the work of being a scholar, making "it easy for a beginning teacher to conclude that failure or struggle is their fault alone and that structural conditions are less influential than the individual's own failings."[49] Perhaps even more discouragingly, when we set out to consult the SoTL in order to try to address our pedagogical challenges, we face certain predictable problems. We find a bewildering number of studies, books, and articles, some or even many of which may seem inapplicable to our individual teaching context.

Additionally, some of them totally contradict each other and yet present their teaching dictums in such an authoritative way that we may begin to question and doubt our own abilities.

As Weimer explains, much of the SoTL aimed at helping new teachers can actually disempower us in our quest to understand our own unique teaching context and to cultivate our own intellectual investigation into teaching and learning:

> The prescriptive nature of the advice creates the impression that teaching is formulaic, a set of rules to be learned and techniques to be mastered. Because most new college teachers feel a certain desperation, they welcome this detailed advice. It feels like just what they need. But is it? Yes and no. The advice does show new faculty a path through the forest, but it doesn't make clear that paths through the forest are multiple. It keeps faculty so focused on the gritty details that they miss that they're even in a forest.[50]

As Weimer points out, the "paths through the forest are multiple," yet teaching and learning advice in SoTL can sound unequivocal. It can quickly become proscriptive rather than supportive, adding to our sense of being stranded all alone, trying to puzzle out our teaching and learning challenges and problems by ourselves. Like Michael Burnham facing the prospect of working undercover in an evil alternate universe, we wonder if we're even going to survive this place all on our own.

Teaching does not need to be, *should* not be, a solitary endeavor. We need SoTL so we can retain and share the intellectual work being achieved by those seeking to foster student learning.[51] We need support because we all need support to be effective teachers. I can't tell you the best way for you to seek that support, nor can I say what exactly that support will look like in your individual teaching context. But I can state unequivocally that when it comes to being an effective teacher, we can help each other. As T'Challa counsels, we need to act as if we are a single tribe.

CHAPTER 5

PRACTICE

I was a different person in those days—arrogant, undisciplined . . .
with far too much ego, but too little wisdom.

—Captain Jean-Luc Picard, "Tapestry,"
Star Trek: The Next Generation

———

I HAVE a recurring dream that I'm a college student again. Sometimes I'm sitting in a classroom, sometimes I'm in a dorm, and sometimes I'm waiting in line at the registrar's, but always I experience a persistent sense of unfairness. "But I already *finished* college," I keep thinking. "I graduated. Why am I back here again?" This dream might simply be a reminder that teaching college students has a certain repetitive quality: every fall yields a new crop of mostly eighteen-year-olds bringing many of the same pedagogical tribulations and triumphs over and over. But I think it's actually more about how becoming an effective college teacher is never a done deal. Effective teachers never finish learning about the science, labor, complexities, frustrations, and rewards of teaching and learning. I dream that I'm back in college because I'm still coming to terms with the fact that as long as I'm teaching I will have to keep figuring out how to best foster student learning. There will be no thesis completed, degree awarded, or doctoral hood bestowed signaling the successful completion of this course of study.

Moreover, once we've accepted the fact that becoming an effective teacher will be a career-long process, and we're ready for support and training to increase our skill and knowledge, we may still face major obstacles to getting that support and finding those opportunities. Demands on faculty are increasing while resources are decreasing, and faculty in all kinds of different teaching situations are "stretched thin," making opportunities to reflect on and learn about effective teaching even scarcer.[1] As Maryellen Weimer asserts, we "tend to trivialize what's involved in the process of growing and developing as teachers," and although continually learning about teaching is essential to effective teaching,

> in too many academic environments, ideas and information about teaching are not everywhere to be gleaned. . . . Most faculty bookshelves do not hold recent books on teaching and learning. Most campus e-mail exchanges do not substantively address teaching-learning topics. Most college libraries do not subscribe to many pedagogical periodicals—understandably, because few faculty read them. Most department meetings do not regularly include discussions of timely teaching topics. . . . For most faculty the regular needed fill-up of new ideas is not as easy as stopping by the neighborhood gas station.[2]

In a wide variety of teaching contexts, new ideas about teaching and learning can be scarce, hindering our access to "regular needed fill-ups" of pedagogical content knowledge.

In addition, SoTL itself can create impediments rather than fostering new teacher learning. It often doesn't sufficiently address the disparate realities of teaching, for example. Also, faculty often "aren't certain how to discern the current debates or historical threads that would help them sort this work into meaningful categories or apply it to their classroom" and furthermore, "the potentially relevant scholarship is simply so abundant that it's almost impossible to keep up."[3] Not to mention all the other factors that can limit our ability to keep learning about effective teaching, such as employment insecurity, dysfunctional departments, systematic discrimination, pressures to publish or get grants, service demands, administrative failures, health issues, and family responsibilities. Most significantly, being able to continue learning about teaching, and to apply what we learn, requires practice.

The Importance of Practice

For people who care about student learning, here's the best and worst news about effective teaching that you will ever hear: no matter who you are or what you teach, you can get better with practice. Nothing will improve our teaching and increase our students' learning more than *doing* it, year after year, term after term, class after class, day after day. This is great news, because our ability to help students learn can always keep improving, just by doing it repeatedly, by consulting the SoTL about recurring pedagogical puzzles and regularly reflecting on what's working and what's not. But it's also bad news, because if we don't have job security and years of experience, there's no replacement—no book we can read, no trick we can do, no technology we can utilize—that can replace experience and practice.

Of course, experience is no guarantor of efficacy. Practice without awareness, feedback, reflection, and support cannot advance knowledge or ability.[4] We all know students who've been doing some academic task for years without sufficient guidance, feedback, and reflection and so have not increased their ability to complete said task successfully. We know that "students who reflect on their learning are better learners than those who do not."[5] The exact same thing is true for teachers and teaching. If we do the same thing for years without critical reflection informed by SoTL, we simply won't be as effective as we would have been if we had approached teaching as an intellectual endeavor worthy of our study and reflection.

Some consistently ineffective college teachers with decades of teaching behind them have convinced themselves that student learning is not their responsibility but rather entirely the students' problem. Just as students who don't do well may be quick to blame an external locus of control, so too do professors who aren't effective often blame an external locus of control: it's the fault of lazy students, evil administrators, or backstabbing colleagues. Just like students, if faculty aren't internally motived to learn about effective teaching, they will have "low expectancies regarding teaching, especially if they believe teaching skill cannot be learned, their sense of self-efficacy is low, or they believe that the environment will not support their efforts."[6]

Like many students, some instructors are fearful—"fearful of even acknowledging a need or desire to improve teaching and learning since any effort to do so carries with it the possibility of failure."[7] Just like students who avoid expending intellectual energy on tasks that seem pointless to them, so too do professors who do not see teaching as meaningful work avoid expending intellectual energy on improving their own teaching efficacy, because it "takes less effort to conclude that students are lazy, unmotivated, or uncaring than it does to assess *why* students are resisting and to reach out to them or make substantive changes to reduce that resistance."[8] Disparate teaching realities and employment insecurity can also chip away at our desire and willingness to improve student learning, and sometimes professors are just so enamored with their own beautiful minds and their scholarly subjects that student learning seems not worth worrying about.

But I believe that many ineffective college teachers are academic nerds who somewhere along the line simply got stuck. It's not that they don't care about student learning but that they were so unprepared for the realities of teaching, so firm in their mistaken belief that earning a living as a PhD would consist solely of Thinking Important Thoughts, that they could never make the necessary transition to teaching students how to do things with that subject. Even more troublingly, while the majority of people teaching college students care very much about student learning, many of us have limited opportunities for painstakingly accruing years of reflective, thoughtful practice. Practice is necessary for effective teaching? No problem! *If* our individual teaching context and employment status afford us the freedom to try lots of different things, to experiment, to admit mistakes and make corrections, to find support and advance our own learning, and then implement what we've learned. But most of us don't have the opportunity to practice without any consequences whatsoever for our students or for ourselves, including our employment status.[9] I wish we had apprenticeships or more widespread rigorous graduate school training in pedagogical content knowledge or mock classrooms on our spaceship's holodeck or some other way to practice teaching with a safety net but *kaiidth*, what is, is.

If we are fortunate enough to be able to accrue practice, faculty still need to be more aware that this is a career-long project because "teacher learning has no end."[10] When I say we need practice, I mean "practice" in all senses of the word. Practice not only as in training how to do it, doing it repeatedly, and getting better—like playing a musical instrument—but also practice as in an activity you undertake on a regular basis at which you hope to keep building skill but accepting that there is no fixed end date and no way you'll ever perfect it and then be done with it. Awareness, preparation, reflection, and support are not finite activities we can methodically complete and then check off a to-do list. We can't work our way through a prescribed set of steps and then, viola! Teaching excellence! Don't look down this road for a finish line. There isn't one.

That's not to say we won't make progress, as Dannelle Stevens and Joanne Cooper point out: "Learning, therefore, is a continuous and cumulative process. Prior learning becomes the fodder for further understanding and insight. . . . Learning is a cycle that perpetuates more learning."[11] Ideally, the more we practice and the longer we practice our pedagogy, the more benefits we'll reap and the more "fodder for further understanding" we accrue. We will be able to increasingly apply what we've learned about effective teaching in our classroom and during interactions with students, remembering "achieving mastery in any domain is a lengthy process that involves acquiring multiple component skills as well as the ability to integrate them fluently and apply them appropriately. Mastery develops in stages."[12] Learning how to teach effectively is indeed "a lengthy process" and even as we acquire "multiple component skills," it takes practice to "integrate them fluently and apply them appropriately."

The more we employ the four pedagogical practices I've described in *Geeky Pedagogy* and the more time we can spend just *doing* them, the better we'll get at effective teaching and advancing our students' learning:

- Awareness: working to be fully aware and accepting of who we are, who our students are, the complexities of identity, and the challenges of learning—and understanding that these realities are always evolving and changing.

- Preparation: approaching teaching as an intellectual endeavor, putting on our professor pants, and carefully planning for interacting with students and conducting classes in order to best foster student learning in our subject—and understanding that preparation is an ongoing process we will do over and over again.
- Reflection: viewing our teaching as an interesting and ongoing intellectual investigation and gathering as much evidence and feedback as possible to consciously and metacognitively explore what's working and what's not; applying the products of reflection to our teaching and learning work; perhaps trying a little gratitude along the way—and understanding that reflection is an ongoing process we will do over and over again.
- Support: finding ways to engage in and learn from the scholarly work on teaching and learning, both in our individual context as well as the field at large; decreasing our isolation in the enterprise of effective teaching, joining a larger conversation about teaching and learning, and increasing our resources for practicing awareness, preparation, and reflection; applying what we've gained and learned to our actual work of teaching and learning—and understanding that this is an ongoing process we will do over and over again.

Each of these practices presupposes that we approach our teaching as something we are always learning and relearning how to do, moving back and forth between reflection, preparation, awareness, and support. It's not a linear process. We won't travel smoothly down a fixed path, passing a certain number of effective teaching milestones until we arrive at last to pedagogical nirvana and are crowned Professor Perfect. There will be numerous detours, setbacks, and side roads. Besides, Professor Perfect doesn't exist.

Geeky professors, however, abound. We nerds thrive in school, and introverts have some natural advantages when it comes to earning an advanced degree. We're the ones most likely to shut ourselves up in the library or the lab or whatever dim solitary place we must inhabit in order to obsessively pursue advanced knowledge in a highly specialized topic. Although these characteristics handicap us in some important ways when we become teachers, as a group we bring one crucial quality to the practice of teaching: if we want to learn about something, then by Grabthar's Hammer, we can sit down and research it. We can focus on, delve into, and study it. We can engage in rigorous debate and evidence-based argument, grind out hour upon hour of dedicated attention, and we will emerge *knowing more about it*. Nobody is better at this than us. Nobody. As Laurie Penny writes about nerd culture's ability to evolve and to embrace racial, gender, and ethnic diversity: "Nerds are brilliant. We are great at learning stuff. We can do anything we put our minds to."[13] Whether it's translating a novel, making sense of the past, creating the internet, mapping the ocean floor, or curing disease, you can count on us. Even what we consider *fun* requires the laborious acquisition of minute, painstaking, and specialized knowledge, as anyone who speaks Klingon will tell you.[14]

However, as we gain knowledge about and understanding of effective teaching and learning, we need to remember that we are studying *our own unique teaching context*. Whatever the SoTL recommends, whatever your mentor tells you, even whatever worked for you in some other teaching context, may or may not work for you in your current localized teaching context.[15] There's no one specific hard and fast method for building our pedagogical practices, no one specific way it must look or one specific thing we must do in all teaching scenarios for all time. This applies to everything from the most sweeping pedagogical theory to any single teaching trick. It applies at every stage of our careers, from our first class to our last.[16] As you become aware of your teaching context, as you read and participate in the SoTL and learn what the research has to say about teaching and learning, as you reflect on your teaching and as you find support for your teaching, you still ultimately have to do whatever it is that works for *you* and advances learning among *your* students.

And then *do it*, as much as you can, because practice—as in repetitive action—is the only way to keep improving. Only by teaching can we become skilled at incorporating our knowledge about effective teaching—knowledge built by awareness, preparation, reflection, and support—into our actual teaching activities. In the words of one group of scholars: "Whereas both novices and experts agree on what qualities

constitute excellent teaching, experts incorporate more of those qualities into their practice of teaching."[17] That is to say, experience is what
helps us close the gap between awareness and our actual teaching in
real life, the gap between preparation and our actual teaching in real
life, the gap between reflection and our actual teaching in real life, and
the gap between knowledge gained by engaging in SoTL and our actual
teaching in real life. It's what makes us experts in our own unique
teaching context.

We also need lots of practice to understand ourselves as teachers.
As Stephen Braden and Deborah Smith assert, "no matter how much
experience one has, techniques, though sometimes useful, are not the
element that assists faculty with connecting to students, rather, it is
knowing and trusting oneself."[18] Very consciously trusting oneself to be
an effective teacher requires us to understand that this is a career-long
endeavor and an intellectually and emotionally demanding undertaking. And knowing oneself is even harder, as Jay Parini summarizes:
"You will have to adapt anything I say here to your own private vision,
to some version of yourself. The essential journey in this profession
is toward self-knowledge; this will involve getting lost in order to get
found, losing your thread, having to revise your sense of reality over
and over, frequently adjusting to new information, new contexts."[19]
The "essential journey toward self-knowledge" is not simple or linear.
It forces us to "revise our sense of reality over and over." In short, it requires a commitment to doing the hard work of real learning, including
feeling confused when we delve into problems and puzzles, and then
repeatedly relearning as our knowledge is tested again and again in the
classroom and during interactions with students.

As I've argued throughout this book, we can make a good start on
expert self-knowledge when we embrace the fact that most of us teaching
college are some variety of nerds, geeks, and introverts. Having fully
accepted my introverted mannerisms, I now make much more of a conscious effort to show students that I am approachable and that I care
about their learning. I now plan for speaking with students casually
before class, knowing ahead of time that this is probably going to be the
hardest part of the class for me to do successfully. When I finally recognized that on some level I resent any intrusion into my office/solitary

Mind Palace, I bought an honest-to-God welcome mat and now, when office hours roll around, I remind myself that it's time to put out the welcome mat literally and figuratively, remembering that teaching and learning are social interactions as well as an intellectual adventure. This doesn't just help me more effectively foster student learning. It also helps me know and accept who I am as a teacher and a person.

Similarly, I'll never forget the big laugh I got in a seminar the first time I joked about my own geekiness. Reflecting back on that moment, I see now how pedagogically effective it was. I wasn't undercutting my authority. On the contrary, I showed students that I could be trusted to guide them because my nerdy knowledge (remember: nerds are *super smart*) reinforced my expertise in the topic. I also demonstrated my enthusiasm for the content and my desire to engage them in the content: "Hey, I'm utterly intrigued by this reading assignment which you, Typical Student, may or may not readily see the utility or purpose of expending your valuable time to try to understand. So watch me model for you what it's like to really grapple with these ideas." It also revealed a professionally appropriate glimpse into who I truly am as a person and teacher. I wasn't faking it or exaggerating it. I *do* love reading about these topics and very much want to facilitate student learning in these topics. I *do* enjoy fostering and encouraging students' intellectual growth. Yes! I *am* a nerd!

I'm still learning how to utilize this self-knowledge effectively. Sometimes I carelessly fall into geek speak that intimidates and confuses students, reinforcing the boundaries between my beloved subjects and the non-nerds trying to learn about it. Sometimes I act the show-off, wielding my immense knowledge over novice learners, forgetting that "teaching depends on what other people [students] think, not what you [Professor Smarty Pants] think."[20] Knowing and planning for being an introvert in a profession where success demands effective communication and interpersonal relations with people who can get angry and emotional doesn't mean that I always achieve effective communication or that I'm always prepared to respond calmly to displays of student emotion. But like every other aspect of teaching and learning, it is getting easier with practice. We must embrace the need for practice because we all need practice for effective teaching, not just for things like class planning and effective lecturing but also awareness, acceptance, cultivating gratitude, productive reflection, and of course coping with student interactions—neutral, negative, positive, and everything in between. Perhaps most importantly, practice *doing it* is the only way to recognize what we've done well and when we've made mistakes.

Making Mistakes

In the *Star Trek: The Next Generation* episode titled "Tapestry," Captain Jean-Luc Picard suffers a grievous injury to his artificial heart. Through flashbacks we learn that Picard received the artificial heart during his callow youth when a stupid bar fight led to his being stabbed. Q, a mischievous omnipotent alien who can bend reality to his whims, sends Picard back in time to fix the misstep. Picard lives out the subsequent alternate life only to discover that mistakes are what make the man. Without the bar fight, he's never forced to confront the limits of his mortality and subsequently seize every opportunity to live a life of adventure seeking out new life and new civilizations among the stars. So Picard demands that Q return him to the original timeline, knowing he will die there when his artificial heart fails, but he will die having known greatness. Spoiler alert: Picard wakes up injured but recovering in sickbay. That crazy Q!

Like Picard musing about his time as a young Starfleet officer, GINs who are fortunate enough to have been teaching a long time, looking back honestly on our early teaching careers, are likely to see an abundance of arrogance (practically a requirement for earning an advanced degree) and a minimum of pedagogical wisdom. To say that I made a few mistakes in the classroom during my egotistical youth would be a gross understatement. But just like every single person who ever tries to learn anything, mistakes are an essential part of becoming good at something. There is just no way to learn how to do something really well without making mistakes in the process.[21] It's one of the ways that learning is hard. Whether we're becoming an effective teacher or the captain of a starship, we *need* to make mistakes, recognize those mistakes, and learn from those mistakes. As Donald Schoffstall writes, "As teachers we all make mistakes, but we must be willing to change and learn from those mistakes just as we implore our students to do."[22] With practice, the mistakes are fewer and further between but as long as we care about student learning and being an effective teacher, we *will* keep learning about teaching and trying new things and, hence, making mistakes.

I can think of some boneheaded bloopers I made just last semester. I chose an ineffective textbook. I should have foreseen the bottleneck first-year students hit when they were doing the research project. I could have made the course content more relevant to students' daily lives. I did some research for a student that I should have made the student do herself. I should have talked less and listened more.[23] However, none of those mistakes derailed the entire class. Why? First, I was *aware* of important teaching and learning realities. Second, I *prepared* for effective teaching and learning. Third, I repeatedly *reflected* on teaching and learning. Fourth, I got *support* on campus and by consulting the SoTL. Experience and practice allowed me to make the necessary adjustments and to chalk up what didn't work to my own learning. Next semester I won't use that textbook, I'll anticipate the bottleneck, I'll try to keep my mouth shut, and so on.

Learning and relearning means doing some things more effectively over time and, yes, making new mistakes as well. But if we're lucky enough to have some employment security and even over the course of a single class, teaching offers repeated opportunities for improvement. Louis J. Gross writes that "an enticing property of teaching regularly is the rejuvenating power of knowing that another 'take' is just a day or two away. There is elation . . . associated with the reflection 'Well, I didn't really get that concept across today, so let's try another tact [sic] on Wednesday.'"[24] Teaching regularly enables us to try another "take." As Christopher Schaberg and Mark Yakich summarize, "This is one of the most exciting parts of the job and yet we often forget to take advantage of it. Not you must change, but you can change, and begin again."[25]

Although there can be a "mind-numbing sameness to parts of teaching's daily grind," there are also always opportunities to start fresh, try again, reinvent, see something differently, and to get better.[26] Parini describes the way that (again, presupposing you enjoy some employment security), the cyclical nature of teaching can be tiring but also energizing:

> I know the feeling: that dread, as one approaches class for the first time in September. It can be difficult to begin again, to invent everything from the ground up, to learn the names of the students, their foibles, their likes and dislikes. There is so much to absorb in a short time. It can make you dizzy with apprehension. . . . [But] it is hard not to like having a job where you can start over every September, shredding the previous year's failures and tossing them out of the window like so much confetti.[27]

With the opportunity to begin again, we have the opportunity to keep learning. Viewing each class, indeed every class meeting, as another opportunity to learn more about teaching and learning in our own unique context, turning teaching and learning into our own intellectual endeavor, goes a long way toward mitigating the apprehension Parini identifies.

Also, don't forget we're striving for "effective," not "superhuman." The pop culture-reinforced stereotype of the naturally gifted teacher who effortlessly makes his (deliberate choice of pronoun) students worship him, and makes students learn seemingly just because they're in his metahuman professorial presence, is sneaky and pernicious. It's there working its destructiveness in our subconscious and setting us up for failure. Robin Williams in *Dead Poets Society*, "O captain! My captain," please get out of my head! Get out of my students' heads too! We cannot be this mythical *perfect* professor, because no matter how effectively we teach and foster student learning, we can't and won't successfully convince every single student we meet to join our geek culture.

Brookfield identifies the tendency of college teachers to become disproportionately focused on those one or two students in every class who seem most resistant to learning, terming it "the trap of conversional obsession" and describing how it can undermine our self-efficacy:

> Conversional obsession is what happens when you become obsessed with converting a small and easily identifiable minority of hardcore, resistant students into becoming enthusiastic advocates for learning.

> You put your whole identity as a competent teacher on the line by
> equating your ability to break through this resistance to produce joy-
> fully committed learners with the sign that you're a proper teacher.[28]

Converting those few students who are determined to resist learning
can powerfully detract us from all the things we are doing effectively in
our classes and all the ways our other students are learning. This, argues
Brookfield, is what makes continual conscious reflection so necessary
for effective teaching, including soliciting frequent feedback from students, which can serve to check our tendency to "put our whole identity
as a competent teacher on the line" when we focus on one or two highly
resistant students. Additionally, I would argue that for this reason alone,
a gratitude practice is necessary for critically reflective teaching because
it helps us keep expanding our focus to include all the students who *are*
learning and the things that are going *right*. We can't find those things
unless we're looking for them.

Teaching Is Hard

We also have to remember that effective teaching is emotionally taxing
as well as both physically and psychically tiring.[29] Brookfield points out
that recognizing the tiring aspects of teaching demonstrates that we are
paying attention (awareness), preparing ourselves, and reflecting on our
experiences: "Experiencing ego-deflating episodes of disappointment
and demoralization is quite normal. Indeed, being aware that we regularly face inherently irresolvable dilemmas in our teaching, and that
we hurt from these, is an important indicator that we are staying awake
and remaining critically alert."[30] Awareness, preparation, reflection, and
seeking support don't magically fix "inherently irresolvable dilemmas
in our teaching" but as Brookfield suggests, sometimes feeling demoral-
ized and disappointed is inevitable when we want to be effective teachers
and we are paying attention to what is happening and reflecting on it.
Moreover, many of the fruits of our labor won't be readily evident to us
because when it comes to teaching, "the relevance and utility of learning
is often not appreciated until long after it has happened and you are long
gone."[31] For all the ways we might be able to measure effective teaching,

we will never fully know the extent to which we may have successfully fostered student learning.

Riding this teaching and learning roller coaster can be emotionally draining. Our nerdy love for whatever geeky topic to which we've devoted so much our lives can effectively fuel our enthusiasm for teaching and learning, but it also makes us vulnerable to burnout because most of our students won't share our passion and it takes different skills and practices to bring those students in and help them do things in and with our subject. Elizabeth Barkley describes this as one of the most significant challenges we face when it comes to engaging students. We chose our "field of scholarly endeavor because somewhere along the line we developed a passion for it," but that's exactly why it's so discouraging when students are bored, unhappy, and disengaged: "They stare at us vacantly or perhaps even hostilely when we attempt to pull them into class discussion, and then bolt for the door like freed prisoners the moment it seems safe to do so."[32] This is more than a little disheartening for nerds who truly want to celebrate and share their love for their subject. We have to prove, again and again, to every new crop of students, exactly why this thing we love is worthy of their time and effort, and exactly how it will improve their mind and their life. That's a tall order for those to whom our subjects are so prodigiously interesting and important.

When we understand how hard learning is—whether learning how to develop a new habit of mind in an unfamiliar discipline like our students have to do, or whether learning how to teach effectively like we have to do all the time—we can more clearly see the entwined tasks of teaching and learning as *everyone's* ongoing effort to keep improving.[33] As Hutchings, Huber, and Ciccone argue, a college teacher utilizes SoTL not only in order to understand new pedagogical techniques and developments in curriculum and assessment, but also to continue "to develop as a *learner about learning* along the way" (original emphasis).[34] Learning anything is never linear, there's always progress then stalled points, steps forward, and steps back. Just like our students, we have to "postpone judgment and tolerate ambiguity" when it comes to effective teaching, and that is *hard*.[35] Just like our own students resist learning, fearful that they are incapable of achieving success or resentful of what they see as pointless or they just plain don't want to make the enormous effort it takes to learn a way of thinking, so too do we faculty resist learning new pedagogical tools and approaches because it is *hard*.

Just like novice learners in our subjects, when it comes to teaching, we have to *do* it in order to learn how to do it well, and just like our students learning anything, when it comes to effective teaching, "it takes a long time to become an effective learner."[36] We can't passively listen to a presentation or read an article and presto chango we know how to do it, because everyone needs repeated practice *doing* whatever it is they're learning how to do.[37] Just like our students, we have to remember that "feeling clueless and unsure isn't a sign you don't belong; it means you're appropriately challenged."[38] After all, "confusion is the first step in learning."[39] Just like our students, we have to believe that we can learn and that we can improve. As Weimer writes: "Why don't faculty take advantage of the fact they are in charge of their development as teachers? Perhaps, like many of their students, they aren't empowered, confident learners when it comes to their own teaching."[40] Understanding that we are capable of learning and improving, accepting the fact that "every teacher is a work in progress, no matter how long they've been at it" enables us to actually then make progress and continue to improve our ability to foster student learning.[41]

To achieve this, we need to nerd out about teaching and learning. We need to approach our teaching work with all the intellectual prowess we bring to bear on our other academic work. Effective teaching requires the same level of professionalism we bring to all our other scholarly pursuits.[42] It's as demanding and as serious an endeavor as our other research: we can't do it half-heartedly.[43] We have to find ways to approach teaching and learning as a series of interesting, mentally engaging puzzles and problems that require our best intellectual attention, using the same academic toolkit that we've accumulated in order to engage in other types of scholarship. As an added benefit, when our brains are absorbed in cognitive tasks like trying to solve a puzzle or explore a problem, our fear centers settle down.[44] Approaching teaching as an intellectual challenge will not only reap rewards in terms of increased skills but will also make us less anxious, less nervous, less afraid that we won't measure up, and thus better enable us to cultivate our own self-efficacy in the classroom and during interactions with students.

You probably arrived at college teaching via your nerdy love of a topic, and then maybe found yourself caring more than you ever thought you could about your students' learning, after so many years of caring almost exclusively about your subject and your research. Making that realization and becoming an effective college teacher isn't easy, and the longer I've been teaching, the more I realize how much I still have to learn—will always have to *keep* learning—about teaching.[45] That's practicing, and the practice of, effective teaching and learning.

Conclusion

> James T. Kirk: "Mr. Sulu. You can, you know, fly this thing, right?"
> Hikaru Sulu: "You kidding me, sir?"
> —*Star Trek Beyond*

For GINs who want to be effective teachers, Sulu in the 2009–2016 rebooted *Star Trek* film franchise is a better role model than Kirk or Spock. Most of us don't have Kirk's sexy bad-boy charisma, and intellectually dominating everyone around us and repressing our human emotions like Spock won't foster student learning. But over the course of the Kelvin Timeline, Sulu gains valuable experience at the helm of the *Enterprise* and becomes a skilled practitioner of his profession, like a teacher in the classroom. He learns from his mistakes—he'll never forget to disengage the external inertial dampener again! He applies his esoteric academic training (studying fencing) to real-life situations (defeating Romulans). When he needs to assert his authority as acting captain, he doesn't hesitate, and everybody knows he means it when Sulu calmly informs the enemy: "If you test me, you will fail."

One moment in *Star Trek Beyond* particularly resonates with me as a teacher. The stranded crew is trying to escape a hostile planet via the abandoned ancient USS *Franklin*. Right before they plummet over a cliff to try to jumpstart the dusty warp drive, Kirk nervously checks with Sulu. "You can fly this thing, right?" Sulu is completely confident, joking "You kidding me, sir?" Yet we can tell that Sulu knows full well he's about to do something dangerous—he exchanges a wry look with Chekov later in the scene—and that getting this bucket of bolts into space is going to take all his skill and experience. He knows what to do but he's also experienced enough to understand that it isn't going to be easy, and although he's the one at the helm, he needs everyone around him to work hard also, including the ship itself.

We who want to foster student learning are the helm officers of our classes. We need Sulu's self-efficacy because we have to know that we can learn and relearn how to foster student learning effectively. We have to know that teaching skill isn't an inborn gift but rather a set of practices we can learn how to do and that we will always keep relearning how to do effectively. We have to accept the realities of our individual teaching contexts. We have to know that preparing as carefully for teaching as we do for our other scholarly work is something we can do when we've implemented our plans with reflection and support, which in its turn leads to increased awareness, improved preparation, and effective instruction and student learning. Most of all, our practice leads to our increased self-efficacy as teachers, something we academic nerds and scholarly geeks and confirmed introverts just can't get from all our book learning.

Knowing we can learn how to be effective teachers, knowing we are effective teachers even as we are always relearning about our teaching and our students' learning: that's the key to steering the ship and to helping our crew do the work they must do in order to succeed. When we're teaching effectively, we don't get the glory of being hotshot Captain Kirk. We can't mind meld our students into knowing how to do things, like Professor Spock might do. We can only steer the ship. Even when we're about to plunge over the side of a mountain not knowing exactly what's going to happen, if we're fully aware, and we've put on our professor pants, reflected, sought support, and we know that we are always learning and relearning how to teach, we can be as cool and effective as Sulu when it's time to boldly go into our classrooms and jump to warp.

GLOSSARY

academic entitlement. Belief that advancing one's learning and earning a good grade should not be difficult or uncomfortable, and that increasing knowledge is the sole responsibility of the teacher, not the learner

actionable feedback. Feedback presented in such a way that the learner can clearly see its utility and readily apply it to future work in order to demonstrate improvement

active learning. Pedagogical approach that emphasizes activity rather than passive reception of information; premised on the idea that learning requires applying and using ideas (not just reading or hearing about them) in meaningful ways

approachability. Teacher's ability to convey to students that students should feel able to interact comfortably one-on-one with the teacher, including asking for clarifications about content and discussing any course-related issues or problems

authenticity. Teaching quality perceived by students as a professor being "genuine"; presenting oneself as a human being rather than aloof and condescending; may include moderate amounts of self-disclosure and willingness to admit mistakes

bottleneck. A predictable and specific point, problem, or stumbling block in student learning in any discipline or class when students generally will not be able to successfully complete the necessary tasks or utilize essential skills; can be cognitive or emotional

classroom management. A teacher's ability to lead students in the classroom and foster a *positive classroom environment*; includes effectively minimizing incivility, inattention, and disengagement

community of inquiry. A pedagogical conceptual model most commonly occurring in *SoTL* about online teaching; emphasizes teachers and students consciously engaging together in collaborative intellectual investigation and learning

concept map. A visual representation of how ideas relate to one other; can range from a highly structured formal diagram to an informal product of brainstorming in small groups or individually

course learning objectives. The intended purpose (what is hoped students will learn) of a set course of study; also sometimes referred to as *student learning objectives* (SLO); can be applied very generally such as program or university learning objectives

decoding the disciplines. Pedagogical model in which teachers work to identify the basic building blocks in a disciplinary way of thinking, beginning with where students will predictably get "stuck" (*bottleneck*) and need specific assistance to move forward

disparate teaching realities. Term used by Roxanna Harlow in a 2003 *Social Psychology Quarterly* article to describe teaching and learning challenges faced by female faculty and all faculty of color that white men who fit the stereotype of "professor" do not face

enthusiasm. A teacher's ability to convey interest in both course content as well as fostering students' ability to successfully learn that content; can be demonstrated in a variety of ways

expert blind spot. Any expert's tendency when teaching to overlook the routine challenges or difficulties *novice learners* encounter in the subject, including underestimating the time it will take to learn certain basic skills or attain foundational knowledge and overestimating student understanding and ability

expert learner. Someone who understands that learning requires active engagement, planning (including effective time management and self-regulation), and reflection, and is highly aware of their own unique learning processes, willing and able to learn from their mistakes, and comfortable with periods of uncertainty

external locus of control. Student or teacher belief that responsibility for the products of teaching and learning are entirely or mostly outside one's own control

external motivation. Teacher or student desire and willingness to improve and develop skills and abilities based on external rewards such as grades (student) or outside pressures to improve efficacy of teaching such as an employment decision (teachers)

faculty learning community. Group of faculty who systematically study teaching and learning topics together; may include peer review

fixed mindset. Teacher or student belief that one's skills and abilities in any one area are set and cannot be substantially improved or developed, first identified by psychologist Carol Dweck

flipped classroom model. A pedagogical approach in which students receive content instruction traditionally delivered in class outside of class meeting time, and class meeting time is devoted to applying concepts, skills, and ideas

formative assessment. Checking and reviewing progress in teaching and learning with *actionable feedback* enabling learner and teacher to demonstrate progress and improvement; includes "low-stakes" assignments or checks on learning towards the summative/final product of teaching and learning, such as a final exam (student) or employment decision (teacher)

geek culture of sharing. Pedagogical approach that emphasizes college teachers' desire and ability to share their expertise with students and enable students to do things in and with their scholarly disciplinary fields; draws on communication scholar Joseph Reagle's research on geek subcultures and various nonacademic discourse about geek culture

geek gatekeeping. Tendency of certain groups of self-identified geeks and nerds to police who gets to claim the title of "geek" or "nerd"; most egregiously used to reinforce rigid gender and racial norms

GIN. Acronym for "geek, introvert, and nerd" (for a descriptive definition of each term, see the introduction)

grading rubric. Assessment tool that details grading standards for components of an assignment

growth mindset. Teacher or student belief that with effort, skills and abilities in any one area can be improved and developed; first identified by psychologist Carol Dweck

immediacy. Teacher ability to clearly communicate full attention or "presence" during class meetings and student interactions; conveys to students a teacher's willingness to engage with a student one-on-one

intrinsic motivation. A teacher or student's desire to learn, improve, and further develop skills and abilities based on an internal desire to learn and improve

learner-centered pedagogy. Structuring teaching around students' own actions, responsibilities, decisions, reflection, and collaboration in learning, in contrast to instructor-centered pedagogy that prioritizes expert delivery of content and passive student reception

low-stakes assignments. Required student work that allows the teacher to give feedback and to assess learning without significant impact on a student's final grade, enabling student to improve skills and performance before completing high-stakes final products such as a final exam

metacognition. Teacher or student ability to reflect on one's own thought processes and learning strategies

microagressions. Unintentional or intentional indirect, and usually subtle, action or statement in the classroom or other interactions between students or between students and a teacher that reinforces discrimination against or stereotype about any group of people

midterm student evaluations of teaching. Assessing student responses to and perceptions of teaching and learning in a class at the midpoint of the semester; enables teacher to make course adjustments and corrections based on student feedback and to address problems and issues before students complete their end-of-the semester *student evaluations of teaching* (SET)

novice learner. Student or teacher new to learning any one subject or to learning generally; characterized by a lack of broad knowledge structures and connections and a dualistic or simplistic approach to knowledge

pedagogical content knowledge. The combination of knowledge about one's field of expertise and knowledge about how to effectively teach others the skills and abilities necessary to successfully engage in one's field of expertise; the ability to apply those skills and make adjustments during actual teaching practices and during reflection

peer observation. Feedback from colleagues or other peers on teaching and learning; can include review of materials such as syllabi or assignments and in-class observations

positive classroom environment. A sense of connection among students and between students and the teacher; class meetings that consistently encourage, support, and motivate the maximum number of students to achieve successful learning and skills building; includes minimizing incivilities, disengagement, and hostilities, and maximizing professional interpersonal relationships; also known as classroom community, class climate, learning community/culture

Professoritis. A common affliction among those who regularly teach college classes; symptoms include pomposity, inflated ego, talking too much and in a condescending manner, not listening enough, and a *fixed mindset* regarding teaching or unwillingness to devote effort to improving one's own teaching and learning; creates an aura around a teacher of unapproachability, distance, and lack of clarity; conveys to students a disinterest in student learning

professor pants. Metaphor for deliberately and consciously planning for teaching and learning as a social interaction by preparing to communicate clearly with students and convey qualities necessary for effective teaching and learning that may not come easily or naturally to *GINs*

rapport. Teacher ability to create and foster positive and trusting interpersonal professional relationships with students; requires communication skills and ability to demonstrate to students a teacher's *approachability* and *immediacy*

reverse course design. Planning course content by beginning with the desired end result, including specific things that students will be able to do at the end of the class that they couldn't do at the beginning, and how those things will be measured and assessed

scaffolding. Curriculum design, including assignments and assessment, that systematically increase student skills and abilities over time by clearly and deliberately building on previous learning

scholarship of teaching and learning (SoTL). Published or otherwise publicly presented and readily available research, presented at conferences, published as blogs or online, etc., undertaken in order to advance knowledge about and understanding of effective teaching and learning; incorporates a variety of evidence and research methods; may be multidisciplinary or aimed at practitioners in a specific field

self-efficacy. Belief in one's own ability to successfully learn and demonstrate learning (student) or belief in one's own ability to successfully foster student learning and to continually keep improving one's teaching efficacy (teacher)

statement of teaching philosophy. A self-reflective document describing a teacher's pedagogical goals and how, in practical terms with concrete examples, the teacher fosters student progress towards those goals and successful learning

student engagement. Broad term referring to range of ways students may be actively working to understand content, develop skills, or apply ideas in a learning environment; may also connote student attention, curiosity, and intrinsic motivation

student evaluations of teaching (SET). Direct feedback from students regarding their perceptions of teaching efficacy and their own learning experiences in a specific course; may include ratings of specific teaching qualities; other terms for this process include student ratings of instruction (SRI), student course evaluations, course evaluations, student perceptions of teaching, student/course opinion surveys

student incivility. Broad term for range of disruptive, disrespectful, hostile, or overtly intimidating student behaviors and actions; can occur during class meetings and during individual interactions with other students or with teachers

student learning outcomes (SLO). Specific knowledge, skills, and abilities (what students learned) as demonstrated by what students can do at the end of a course of study; learning that is observable, assessable, and measurable by teachers

summative assessment. An "end product" review and evaluation of teaching and learning such as a final exam (student) or employment decision review (teacher)

teacher presence. A teacher's ability to command attention, communicate caring, and foster students' academic engagement and interpersonal connectedness in a classroom; communicated both verbally as well as nonverbally to students

teaching circle. A formal or informal group of faculty who meet on a regular basis to discuss specific issues associated with effective teaching and advancing student learning in their localized teaching contexts; coined by Pat Hutchings in 1996

teaching journal. An individual record of a teacher's own unique teaching experiences undertaken for the purpose of self-reflection on pedagogical puzzles and problems a teacher encounters, and preparation for applying those insights to one's teaching practices

teaching persona. A metaphor for how every teacher consciously or unconsciously conveys certain teaching and personal qualities to students; sometimes misunderstood as a false front or purely performative aspect of teaching, but more accurately a combination of one's teaching *authenticity*, communication with students, and deliberate effort to foster interpersonal skills required for effective teaching and learning in our unique teaching context

teaching portfolio. The collected documentation of a teacher's efficacy, including but not limited to teaching materials such as syllabi and assignments, examples of student work or other documented student learning, *statement of teaching philosophy*, *SET*, and reflective statements; can be used when seeking employment and for *summative assessment*

teaching squares. A formal or informal group of four faculty organized in order to provide peer feedback, including class visits, and to facilitate reflection; not linked to employment decisions or *summative assessment*

threshold concepts. Significant ideas or understandings that create moments of transition in a learner's progress toward skillful mastery of a subject and results in transformation; first identified by Erik Myer and Ray Land in 2003

transparency. Consistently ensuring that students understand the reasons for one's pedagogical techniques by communicating rationales; clearly communicating all course expectations; can also refer to conversation among teachers about improving teaching and learning

NOTES

Introduction

1. Jay Parini, *The Art of Teaching* (New York: Oxford University Press, 2005), 61. For citations on pedagogical training in graduate school, see "Introduction Bibliographic Essay," available for download at geekypedagogy.com.

2. Douglass J. Wilde, *Jung's Personality Theory Quantified* (New York: Springer, 2011), 8.

3. Michael Godsey, "Why Introverted Teachers Are Burning Out," *The Atlantic*, January 25, 2016, https://www.theatlantic.com/education /archive/2016/01/why-introverted-teachers-are-burning-out/425151.

4. Susan Cain, *Quiet: The Power of Introverts in a World That Can't Stop Talking* (New York: Crown Publishing, 2012). For further citations, see "Introduction Bibliographic Essay," geekypedagogy.com.

5. "The image of the nerd persists in our culture because of the richness of references, and the plethora of narratives to which it connects. Embodied in the nerd are stories about economics, technology, gender, and race. All of these topics continue to be sites of power, inequalities, contestation, and controversy." Lori Kendall, "'White and Nerdy': Computers, Race, and the Nerd Stereotype," *The Journal of Popular Culture* 44, no. 3 (2011): 519.

6. Jessica Bennett and Jennie Yabroff trace "geek" and "nerd" to post-WWII tech school humor magazines. "Revenge of the Nerdette," *Newsweek*, June 16, 2008, 44–49. Others reference early 1900s radio amateurs, sci-fi fan clubs in the 1920s and 1930s, and 1940s polytechnic institutes. Kathryn E. Lane, "How Was the Nerd or

Geek Born?" in *Age of the Geek: Depictions of Nerds and Geeks
in Popular Media*, ed. Kathryn E. Lane (New York: Palgrave
Macmillan, 2018), 3. See also Ron Eglash, "Race, Sex, and Nerds:
From Black Geeks to Asian American Hipsters," *Social Text* 20,
no. 2 (Summer 2002): 50–51; Benjamin Nugent, *American Nerd:
The Story of My People* (New York: Scribner, 2008), 39–42, 57–59.
Posted online in 1996 by self-identified geeks, "The Geek Code"
delineated who could claim the title of "geek." Joseph Reagle, "Geek
Policing: Fake Geek Girls and Contested Attention," *International
Journal of Communication* 9 (2015): 2865. On a similar "Nerdity
Test," see Anastasia Salter and Bridget Bodgett, *Toxic Geek
Masculinity in Media: Sexism, Trolling, and Identity Policing* (New
York: Palgrave Macmillan, 2017), 6–7; Lori Kendall, "Nerd Nation:
Images of Nerds in U.S. Popular Culture," *International Journal of
Cultural Studies* 2, no. 2 (1999): 262. For further discussion about
geeks and nerds, including representations in popular culture
and geek "gatekeeping," see "Introduction Bibliographic Essay,"
geekypedagogy.com.

7.   Eleanor Amaranth Lockhart, "Nerd/Geek Masculinity: Technocracy,
Rationality, and Gender in Nerd Culture's Countermasculine
Hegemony," PhD diss., Texas A&M University, 2015, 4; Laurie Penny,
"The Problem with Nerd Entitlement," *New Statesmen*, January
9–15, 2015, 14; Christine Quail, "Nerds, Geeks, and the Hip/Square
Dialectic in Contemporary Television," *Television and New Media* 12,
no. 5 (2011): 464–65; Angela Willey and Banu Subramaniam, "Inside
the Social World of Asocials: White Nerd Masculinity, Science, and
the Politics of Reverent Disdain," *Feminist Studies* 43, no. 1 (2017):
25. On early depictions of nerds as Jewish, see Johnathan Charles
Flowers, "How Is It Okay to Be a Black Nerd?" in Lane, *Age of the
Geek*, 172; Nugent, *American Nerd*, 81–88.

8.   Lockhart describes such attempts as activists working to "retake
geek culture." "Nerd/Geek Masculinity," 151–52. See also Lauren
Alfrey and France Winddance Twine, "Gender-Fluid Geek Girls:
Negotiating Inequality Regimes in the Tech Industry," *Gender and
Society* 31, no. 1 (February 2017): 28–50; Mary Bucholtz, "Geek
Feminism," in *Gendered Practices in Language*, ed. Sarah Benor et al.

(Stanford: CSLI Publications, 2002); Heather Cabot and Samantha Walravens, *Geek Girl Rising: Inside the Sisterhood Shaking Up Tech* (New York: St. Martin's Press, 2017); Kameron Hurley, *The Geek Feminist Revolution* (New York: Tor, 2016); Bao Phi, "What It's Like to Be a N. O. C. (Nerd of Color)," *io9*, August 4, 2010, https://io9 .gizmodo.com/5604617/what-its-like-to-be-an-noc-nerd-of-color. See also *Riot Nrrd*, http://www.riotnrrdcomics.com/links. Two examples of fictional nerds who illustrate the diversification of nerds and geeks are Elena Alvarez (Netflix, *One Day at a Time*), a lesbian Latinx Dr. Who fan, and Nomi Marks, a queer transgender hacker (Netflix, *Sense8*).

9.   Mary Bucholtz, "The Whiteness of Nerds: Superstandard English and Racial Markedness," *Journal of Linguistic Anthropology* 11, no. 1 (2001): 84; Flowers, "How Is It Okay to Be a Black Nerd?" 174–75.

10.   David Gillota, "Black Nerds: New Directions in African American Humor," *Studies in American Humor* 28 (2013): 17–30; Mekeisha Madden Toby, "The Rise of the Black Nerd in Pop Culture," *CNN Online*, March 31, 2012, http://www.cnn.com/2012/03/31/showbiz /rise-of-black-nerds/index.html. Some prominent public intellectuals are self-identified blerds, such as Neil deGrasse-Tyson, who joined Larry Wilmore in a *Nightly Show* segment called "Blerd-Off 2015." Examples of fictional blerds on TV include Dr. Chris Turk (*Scrubs*), sometimes referenced as the first to use the term "blerd"; Burton "Gus" Guster (*Psych*); Andre Johnson Jr. (*Black-ish*); Lucas Sinclair (*Stranger Things*); and Chidi Anagonye (*The Good Place*).

11.   Ta-Nehisi Coates, "Why Ta-Nehisi Isn't a 'Black Nerd,'" *The Atlantic*, July 9, 2008, https://www. theatlantic.com/entertainment /archive/2008/07/ why-ta-nehisi-isn-apos-t-a-quot-black-nerd-quot /5008.

12.   As quoted in Beatriz Valenzuela, "Comic-Con 2017: Black Nerds, or Blerds, Describe the Challenge of Diversity in Geek Culture," *San Bernardino County Sun*, July 22, 2017, https://www.ocregister .com/2017/07/21/comic-con-2017-black-nerds-or-blerds-describe -the-challenge-of-diversity-in-geek-culture. See also "The Blerd Is Out: Indigenous People Can Be Total Nerds Too," *The Age* (Melbourne, Australia), November 24, 2016, http://lexisnexis.com;

Keshia McEntire, "Black and Nerdy: Blerd Club Brings Black Nerd Culture to Indy," *Indianapolis Recorder*, December 8, 2016, http://www.indianapolisrecorder.com.

13.   Noah Berlatsky, "'Fake Geek Girls' Paranoia Is about Male Insecurity, Not Female Duplicity," *The Atlantic*, January 22, 2013, https://www.theatlantic.com/sexes/archive/2013/01/fake-geek-girls-paranoia-is-about-male-insecurity-not-female-duplicity/267402/; Joseph Reagle, "Nerd vs. Bro: Geek Privilege, Idiosyncrasy, and Triumphalism," *First Monday* 23, no. 1 (January 2018), http://dx.doi.org/10.5210/fm.v23i1.7879; Katie Spies, "Gatekeeping: How Women Are Kept Out Of Nerd Culture," *Odyssey*, April 19, 2016, https://www.theodysseyonline.com/gatekeeping-women-nerd-culture.

14.   Reagle, "Geek Policing." See also Kristina Busse, "Geek Hierarchies, Boundary Policing, and the Gendering of the Good Fan," *Participations* 10, no. 1 (2013): 73–91; Salter and Blodgett, *Toxic Geek Masculinity in Media*, 11–12.

15.   Erika L. Sánchez, "The Origin of a Latina Nerd," *Huffington Post*, June 13, 2012, https://www.huffingtonpost.com/erika-l-sanchez/the-origin-of-a-latina-ne_b_1589666.html.

16.   Tricia Berry, "'Geek' Be Gone: Word Could Be Turning Girls Off to STEM," *Chicago Tribune*, December 7, 2017, LS 7; Katherine Losse, *The Boy Kings: A Journey into the Heart of the Social Network* (New York: Free Press, 2012); Liza Mundy, "Why Is Silicon Valley So Awful to Women?" *The Atlantic*, April 2017, 60–73; Ralph Potts, "'Geeks' Only: Understanding the Geek Culture in the IT Sector to Explain Cultural Barriers," PhD diss., Northcentral University, 2018; Salter and Blodgett, *Toxic Geek Masculinity in Media*, 13.

17.   On the decreasing power of nerd stereotypes, see Tracy Cross, "Nerds and Geeks: Society's Evolving Stereotypes of Our Students with Gifts and Talents," *Gifted Child Today* 28, no. 4 (Fall 2005): 26–27, 65; Glen Weldon, "How We Nerd Now," *The Washingtonian*, August 2016, 15–16. On how "nerd" remains a derogatory label, see Dave Anderegg, *Nerds: How Dorks, Dweebs, Techies, and Trekkies Can Save America and Why They Might Be Our Last Hope* (New York: Tarcher/Penguin, 2011), 2–3, 13, 15, 66, 262–63; Katrin Rentzsch, Astrid Schutz, and Michela Schroder-Abe, "Being Labeled Nerd:

Factors That Influence the Social Acceptance of High-Achieving Students," *Journal of Experimental Education* 79, no. 2 (2011): 143–68. Nerd stereotypes may negatively impact young people of color especially. See Jaun Carillo, *Barrio Nerds: Latino Males, Schooling, and the Beautiful Struggle* (Rotterdam: Sense Publishing, 2016); Willow Lung-Amam, "'Dumb White Kids' and 'Asian Nerds': Race and Ethnic Relations in Silicon Valley," in *Transcultural Cities: Border-Crossing and Placemaking*, ed. Jeffery Hou (New York: Taylor and Francis, 2013); Ebony McGee, K. Bhoomi Thakore, and Sandra LaBlance, "The Burden of Being 'Model': Racialized Experiences of Asian STEM College Students," *Journal of Diversity in Higher Education* 10, no. 3 (September 2017): 253–70; Sameer Pandya, "Freaks and Geeks: On the Provisional Citizenship of Indian American Spelling Bee Winners," *Journal of Asian American Studies* 20, no. 2 (June 2017): 245–63; Qin Zhang, "Asian Americans beyond the Model Minority Stereotype: The Nerdy and the Left Out," *Journal of International and Intercultural Communication* 3, no. 1 (February 2010): 20–37. Gerald Graff points out that the "vast gulf between the nerds and the popular crowd or jocks" that he experienced growing up in the 1950s has lessened but also that the "triumphant nerds" in films such as *Good Will Hunting* "are usually computer geeks and technical scientists, not philosophical or cultural thinkers." Gerald Graff, *Clueless in Academe: How Schooling Obscures the Life of the Mind* (New Haven: Yale University Press, 2003), 40–41.

18.   Cory Casciato, "How to Make a Geek: Nurture Nerdiness," *Westworld*, June 12, 2014, http://www.westword.com/arts/how-to-make-a-geek-nurture-nerdiness-5795488.

19.   Lane, "How Was the Nerd or Geek Born?" in Lane, *Age of the Geek*, 3.

20.   J. A. McArthur, "Digital Subculture: A Geek Meaning of Style," *Journal of Communication Inquiry* 33, no. 1 (2009): 62.

21.   Reagle, "Geek Policing," 2866, 2874.

22.   Tom Rogers, "Let's Celebrate Nerdiness!" *Newsweek*, December 11, 2000: 14.

23.   Leslie Simon, *Geek Girls Unite: How Fangirls, Bookworms, Indie Chicks, and Other Misfits Are Taking Over the World* (New York: HarperEntertainment, 2011), 3.

24.   Jessica Bodner, "A Nerd, a Geek, and a Hipster Walk into a Bar," in
       Lane, *Age of the Geek*, 23–24.

25.   Donald Glover, as quoted in Toby, "The Rise of the Black Nerd in Pop
       Culture."

26.   Michael Flachmann, "Great Teachers and Dead Sharks," in *The Art
       of College Teaching: 28 Takes*, ed. Marilyn Kallet and April Morgan
       (Knoxville: The University of Tennessee Press, 2005), 45.

27.   See for example Jessamyn Neuhaus, *Housework and Housewives
       in American Advertising: Married to the Mop* (New York: Palgrave
       Macmillan, 2011) and *Manly Meals and Mom's Home Cooking:
       Cookbooks and Gender in Modern America* (Baltimore: Johns
       Hopkins University Press, 2003). To see my complete vita, visit
       geekypedagogy.com.

28.   Michele DiPietro and Marie Norman, "Using Learning Principles
       as a Theoretical Framework for Instructional Consultations,"
       International Journal for Academic Development 19, no. 4 (2014): 285.
       See also Susan Ambrose et al., *How Learning Works: Seven Research-
       Based Principles for Smart Teaching* (San Francisco: Jossey-Bass,
       2013), 99–103.

29.   One fruitful approach to this common problem is "decoding the
       disciplines," articulated by Joan Middendorf and David Pace, which
       "arose from the realization that there is a disciplinary unconscious,
       automatic moves learned tacitly by the expert." Leah Shopkow et al.,
       "The History Learning Project 'Decodes' a Discipline: The Union
       of Teaching and Epistemology," in Kathleen McKinney, ed., *The
       Scholarship of Teaching In and Across the Disciplines* (Bloomington:
       Indiana University Press, 2013), 93. See also Janice Miller-Young
       and Jennifer Boman, *Using the Decoding the Disciplines Framework
       for Learning across Disciplines* (New York: John Wiley and Sons,
       2017); David Pace, *The Decoding the Disciplines Paradigm: Seven
       Steps to Increased Student Learning* (Bloomington: Indiana
       University Press, 2017).

30.   David Sedaris, *Me Talk Pretty One Day* (New York: Little, Brown and
       Company, 2000), 85.

31.   Reagle, "Geek Policing," 2864.

32. Ken Bain, *What the Best College Teachers Do* (Cambridge: Harvard University Press, 2004), 17. On teaching as an intellectual activity and scholarly teaching, see Dan Bernstein, "Now Is a Good Time to Recognize Teaching as Serious Intellectual Work," *InSight: A Journal of Scholarly Teaching* 11 (2016): 9–14; Ernest L. Boyer et al. *Scholarship Reconsidered: Priorities of the Professoriate, Expanded Edition* (San Francisco: Jossey-Bass, 2015); Charles Glassick, Mary Taylor Huber, and Gene Maeroff, *Scholarship Assessed: Evaluation of the Professoriate* (San Francisco: Jossey-Bass, 1997); Carolin Kreber, ed., *Scholarship Revisited: Perspectives on the Scholarship of Teaching* (San Francisco: Jossey-Bass, 2001); Mary Taylor Huber and Pat Hutchings, *The Advancement of Learning: Building the Teaching Commons* (San Francisco: Jossey Bass, 2005); Paul Savory, Amy Nelson Burnett, and Amy Goodburn, *Inquiry into the College Classroom: A Journey toward Scholarly Teaching* (Bolton, MA: Anker Publishing, 2007); Lee S. Shulman, *Teaching as Community Property: Essays on Higher Education* (San Francisco: Jossey Bass, 2009).

33. "The purpose of higher education is not to demonstrate my expertise to students but rather help them build their own expertise." Kevin Gannon, "Lecture-Based Pedagogy and the Pitfalls of Expertise," *The Tattooed Professor* (blog), January 16, 2018, http://www.thetattooedprof.com/2018/01/16/lecture-based-pedagogy-and-the-pitfalls-of-expertise.

34. Reagle, "Geek Policing," 2862. See also Benjamin Woo, "Nerds, Geeks, Gamers, and Fans: Doing Subculture at the Edge of the Mainstream," in *The Borders of Subculture: Resistance and the Mainstream*, ed. Alexander Dhoest et al. (New York: Routledge, 2015).

35. Leonardo Flores, "Towards a Geek Pedagogy: A Manifesto," *Leonardoflores.net* (blog), January 7, 2016, http://leonardoflores.net/blog/towards-a-geek-pedagogy-a-manifesto/; Heather Wolpert-Gawron, "Creating a Geek Culture in the Classroom," *Edutopia Blog*, August 11, 2015, https://www.edutopia.org/blog/creating-geek-culture-classroom-heather-wolpert-gawron.

36. Wil Wheaton, "Being a Nerd Is Not about What You Love, It's How

You Love It," *Wil Wheaton Dot Net* (blog), April 30, 2013, http://
wilwheaton.net/2013/04/being-a-nerd-is-not-about-what-you-love
-its-about-how-you-love-it.

37.   As quoted in Bodner, "A Nerd, A Geek, and Hipster Walk into a Bar,"
       27–28.

38.   Flachmann, "Great Teachers and Dead Sharks," 45.

39.   Robert Rotenberg, *The Art and Craft of College Teaching: A Guide
       for New Professors and Graduate Students,* Second Edition (Walnut
       Creek, CA: Left Coast Press, 2010), 49–50.

40.   Reagle, "Geek Policing," 2873.

41.   To be sure, students sometimes view effective college teachers
       as almost magically infused with superhuman charisma: "The
       metaphors used by graduates to describe their favorite teachers
       spring not from the language of information exchange, but from
       religion—or love: inspiration, revelation, passion, enthusiasm,
       charisma, transformation. . . . Professors are invested with the power
       of the shaman, blowing life into dead subjects and making students
       blossom; they are viewed as prophets who change lives." James R.
       Acker, "Class Acts: Outstanding College Teachers and the Difference
       They Make," *Criminal Justice Review* 28, no. 2 (Autumn 2003): 221.
       I'm not discounting this perception on the part of students, but for
       faculty it can undermine teaching self-efficacy. See Bain, *What the
       Best College Teachers Do,* 173; Jennifer McCrikerd, "Understanding
       and Reducing Faculty Reluctance to Improve Teaching," *College
       Teaching* 60 (2012): 56–64.

42.   Highly effective teachers utilize "organization, clarity, enthusiasm,
       knowledge and love of content," which "look a lot more like
       acquirable skills than divine gifts." Maryellen Weimer, *Inspired
       College Teaching: A Career-Long Resource for Professional Growth*
       (San Francisco: Jossey-Bass, 2010), 151–52, 6.

43.   In one survey, 70% of Americans "thought the ability to teach
       was more the result of innate talent than training." "Teaching the
       Teachers," *The Economist,* July 11, 2016, http://www.economist.com
       /news/briefing/21700385-great-teaching-has-long-been-seen-innate
       -skill-reformers-are-showing-best.

44.   "Career counselors and popular films may portray teachers as

transformative heroes skillfully navigating classroom dilemmas to empower previously skeptical students, but actual teacher narratives emphasize much more how teaching is riddled with irresolvable dilemmas and complex uncertainties." Stephen D. Brookfield, *The Skillful Teacher: On Technique, Trust, and Responsiveness in the Classroom*, Third Edition (San Francisco: Jossey-Bass, 2015), 2. For further citations on popular representations of teachers see "Introduction Bibliographic Essay," geekypedagogy.com.

45. Self-efficacy is "a person's belief in their ability to succeed at a particular task or in a specific situation." Vincent Tinto, "Reflections on Student Persistence," *Student Success* 8, no. 2 (July 2017): 2. Megan Tschannen-Morah and Anita Woolfolk Hoby define teacher self-efficacy as a teacher's own "judgment of his or her capabilities to bring about desired outcomes of student engagement and learning, even among those students who may be difficult or unmotivated." "Teacher Efficacy: Capturing an Elusive Concept," *Teaching and Teacher Education* 17 (2001): 783.

46. Todd Zakrajsek reminded me of this point during his EBT Talk, Annual Lilly Conference on College Teaching and Learning, Bethesda, MD, June 3, 2017. College instructors who are focused more on student learning generally than specific subject content may feel more positive about teaching and have greater self-efficacy. See Liisa Postareff and Sari Lindblom-Ylänne, "Emotions and Confidence within Teaching in Higher Education," *Studies in Higher Education* 36, no. 7 (November 2011): 799–813.

47. As quoted in Garry Hoban, "Using a Reflective Framework to Study Teaching-Learning Relationships," *Reflective Practice* 1, no. 2 (2000): 165.

48. Another good definition of effective teaching is "selecting the materials, resources, teaching strategies and assignments that have the greatest potential to contribute to student learning." Michael Komos, "'Thanks for Asking': Adjunct Faculty Members' Views of Effective Teaching," *Journal on Excellence in College Teaching* 24, no. 4 (2013): 133. A succinct definition similar to mine is Wilbert J. McKeachie's: "the extent to which a professor enables students to execute their academic objectives." As quoted in Aaron Richmond

et al., "*a* + (b$_1$) Professor–Student Rapport + (b$_2$) Humor + (b$_3$) Student Engagement = (Ŷ) Student Ratings of Instructors," *Teaching of Psychology* 42, no. 2 (2015): 119.

49.   SoTL based on empirical research undertaken with the tools of scientific inquiry is valuable, but "scholarship that reports research results is less effective at improving practice; it is not easy to read and the implications of its findings are not always clear or applicable." Maryellen Weimer, *Enhancing Scholarly Work on Teaching and Learning: Professional Literature That Makes a Difference* (San Francisco: Jossey-Bass, 2006), 158–59.

50.   Brookfield, *The Skillful Teacher*, 265; Weimer, *Inspired College Teaching*, xii.

51.   Pat Hutchings, Mary Taylor Huber, Anthony Ciccone, *The Scholarship of Teaching and Learning Reconsidered: Institutional Integration and Impact* (San Francisco: Jossey-Bass, 2011), 29.

52.   Educational consultants Michele DiPietro and Marie Norman argue that faculty who wish to improve their teaching often mistakenly believe that it is a matter of a few "quick tips" or that there's an easy "magic solution" for effective teaching. "Using Learning Principles as a Theoretical Framework for Instructional Consultations," 278. They counter this tendency by "providing instructors with an overarching framework to organize their knowledge of teaching" (284). *Geeky Pedagogy* offers another type of overarching framework created for the same type of application.

53.   L. Dee Fink, *Creating Significant Learning Experiences,* Revised and Updated Edition (San Francisco: Jossey-Bass, 2013), 216–17.

Chapter 1

1.   Elizabeth Minnich, Laura Gardner, and Brenda Sorkin term this "present teaching." "In the Presence of Teaching: Reflections from a Project," *Change: The Magazine of Higher Learning* 48, no. 3 (May–June 2016): 60–66. See also Daniel P. Barbezat and Mirabai Bush, *Contemplative Practices in Higher Education: Powerful Methods to Transform Teaching and Learning* (San Francisco, CA: Jossey-Bass, 2014); Beth Berila, *Integrating Mindfulness into Anti-Oppression*

Pedagogy: Social Justice in Higher Education (New York: Routledge, 2016); Paula Gardner and Jill Grose, "Mindfulness in the Academy: Transforming Our Work and Ourselves 'One Moment at a Time,'" *Collected Essays on Learning and Teaching* 8 (January 2015): 35–46; Mei Hoyt, "Teaching with Mindfulness: The Pedagogy of Being-with/ for and Without Being-with/for," *Journal of Curriculum Theorizing* 31, no. 1 (2016): 126–42; Tim Lomas et al., "The Impact of Mindfulness on the Wellbeing and Performance of Educators: A Systematic Review of the Empirical Literature," *Teaching and Teacher Education* 61 (January 2017): 132–41; Ira Rabois, *Compassionate Critical Thinking: How Mindfulness, Creativity, Empathy, and Socratic Questioning Can Transform Teaching* (Lanham, MA: Rowman and Littlefield, 2016). For further citations, see "Chapter 1 Bibliographic Essay," available for download at geekypedadogy.com.

2.   See for example Anonymous, "Surviving Institutional Racism in Academe," *Inside Higher Ed,* November 17, 2017, https://www .insidehighered.com/advice/2017/11/17/faculty-member-offers -lessons-shes-learned-about-institutional-racism-essay.

3.   Sylvia R. Lazos, "Are Student Teaching Evaluations Holding Back Women and Minorities? The Perils of 'Doing' Gender and Race in the Classroom," in *Presumed Incompetent: The Intersections of Race and Class for Women in Academia*, ed. Gabriella y Muhs Gutiérrez et al. (Boulder: University Press of Colorado, 2012), 175, 177. See also Joel Nadler, Seth Berry, and Margaret Stockdale, "Familiarity and Sex Based Stereotypes on Instant Impressions of Male and Female Faculty," *Social Psychology of Education: An International Journal* 16, no. 3 (September 2013): 517–39.

4.   Roxanna Harlow, "'Race Doesn't Matter, But . . . ' The Effect of Race on Professors' Experiences and Emotion Management in the Undergraduate College Classroom," *Social Psychology Quarterly* 66, no. 4 (2003): 348.

5.   For further discussion of embodied identity and disparate teaching realities, see "Chapter 1 Bibliographic Essay," geekypedagogy.com.

6.   "Research shows that both minorities and women are presumed to be incompetent as soon as they walk in the door." Lazos, "Are Student Teaching Evaluations Holding Back Women and Minorities?" 177.

See also Brettjet Cody, "Fragmented Exchanges: The Impact of Cultural Mistrust on Student Faculty Interaction in a Predominantly White University," *Journal of Pan African Studies* 11, no. 3 (December 2017): 3–16; A. Yemisi Jimoh and Charlene Johnson, "Racing into the Academy: Pedagogy and Black Faculty," in *Race in the College Classroom: Pedagogy and Politics*, ed. Bonnie Tusmith and Maureen T. Reddy (New Brunswick, NJ: Rutgers University Press, 2002), 295; Katherine Grace Hendrix, "'She must be trippin': The Secret of Disrespect from Students of Color toward Faculty of Color," *New Directions for Teaching and Learning* 110 (Summer 2007): 89–96; Ginger Ko, "The Case for Humanities Training: A Woman of Color Teaching Social Justice in a Predominantly White Institution," *Theory in Action* 8, no. 4 (October 2015): 55–65. Having mostly K–12 female teachers appears to make college students less able to perceive female faculty as equipped with the same expertise as male professors. Bradley E. Cox, "Pedagogical Signals of Faculty Approachability: Factors Shaping Faculty-Student Interaction outside the Classroom," *Research in Higher Education* 51 (2010): 785.

7.   Kevin Everod Quashi, "Fear and the Professorial Center," in *Race in the College Classroom*, 96.

8.   As quoted in Mary-Antoinette Smith, "Free at Last! No More Performance Anxieties in the Academy 'Cause Stepin Fetchit Has Left the Building," in Muhs Gutiérrez et al., *Presumed Incompetent*, 414.

9.   Lucila Vargas, "Introduction," in *Women Faculty of Color in the White Classroom: Narratives on the Pedagogical Implications of Teacher Diversity*, ed. Lucile Vargas (New York: Peter Lang, 2002), 7, 20.

10.   Vargas, "Introduction," 18.

11.   Gary Perry et al., "Maintaining Credibility and Authority as an Instructor of Color in Diversity-Education Classrooms: A Qualitative Inquiry," *The Journal of Higher Education* 80, no. 1 (January/February 2009): 89. See also Christine A. Stanley, *Faculty of Color: Teaching in Predominantly White Colleges and Universities* (Bolton, MA: Anker Publishing Company, 2006), 21.

12.   Mia Alexander-Snow, "Dynamics of Gender, Ethnicity, and Race in Understanding Classroom Incivility," *New Directions for Teaching*

and Learning 99 (Fall 2004): 21–31; Chavella Pittman, "Race and Gender Oppression in the Classroom: The Experiences of Women Faculty of Color with White Male Students," *Teaching Sociology* 38, no. 3 (July 2010): 183–96.

13. Jennifer Ho, "When the Political Is Personal: Life on the Multiethnic Margins," in Tusmith and Reddy, *Race in the College Classroom*, 63.

14. Harlow, "'Race Doesn't Matter, But . . . ,'" 362.

15. Juanita Johnson-Bailey and Ming-Yeh Lee, "Women of Color in the Academy: Where's Our Authority in the Classroom?" *Feminist Teacher* 15, no. 2 (2005): 113.

16. Dolly Chugh, Katherine L. Milkman, and Dodupe Akinola, "Professors Are Prejudiced, Too," *New York Times*, May 11, 2014, SR14; Shaun Harper and Charles Davis, "Eight Actions to Reduce Racism in College Classroom: When Professors Are Part of the Problem" *Academe* 102, no. 6 (November–December 2016): 31–34; Scott Jaschik, "Who Is Stereotyped Now?" *Inside Higher Ed,* May 8, 2015, https://www.insidehighered.com/news/2015/05/18/duke -professors-comments-black-students-anger-many; Fernando Zamudio Suréz, "How to Teach Professors to Avoid Implicit Bias," *The Chronicle of Higher Education,* November 11, 2016, A28–29.

17. Terry Doyle and Todd Zakrajsek, *The New Science of Learning: How to Learn in Harmony with Your Brain* (Sterling, VA: Stylus, 2013), 13. For further citations about the research on learning, see "Chapter 1 Bibliographic Essay," geekypedagogy.com.

18. Diane Cummings Persellin and Mary Blythe Daniels, *A Concise Guide to Improving Student Learning: Six Evidence-Based Principles and How to Apply Them* (Sterling, VA: Stylus, 2014), 2.

19. Anton O. Tolman, Andy Sechler, and Shea Smart, "Defining and Understanding Student Resistance," in *Why Students Resist Learning: A Practical Model for Understanding and Helping Students*, ed. Anton O. Tolman and Janine Kremling (Sterling, VA: Stylus, 2017), 44.

20. Susan Ambrose et al., *How Learning Works: Seven Research-Based Principles for Smart Teaching* (San Francisco: Jossey-Bass, 2010), 45.

21. Ambrose et al., *How Learning Works*, 51.

22. Peter Brown, Henry Roediger II, and Mark McDaniel, *Make It Stick:*

The Science of Successful Learning (Cambridge: Harvard University Press, 2014), 226.

23.   "Teachers often underestimate the power of students' tacit beliefs about knowing in preventing them from integrating new concepts and ways of thinking into what they already know—or worse, think they know." Linda Hodges and Katherine Stanton, "Translating Comments on Student Evaluations into the Language of Learning," *Innovative Higher Education* 31 (2007): 284.

24.   Alexander Doty, "'My Beautiful Wickedness': *The Wizard of Oz* as Lesbian Fantasy," in *Hop on Pop: The Politics and Pleasure of Popular Culture*, ed. Henry Jenkins, Tara McPherson, and Jane Shattuc (Durham: Duke University Press, 2002), 143.

25.   See for example Joan Middendorf and Leah Shopkow, *Overcoming Student Learning Bottlenecks: Decode the Critical Thinking of Your Discipline* (Sterling, VA: Stylus, 2018).

26.   Michael Thomas Flanagan, "Threshold Concepts: Undergraduate Teaching, Postgraduate Training, and Professional Development," *Threshold Concepts*, no date, http://www.ee.ucl.ac.uk/~mflanaga /thresholds.html.

27.   Ray Land, "Threshold Concepts and Troublesome Knowledge: A Transformational Approach to Learning" (keynote, Annual Lilly International Conference on College and University Teaching and Learning, Bethesda, MD, May 31, 2014). See also Ray Land, Jan H. F. Meyer, and Michael T. Flanagan, eds., *Threshold Concepts in Practice* (Rotterdam, Netherlands: Sense Publishers, 2016); Jan H. F. Meyer and Ray Land, eds., *Overcoming Barriers to Student Understanding: Threshold Concepts and Troublesome Knowledge* (New York: Routledge, 2006); Jan H. F. Meyer, Ray Land, and Caroline Baillie, eds., *Threshold Concepts and Transformational Learning* (Rotterdam, Netherlands: Sense Publishers, 2010).

28.   Elizabeth F. Barkley, *Student Engagement Techniques: A Handbook for College Faculty* (San Francisco: Jossey-Bass, 2010), 7. See also Edward W. Taylor and Patricia Cranton, *The Handbook of Transformative Learning: Theory, Research, and Practice* (San Francisco: Jossey-Bass, 2013).

29.   Ambrose et al., *How Learning Works*, 3–6.

30.   Doyle and Zakrajsek, *The New Science of Learning*, 35–44; Greta G. Freeman and Pamela D. Wash, "You Can Lead Students to the Classroom and You Can Make Them Think: Ten Brain-Based Strategies for College Teaching and Learning Success," *Journal on Excellence in College Teaching* 42, no. 3 (2013): 108.

31.   Nancy Dorion-Maillet, "If I Tell Them, They Will Learn," in *Teaching Mistakes from the Classroom* (Madison, WI: Magna Publications, 2010), 10. See also Kathleen F. Gabriel, *Teaching Unprepared Students: Strategies for Promoting Success and Retention in Higher Education* (Sterling, VA: Stylus, 2008), 22; Maryellen Weimer, *Inspired College Teaching: A Career-Long Resource for Professional Growth* (San Francisco: Jossey-Bass, 2010), 161.

32.   James E. Zull, *The Art of Changing the Brain: Enriching Teaching by Exploring the Biology of Learning* (Sterling, VA: Stylus, 2002), 101–2, 108–9; Stacy Bailey, "This Is Your Brain on College: Educating Students with the Brain in Mind," *CEA Critic* 76, no. 3 (November 2014): 270.

33.   Doyle and Zakrajsek, *The New Science of Learning*, 13.

34.   Brown, Roediger, II, and McDaniel, *Make It Stick*, 4. Mathematician Manu Kapur identified "productive struggle" as necessary for learning. See Douglas Fisher and Nancy Frey, "The Importance of Struggle," *Educational Leadership* 74, no. 8 (May 2017): 85–86. Another term is "desirable difficulties." Persellin and Daniels, *A Concise Guide to Improving Student Learning*, 3.

35.   See for example Sarah Rose Cavanagh, *The Spark of Learning: Energizing the College Classroom with the Science of Emotion* (Morgantown: West Virginia University Press, 2016); Mary Sunderland, "Taking Emotion Seriously: Meeting Students Where They Are," *Science and Engineering Ethics* 20, no. 1 (March 2014): 183–95.

36.   Anindito Aditomo, "Students' Response to Academic Setback: 'Growth Mindset' as a Buffer against Demotivation," *International Journal of Educational Psychology* 4, no. 2 (June 2015): 198–222; Janice Wiersema et al., "Mindset about Intelligence and Meaningful and Mindful Effort: It's Not My Hardest Class Any More!" *Learning Communities: Research and Practice* 3, no. 2 (2015): http://

washingtoncenter.evergreen.edu/lcrpjournal/vol3/iss2/3. Some recent scholarship questions the role of mindset in academic success. See Štěpán Bahník and Marek Branka, "Growth Mindset Is Not Associated with Scholastic Aptitude in a Large Sample of University Applicants," *Personality and Individual Differences* 117 (October 2017): 139–43.

37.   T. Scott Bledsoe and Janice C. Baksin, "Recognizing Student Fear: The Elephant in the Classroom," *College Teaching* 62 (2014): 32; Zull, *The Art of Changing the Brain*, 59.

38.   Aaron S. Richmond, Guy A. Boysen, and Regan A. R. Gurung, *An Evidence-Based Guide to College and University Teaching: Developing the Model Teacher* (New York: Routledge, 2016), 40.

39.   Cheryl Albers, "Teaching: From Disappointment to Ecstasy," *Teaching Sociology* 37 (July 2009): 269. See also Maryellen Weimer, *Learner-Centered Teaching: Five Key Changes to Practice*, Second Edition (San Francisco: Jossey-Bass, 2013), 203.

40.   Hodges and Stanton, "Translating Comments on Student Evaluations into the Language of Learning," 284.

41.   Hodges and Stanton, "Translating Comments on Student Evaluations into the Language of Learning," 284. See also Joshua Eyler, *How Humans Learn: The Science and Stories behind Effective College Teaching* (West Virginia University Press, 2018).

42.   Dannelle D. Stevens and Joanne E. Cooper, *Journal Keeping: How to Use Reflective Writing for Effective Learning, Teaching, Professional Insight, and Positive Change* (Sterling, VA: Stylus, 2009), 21.

43.   Michele DiPietro and Marie Norman, "Using Learning Principles as a Theoretical Framework for Instructional Consultations," *International Journal for Academic Development* 19, no. 4 (2014): 284–85.

44.   Claire B. Potter, "If I could stick my pen in my heart/and spill it all over the stage: Teaching Evaluations," *Tenured Radical* (blog), *The Chronicle of Higher Education*, January 11, 2011, http://www.chronicle.com/blognetwork/tenuredradical/2011/01/if-i-could-stick-my-pen-in-my-heartand.

45.   Allison Buskrik-Chohen, "Using Generational Theory to Rethink Teaching in Higher Education," *Teaching in Higher Education* 21, no. 1 (January 2016): 25–36. For further citations on generational

studies, including students' use of personal technology, see "Chapter 1 Bibliographic Essay," geekypedagogy.com.

46.   See especially Jean M. Twenge, *iGen: Why Today's Super-Connected Kids Are Growing Up Less Rebellious, More Tolerant, Less Happy—and Completely Unprepared for Adulthood* (New York: Atria Books, 2017), 49–50. See also Juyeon Ahn and Yoonhyuk Jung, "The Common Sense of Dependence on Smartphone: A Comparison between Digital Natives and Digital Immigrants," *New Media and Society* 18, no. 7 (August 2016): 1236–56; Anastasia Elder, "College Students' Cell Phone Use, Beliefs, and Effects on Their Learning," *College Student Journal* 47, no. 4 (Winter 2013): 585–92; Aaron W. Kates, Huang Wu, and Chris Coryn, "The Effects of Mobile Phone Use on Academic Performance: A Meta-Analysis," *Computers and Education* 127 (December 2018): 107–112; James A. Roberts et al., "The Invisible Addiction: Cell-Phone Activities and Addiction among Male and Female College Students," *Journal of Behavioral Addictions* 3, no. 4 (December 2014): 254–65; Seungyeon Lee et al., "The Effects of Cell Phone Use and Emotion-Regulation Style on College Students' Learning," *Applied Cognitive Psychology* 31, no. 3 (May–June 2017): 360–66. See also Diane Frances, "Cell Phones as Cigarettes," *The American Interest*, May 23, 2018, https://www.the -american-interest.com/2018/05/23/cell-phones-as-cigarettes.

47.   Bryce Airwood et al., *To My Professor: Student Voices for Great College Teaching* (Canton, MI: Read the Spirit Books, 2016), 191–96; Sarah Goldrick-Rab, *Paying the Price: College Costs, Financial Aid, and the Betrayal of the American Dream* (Chicago: University of Chicago Press, 2016); Arthur Levine, *Generation on a Tightrope: A Portrait of Today's College Student* (San Francisco: Jossey-Bass, 2012).

48.   Twenge, *iGen*, 307.

49.   Rebecca Cox, *The College Fear Factor: How Students and Professors Misunderstand Each Other* (Cambridge, MA: Harvard University Press, 2009), 41.

50.   Stephen Lippman, Ronald E. Bulanda, and Theodore C. Wagenaar, "Student Entitlement: Issues and Strategies for Confronting Entitlement in the Classroom and Beyond," *College Teaching* 57,

no. 4 (Fall 2009): 197; Sarah Sohr-Preston and Stefanie Boswell, "Predicting Academic Entitlement in Undergraduates," *International Journal of Teaching and Learning in Higher Education* 27, no. 2 (2015): 183. See also Zachary Goldman and Matthew Martin, "Millennial Students in the College Classroom: Adjusting to Academic Entitlement," *Communication Education* 65, no. 3 (July 2016): 365–67.

51. Thomas Schaefer, "The *You Owe Me!* Mentality: A Student Entitlement Perception Paradox," *Journal of Learning in Higher Education* 9, no. 1 (Spring 2013): 8; Lippman, Bulanda, and Wagenaar, "Student Entitlement," 197. See also Antonio Laverghetta, "The Relationship between Student Anti-Intellectualism, Academic Entitlement, Student Consumerism, and Classroom Incivility in a Sample of College Students," *College Student Journal* 52, no. 2 (Summer 2018): 278–82.

52. Zachary W. Goldman et al., "What Do College Students Want? A Prioritization of Instructional Behaviors and Characteristics," *Communication Education* 66, no. 3 (2017): 280.

53. Anton O. Tolman, Andy Sechler, and Shea Smart, "Obstacles, Biases, and the Urgent Need to Understand the Social Cost of Resistance," in Tolman and Kremling, *Why Students Resist Learning*, 49. I should note that faculty may *overestimate* the presence of academic entitlement. See Debra Lemke, Jeff Marx, and Lauren Dundes, "Challenging Notions of Academic Entitlement and Its Rise among Liberal Arts College Students," *Behavioral Sciences* 7, no. 4 (December 2017): 1–18.

54. Preston and Boswell, "Predicting Academic Entitlement in Undergraduates," 184. Students who exhibit academic entitlement may also be measurably unhappier than other students. Rebekah H. Reysen, Suzanne Degges-White, and Matthew B. Reysen, "Exploring the Interrelationships among Academic Entitlement, Academic Performance, and Satisfaction with Life in a College Student Sample," *Journal of College Student Retention: Research, Theory, and Practice* (October 2017): https://doi.org/10.1177/1521025117735292.

55. Stefanie S. Boswell, "I *Deserve* Success: Academic Entitlement Attitudes and Their Relationships with Course Self-Efficacy, Social

Networking, and Demographic Variables," *Social Psychology Education* 15 (2012): 356.

56.   Cathleen Kennedy, "Ten Surprises about Teaching," in *The Art of College Teaching: 28 Takes*, ed. Marilyn Kallet and April Morgan (Knoxville: The University of Tennessee Press, 2005), 9.

57.   Christopher Manor et al., "Foundations of Student-Faculty Partnerships in the Scholarship of Teaching and Learning: Theoretical and Developmental Considerations," in *Engaging Student Voices in the Study of Teaching and Learning*, ed. Carmen Werder and Megan M. Otis (Sterling, VA: Stylus, 2010), 10.

58.   Lippman, Bulanda, and Wagenaar, "Student Entitlement," 197; Schaefer, "The *You Owe Me!* Mentality," 89.

59.   Airwood, *To My Professor*, 32; Ambrose et al., *How Learning Works*, 180–87; Dave Berque, "Teaching as a Balancing Act: Strategies for Managing Competing Objectives," in Kallet and Morgan, *The Art of College Teaching*, 101–2; Zac D. Johnson and Sara LaBelle, "An Examination of Teacher Authenticity in the College Classroom," *Communication Education* 66, no. 4 (2017): 430; Stephen Lippman, "Facilitating Class Sessions for Ego-Piercing Engagement," in *New Directions for Teaching and Learning* no. 135 (Fall 2013): 45; Persellin and Daniels, *A Concise Guide to Improving Student Learning*, 16; Laurie Richlen, *Blueprint for Learning: Constructing College Courses to Facilitate, Assess, and Document Learning* (Sterling, VA: Stylus, 2006), 12; Richmond, Boysen, and Gurung, *An Evidence-Based Guide to College and University Teaching*, 62; Robert Rotenberg, *The Art and Craft of College Teaching: A Guide for New Professors and Graduate Students*, Second Edition (Walnut Creek, CA: Left Coast Press, 2010), 57–64.

60.   Katrina Zook, "Assumptions I Made in the Past and How I Come to Know My Students Now," in *Teaching Mistakes from the Classroom*, 116–17; Thomas F. Hawk and Paul R. Lyons, "Please Don't Give Up on Me: When Faculty Fail to Care," *Journal of Management Education* 32, no. 3 (June 2008): 344; Marilla D. Svinicki, *Learning and Motivation in the Postsecondary Classroom* (San Francisco: Anker Publishing Company, 2004), 187.

61.   Liz Grauerholz and Eric Main, "Fallacies of SOTL: Rethinking

How We Conduct Our Research," in *The Scholarship of Teaching In and Across the Disciplines*, ed. Kathleen McKinney (Bloomington: Indiana University Press, 2013), 156.

62.   Because "texting," as in "putting one's fingers on one's phone and actively typing" isn't *at all* the same thing as "just looking" at one's phone, as "Megan" argued adamantly and indignantly, when I asked her to please stop texting in class. The moral of this sad story? We have to be prepared to calmly and in a noncondescending way explain all our course policies well before we get sucked into a dumb and unwinnable argument about the difference between "looking with eyes" versus "thumb movements."

63.   Introvert Life, Twitter post, October 10, 2016, 2:24 p.m., https://twitter.com/introvertliving/status/785591932026130433?lang=en.

64.   Stephen W. Braden and Deborah N. Smith, "Managing the College Classroom: Perspectives from an Introvert and an Extrovert," *College Quarterly* 9, no. 1 (2006): https://eric.ed.gov/?id=EJ835334; Anne Guarnera, "Self-Care for the Introverted TA," *GradHacker* (blog), *Inside Higher Ed*, April 19, 2016, https://www.insidehighered.com/blogs/gradhacker/self-care-introverted-ta; Erika Vause, "Beyond First-Day Jitters: Teaching While Introverted, Shy, or Both," *Perspectives on History*, March 2016, https://www.historians.org/publications-and-directories/perspectives-on-history/march-2016/beyond-first-day-jitters-teaching-while-introverted-shy-or-both; Amir Mahdavi Zafarghandi, Sepideh Salehi, and Masoud Khalil Sabet, "The Effects of EFL Teachers' Extrovert and Introvert Personality on Their Instructional Immediacy," *International Journal of Applied Linguistics and English Literature* 5, no. 1 (January 2016): 57–64. For further citations on being an introvert in academia, see "Chapter 1 Bibliographic Essay," geekypedagogy.com.

65.   Stephen Brookfield, *The Skillful Teacher: On Technique, Trust, and Responsiveness in the Classroom*, Third Edition (San Francisco: Jossey-Bass, 2015), 272.

66.   Brian R. Little, "Acting Out of Character in the Immortal Profession: Toward a Free Trait Agreement," *Academic Matters*, April–May 2010, http://www.academicmatters.ca/2010/04/acting-out-of-character-in-the-immortal-profession-toward-a-free-trait-agreement.

67. "For many professors, solitude helps to replenish" energy, so "finding time alone is essential for refueling." Richard E. Lyons, Meggin McIntosh, Marcella L. Kysilka, *Teaching College in an Age of Accountability* (Boston: Allyn and Bacon/Pearson, 2003), 269.

68. Michael Houlihan et al., "Personality Effects on Teaching Anxiety and Teaching Strategies in University Professors," *Canadian Journal of Higher Education* 39, no. 1 (2009): 61.

69. Elsie Ameen, Daryl Guffey, and Cynthia Jackson, "Evidence of Teaching Anxiety among Accounting Educators," *Journal of Education for Business* 78, no. 1 (September/October 2002): 20.

70. Maggie Berg and Barbara K. Seeber, *The Slow Professor: Challenging the Culture of Speed in the Academy* (Toronto: University of Toronto Press, 2016), 42.

71. John Hanc, "Teaching Professors to Become Better Teachers," *New York Times*, June 23, 2016, F5; Minnich, Gardner, and Sorkin, "In the Presence of Teaching: Reflections from a Project," 61.

Chapter 2

1. Marilla D. Svinicki, Willbert J. McKeachie, et al., *McKeachie's Teaching Tips: Strategies, Research, and Theory for College and University Teachers*, Fourteenth Edition (Belmont, CA: Wadsworth Cengage Learning, 2014), 181. See also L. Dee Fink, *Creating Significant Learning Experiences, Revised and Updated* (San Francisco: Jossey-Bass, 2013), 114; Richard E. Lyons, Meggin McIntosh, Marcella L. Kysilka, *Teaching College in an Age of Accountability* (Boston: Allyn and Bacon/Pearson, 2003), 59–60.

2. For further discussion of employment status in academia, see "Chapter 2 Bibliographic Essay," available for download at geekypedagogy.com.

3. Lisa Carloye, "Mini-Case Studies: Small Infusions of Active Learning for Large-Lecture Courses," *Journal of College Science Teaching* 46, no. 6 (July–August 2017): 63–67; Christine Harrington and Todd Zakrajsek *Dynamic Lecturing: Research-Based Strategies to Enhance Lecture Effectiveness* (Sterling, VA: Stylus, 2017); Linlin Luo, Kenneth Kiewra, and Lydia Samuelson, "Revising Lecture

Notes: How Revision, Pauses, and Partners Affect Note Taking and Achievement," *Instructional Science* 44, no. 1 (February 2016): 45–67; Jennifer Waldeck and Maryellen Weimer, "Sound Decision Making about the Lecture's Role in the College Classroom," *Communication Education* 66, no. 2 (April 2017): 247–50.

4. Paul Umbach, "Faculty Cultures and College Teaching," in *The Scholarship of Teaching and Learning in Higher Education: An Evidence-Based Perspective*, ed. Raymond Perry and John Smart (The Netherlands: Springer, 2007), 263–317.

5. On active learning, see *Active Learning: A Practical Guide for College Faculty* (Madison, WI: Magna Publications, 2017) and Elizabeth F. Barkley, *Student Engagement Techniques: A Handbook for College Faculty* (San Francisco: Jossey-Bass, 2010). On learner-centered pedagogy, see Terry Doyle, *Learner-Centered Teaching: Putting the Research on Learning into Practice* (Sterling, VA: Stylus, 2011) and Maryellen Weimer, *Learner-Centered Teaching: Five Key Changes to Practice*, Second Edition (San Francisco: Jossey-Bass, 2013). On flipped classrooms, see Carl Reidseman et al., *The Flipped Classroom: Practice and Practices in Higher Education* (The Netherlands: Springer, 2017) and Robert Talbert, *Flipped Learning: A Guide for Higher Education Faculty* (Sterling, VA: Stylus, 2017). For further citations on active learning, learner-centered pedagogy, and flipped classrooms, see "Chapter 2 Bibliographic Essay," geekypedagogy.com.

6. P. H. Phelps, as quoted in Weimer, *Learner-Centered Teaching*, 7.

7. Sid Brown, *A Buddhist in the Classroom* (Albany: SUNY Press, 2008), 17.

8. Cheryl Albers, "Teaching: From Disappointment to Ecstasy," *Teaching Sociology* 37 (July 2009): 274. See also Elsie Ameen, Daryl Guffey, and Cynthia Jackson, "Evidence of Teaching Anxiety among Accounting Educators," *Journal of Education for Business* 78, no. 1 (September/October 2002): 17; Gokcen Aydin, "Personal Factors Predicting College Student Success," *Eurasian Journal of Educational Research* 69 (2017): 97; Janie H. Wilson, Shauna B. Wilson, and Angela M. Legg, "Building Rapport in the Classroom and Student Outcomes," in *Evidence-Based Teaching for Higher Education*, ed. Beth M. Schwartz and Regan A. R. Gurung (Washington, DC:

American Psychological Association, 2012), 28; Jenna Van Sickle, "Discrepancies between Student Perception and Achievement of Learning Outcomes in the Flipped Classroom," *Journal of the Scholarship of Teaching and Learning* 16, no. 2 (April 2016): 34.

9.   Liz Grauerholz and Eric Main, "Fallacies of SOTL: Rethinking How We Conduct Our Research," in *The Scholarship of Teaching In and Across the Disciplines*, ed. Kathleen McKinney (Bloomington: Indiana University Press, 2013), 155. See also Meera Komarragu, Sergey Musulkin, and Gargi Bhattacharya, "Role of Student-Faculty Interactions in Developing College Students' Academic Self-Concept, Motivation, and Achievement," *Journal of College Student Development* 51, no. 3 (2010): 333.

10.   Danuta Gabrys-Barker, "Success: From Failure to Failure with Enthusiasm," *Studies in Second Language and Teaching* 4, no. 2 (2014): 304.

11.   Janine Kremling, Colt Rothlisberger, and Shea Smart, "Negative Classroom Experiences," in *Why Students Resist Learning: A Practical Model for Understanding and Helping Students,* ed. Anton O. Tolman and Janine Kremling (Sterling, VA: Stylus, 2017), 129.

12.   See Robert T. Tauber and Cathy Sargent Mester, *Acting Lessons for Teachers: Using Performance Skills in the Classroom*, Second Edition (Westport, CT: Praeger, 2007).

13.   James M. Lang, "Crafting a Teaching Persona," *The Chronicle of Higher Education*, February 2007, C2; Lad Tobin, "Self-Disclosure as a Strategic Teaching Tool: What I Do—and Don't—Tell My Students," *College English* 73, no. 2 (November 2010): 196–206; Caroline Walker and Alan Gleaves, "Constructing the Caring Higher Education Teacher: A Theoretical Framework," *Teaching and Teacher Education* 54 (February 2016): 65–76; Rob Kelly, "Convey Your Online Teaching Persona," *Online Classroom* (January 2010): 8.

14.   Aaron S. Richmond, Guy A. Boysen, and Regan A. R. Gurung, *An Evidence-Based Guide to College and University Teaching: Developing the Model Teacher* (New York: Routledge, 2016), 16–17.

15.   Weimer, *Learner-Centered Teaching,* 156.

16.   Ken Bain, *What the Best College Teachers Do* (Cambridge: Harvard University Press, 2004), 18.

17.   Beth Dietz, "Translating Immediacy Behavior in the Online
      Classroom," *AURCO Journal* 23 (Spring 2017): 42–48; Steven A.
      Meyers et al., "How Do Faculty Experience and Respond to
      Classroom Conflict?" *International Journal of Teaching and
      Learning in Higher Education* 18, no. 3 (2006): 180; Janie Wilson
      and Kelli Taylor, "Professor Immediacy as Behaviors Associated
      with Liking Students," *Teaching of Psychology* 28, no. 2 (2001):
      136–38.

18.   Don Huffard, "Presence in the Classroom," *New Directions for
      Teaching and Learning* 140 (Winter 2014): 11–21; Michèle Irwin and
      John P. Miller, "Presence of Mind: A Qualitative Study of Meditating
      Teachers," *Journal of Transformative Education* 14, no. 2 (April
      2016): 86–97; Laura Weaver and Mark Wilding, *The 5 Dimensions of
      Engaged Teaching: A Practical Guide for Educators* (Bloomington, IN:
      Solution Tree Press, 2013).

19.   Stephen Brookfield, *The Skillful Teacher: On Technique,
      Responsiveness, and Trust in the Classroom*, Third Edition (San
      Francisco: Jossey-Bass, 2015), 179.

20.   Gabrys-Barker, "Success," 305.

21.   Patricia Kohler-Evans and Candice Barnes, "Witness the Struggle:
      The Gifts of Presence, Silence, and Choice," in *Essential Teaching
      Principles: A Resource Collection for Adjunct Faculty*, ed. Maryellen
      Wiemer (Madison, WI: Magna Publications, 2016), 140.

22.   For further citations on instructor presence and COI, see "Chapter 2
      Bibliographic Essay," geekypedagogy.com.

23.   See Bradley Cox et al., "Pedagogical Signals of Faculty
      Approachability: Factors Shaping Faculty-Student Interaction
      Outside the Classroom," *Research in Higher Education* 51, no. 8
      (December 2010): 767–88; Ashley Grantham, Emily Erin Robinson,
      and Diane Chapman, "'That Truly Meant a Lot to Me': A Qualitative
      Examination of Meaningful Faculty-Student Interactions," *College
      Teaching* 63, no. 3 (July–September 2015): 125–32; V. J. Hall,
      "Exploring Teacher-Student Interactions: Communities of Practice,
      Ecological Learning Systems—or Something Else?" *Journal of
      Further and Higher Education* 41, no. 2 (2017): 120–32.

24.   Thomas Benton, "Shyness and Academe," *The Chronicle of Higher*

Education, May 24, 2004, http://www.chronicle.com/article
/ShynessAcademe/44632.

25.   Elizabeth Renter, "Why Nice Doctors Are Better Doctors," *U.S. News
and World Report*, April 20, 2015, https://health.usnews.com/health
-news/patient-advice/articles/2015/04/20/why-nice-doctors-are
-better-doctors.

26.   Laurie Richlen, *Blueprint for Learning: Constructing College Courses
to Facilitate, Assess, and Document Learning* (Sterling, VA: Stylus,
2006), 35; Richmond, Boysen, and Gurung, *An Evidence-Based
Guide to College and University Teaching*, 60–61. See also Janie H.
Wilson, Rebecca G. Ryan, and James L. Pugh, "Professor-Student
Rapport Scale Predicts Outcomes," *Teaching of Psychology* 37 (2010):
246–51.

27.   Jared W. Keeley, Emad Ismail, and William Buskit, "Excellent
Teachers' Perspectives on Excellent Teaching," *Teaching of Psychology*
43, no. 3 (2016): 175.

28.   Students have identified "talks to students outside of class" as a
characteristic of an "ideal" college professor. L. Kimberly Epting
et al., "Student Perspectives on the Distinction between Ideal and
Typical Teachers," *Teaching of Psychology* 31, no. 3 (2004): 182.
See also Dave Berque, "Teaching as a Balancing Act: Strategies for
Managing Competing Objectives," in *The Art of College Teaching:
28 Takes*, ed. Marilyn Kallet and April Morgan (Knoxville: The
University of Tennessee Press, 2005), 106; Zac D. Johnson and Sara
LaBelle, "An Examination of Teacher Authenticity in the College
Classroom," *Communication Education* 66, no. 4 (2017): 429.

29.   Kathleen F. Gabriel, *Teaching Unprepared Students: Strategies for
Promoting Success and Retention in Higher Education* (Sterling, VA:
Stylus, 2008), 51; Richmond, Boysen, and Gurung, *An Evidence-
Based Guide to College and University Teaching*, 69.

30.   William Buskit and Bryan K. Saville, "Rapport-Building: Creating
Positive Emotional Contexts for Enhancing Teaching and Learning,"
in *Lessons Learned, Volume 2: Practical Advice for the Teaching
of Psychology*, ed. Baron Perlman, Lee I. McCann, and Susan H.
McFadden (Washington, DC: American Psychological Society,
2004), 152–54.

31.   Barkley, *Student Engagement Techniques*, 82.

32.   Elisha Babad, "Teachers' Nonverbal Behavior and Its Effects on
       Students," in Perry and Smart, *The Scholarship of Teaching and
       Learning in Higher Education*, 211–15; Aju Jacob Fenn, "Student
       Evaluation Based Indicators of Teaching Excellence from a Highly
       Selective Liberal Arts College," *International Review of Economics
       Education* 18 (January 2015):11–24; Sabine Hoidn, *Student-Centered
       Learning Environments in Higher Education Classrooms* (New York:
       Palgrave Macmillan, 2017), 110–11; Mareike Kunter et al., "Teacher
       Enthusiasm: Dimensionality and Context Specificity," *Contemporary
       Educational Psychology* 36, no. 4 (2011): 289–301; Debra Meyer and
       Julianne Turner, "Re-conceptualizing Emotion and Motivation to
       Learn in Classroom Contexts," *Educational Psychology Review* 18
       (2006): 377–90; Maryellen Weimer, *Inspired College Teaching: A
       Career-Long Resource for Professional Growth* (San Francisco: Jossey-
       Bass, 2010), 39–40.

33.   Regan A. R. Gurung and Beth M. Schwartz, *Optimizing Teaching
       and Learning: Practicing Pedagogical Research* (Malden, MA:
       Wiley Blackwell, 2009), 30. See also James R. Acker, "Class Acts:
       Outstanding College Teachers and the Difference They Make,"
       Criminal Justice Review 28, no. 2 (Autumn 2003): 215, 217; Keeley,
       Ismail, and Buskit, "Excellent Teacher's Perspectives on Excellent
       Teaching," 177.

34.   Richlen, *Blueprint for Learning*, 35.

35.   Melanie M. Keller et al., "Teacher Enthusiasm: Reviewing and
       Redefining a Complex Construct," *Educational Psychology Review* 28
       (2016): 749. This literature review concludes that approximately four
       decades of research proves that enthusiasm is important to effective
       teaching and learning but that "there is no agreed-upon definition of
       teacher enthusiasm" (754).

36.   Weimer, *Learner-Centered Teaching*, 157.

37.   Weimer, *Learner-Centered Teaching*, 157.

38.   Weimer, *Inspired College Teaching*, 30.

39.   Richlin, *Blueprint for Learning*, 36.

40.   Kremling, Rothlisberger, and Smart, "Negative Classroom

Experiences," in Tolman and Kremling, *Why Students Resist Learning*, 130.

41.   Johnson and LaBelle, "An Examination of Teacher Authenticity in the College Classroom," 423.

42.   Johnson and LaBelle, "An Examination of Teacher Authenticity in the College Classroom," 436. See also Fabian Canizzo, "'You've got to love what you do': Academic Labour in a Culture of Authenticity," *Sociological Review* 66, no. 1 (January 2018): 91–106; Patricia Cranton, ed., *Authenticity in Teaching* (San Francisco: Jossey-Bass, 2006); Pedro De Bruyckere and Paul A. Kirschner, "Measuring Teacher Authenticity: Criteria Students Use in Their Perception of Teacher Authenticity," *Cogent Education* 4, no. 1 (December 2017), doi: 10.1080/2331186X.2017.1354573; Akram Ramezanzadeh et al., "Authenticity in Teaching: A Constant Process of Becoming," *Higher Education* 73, no. 2 (February 2017): 299–315. For critiques, see Lauren Bialystok, "Should Teachers Be Authentic?" *Ethics and Education* 10, no. 3 (November 2015): 313–26; Damien Page, "The Surveillance of Teachers and the Simulation of Teaching," *Journal of Education Policy* 32, no. 1 (January 2017): 1–13.

43.   Johnson and LaBelle, "An Examination of Teacher Authenticity in the College Classroom," 430.

44.   W. J. McKeachie, "Good Teaching Makes a Difference—And We Know What It Is," in Perry and Smart, *The Scholarship of Teaching and Learning in Higher Education*, 463.

45.   Cathy Sargent Mester and Robert T. Tauber, "Acting Lessons for Teachers: Using Performance Skills in the Classroom," in *Lessons Learned: Practical Advice for the Teaching of Psychology*, ed. Baron Perlman, Lee I. McCann, and Susan H. McFadden (Washington, DC: American Psychological Society, 2008), 158.

46.   Susan Ambrose et al., *How Learning Works: Seven Research-Based Principles for Smart Teaching* (San Francisco: Jossey-Bass, 2010), 214.

47.   Jamie Taxer and Anne C. Franzel, "Inauthentic Expression of Enthusiasm: Exploring the Cost of Emotional Dissonance," *Learning and Instruction* 53 (February 2018): 74–88.

48.   Keller, "Teacher Enthusiasm," 750.

49.   This won't work if they're all staring at their phones. A hole in the
       space-time continuum could suddenly rip open up at the lectern,
       sucking you out into an endless void beyond all known reality
       and students still won't look up from their phones. So if you try
       this, make sure you've also clearly signaled to students that class is
       beginning and that you expect the class meeting to be a no-phone
       zone.

50.   Maggie Berg and Barbara K. Seeber, *The Slow Professor: Challenging
       the Culture of Speed in the Academy* (Toronto: University of Toronto
       Press, 2016), 42.

51.   Mester and Tauber, "Acting Lessons for Teachers," 158.

52.   Angelo Caranfa, "Silence as the Foundation of Learning," *Educational
       Theory* 54, no. 2 (Spring 2004): 211. For further citations on silent
       pedagogy, see "Chapter 2 Bibliographic Essay," geekypedagogy.com.

53.   Ronald Berk, *Humor as an Instructional Defibrillator: Evidence-
       Based Techniques in Teaching and Assessment* (Sterling, VA: Stylus,
       2002); Fuzhan Nasiri and Fereshteh Mafakheri, "Higher Education
       Lecturing and Humor: From Perspectives to Strategies," *Higher
       Education Studies* 5, no. 5 (2015): 26–31; Michel Tews et al., "Fun in
       the College Classroom: Examining Its Nature and Relationship with
       Student Engagement," *College Teaching* 63, no. 1 (January–March
       2015): 16–26; Alan Seidman, "I'm Not Joking. But Maybe I Should
       Start?" *Reading Improvement* 53, no. 1 (Spring 2016): 17–22. On the
       complexities of effective humor around issues of embodied identity,
       see Ellie Fitts Fulmer and Nia Nunn Makepeace, "'It's Okay to Laugh,
       Right?': Toward a Pedagogy of Racial Comedy in Multicultural
       Education," *Perspectives on Urban Education* 12, no. 1 (Fall 2015):
       38–53; Garry Jones and Colleen McGloin, "Pedagogy, Pleasure,
       and the Art of Poking Fun," *AlterNative: An International Journal
       of Indigenous Peoples* 12, no. 5 (2016): 527–40; Johnathan Rossing,
       "Emancipatory Racial Humor as Critical Public Pedagogy: Subverting
       Hegemonic Racism," *Communication, Culture and Critique* 9, no. 4
       (December 2016): 614–32.

54.   Berg and Seeber, *The Slow Professor*, 44.

55.   Timothy M. Diette and George W. Kester, "Student Course
       Evaluations: Key Determinants of Teaching Effectiveness Ratings

in Accounting, Business and Economics Courses at a Small Private Liberal Arts College," *Journal of the Academy of Business Education* 16 (Winter 2015): 207; John R. Slate et al., "Views of Effective Faculty: A Mixed Analysis," *Assessment and Evaluation in Higher Education* 36, no. 3 (2011): 336.

56.   Zachary W. Goldman et al., "What Do College Students Want? A Prioritization of Instructional Behaviors and Characteristics," *Communication Education* 66, no. 3 (2017): 290–91.

57.   Stephen Lippman, Ronald E. Bulanda, and Theodore C. Wagenaar, "Student Entitlement: Issues and Strategies for Confronting Entitlement in the Classroom and Beyond," *College Teaching* 57, no. 4 (Fall 2009): 15.

58.   "The central role of the teacher as a communicator needs more attention, effort, and skill in training." Kim Orton, "Reflective Practice: What's the Problem?" *Education Today* 64, no. 3 (Autumn 2014): 27.

59.   Richmond, Boysen, and Gurung, *An Evidence-Based Guide to College and University Teaching*, 159.

60.   Murat Balkis, "Academic Procrastination, Academic Life Satisfaction, and Academic Achievement: The Mediation Role of Rational Beliefs about Studying," *Journal of Cognitive & Behavioral Psychotherapies* 13, no. 1 (March 2013): 57–74; Lauren Hensley, "The Draws and Drawbacks of College Students' Active Procrastination," *Journal of College Student Development* 57, no. 4 (May 2016): 465–71; Kamden Strunk, Forrest Lane, and Mwarumba Mwavita, "Changes in Time-Related Academic Behaviour Are Associated with Contextual Motivational Shifts," *Educational Psychology* 38, no. 2 (February 2018): 203–20; Lisa Zarick and Robert Stonebraker, "I'll Do It Tomorrow: The Logic of Procrastination," *College Teaching* 57, no. 4 (Fall 2009): 211–15.

61.   "We are all too familiar with faculty who write their syllabus at the last minute." Michele DiPietro and Marie Norman, "Using Learning Principles as a Theoretical Framework for Instructional Consultations," *International Journal for Academic Development* 19, no. 4 (2014): 288.

62.   Judith Grunet O'Brien, Barabra J. Millis, and Margaret W. Cohen,

The Course Syllabus: A Learning-Centered Approach, Second Edition (San Francisco: Jossey-Bass, 2008); Christine M. Harrington and Melissa Thomas, *Designing a Motivational Syllabus: Creating a Learning Path for Student Engagement* (Sterling, VA: Stylus, 2018); Mary Jon Ludy et al., "Student Impressions of Syllabus Design: Engaging Versus Contractual Syllabus," *International Journal for the Scholarship of Teaching and Learning* 10, no. 2 (July 2016): https:// doi.org/10.20429/I jsotl.2016.100206.

63.   Linda B. Nilson, *The Graphic Syllabus and the Outcomes Map: Communicating Your Course* (San Francisco: Jossey-Bass, 2007), 7.

64.   Bain, *What the Best College Teachers Do*, 49.

65.   Arizona State, "What Is the Difference between Course Objectives and Learning Outcomes?" no date, https://provost.asu.edu/sites /default/files/page/1595/student-learning-outcomes_11-2018 .pdf; DePaul University Teaching Commons, "Course Objectives and Learning Outcomes," no date, https://resources.depaul.edu/teaching -commons/teaching-guides/course-design/Pages/course-objectives -learning-outcomes.aspx. I should note that some scholars question whether SLO really foster authentic student learning. See for example Anton Havnes and Tine Sophie Prøitz, "Why Use Learning Outcomes in Higher Education? Exploring the Grounds for Academic Resistance and Reclaiming the Value of Unexpected Learning," *Educational Assessment, Evaluation and Accountability* 28, no 3. (August 2016): 205–23. On employment status and SLO, see Jennifer Danley-Scott, "The Other Half: Non-Tenure Track Faculty Thoughts on Student Learning Outcomes," *Research and Practice in Assessment* 19, no. 1 (Summer 2014): 31–44.

66.   Kevin Jack Hagopian, "Rethinking the Structural Architecture of the College Classroom," in *New Directions for Teaching and Learning* no. 135 (Fall 2013): 15.

67.   Linda C. Hodges and Katherine Stanton, "Translating Comments on Student Evaluations into the Language of Learning," *Innovative Higher Education* 31 (2007): 285.

68.   Hodges and Stanton, "Translating Comments on Student Evaluations into the Language of Learning," 282.

69. Hodges and Stanton, "Translating Comments on Student Evaluations into the Language of Learning," 282.

70. Marilla D. Svinicki, *Learning and Motivation in the Postsecondary Classroom* (San Francisco: Anker Publishing Company, 2004), 91.

71. Brookfield, *The Skillful Teacher*, 222.

72. Angela Proviteria McGlynn, *Teaching Today's College Students: Widening the Circle of Success* (Madison, WI: Atwood Publishing, 2007), 111.

73. Hagopian, "Rethinking the Structural Architecture of the College Classroom," 13. See also Acker, "Class Acts," 218.

74. Weimer, *Inspired College Teaching*, 157.

75. Ruth B. Small, "About Motivation," in *University Teaching: A Reference Guide for Graduate Students and Faculty*, Second Edition, ed. Stacey Lane Tice et al. (Syracuse: Syracuse University Press, 2005), 36–37; Regan A. R. Gurung, Nancy L. Chick, and Aeron Haynie, eds., *Exploring Signature Pedagogies: Approaches to Teaching Disciplinary Habits of Mind* (Sterling, VA: Stylus, 2009), xiii.

76. Ambrose et al., *How Learning Works*, 83.

77. Vincent Tinto, "Reflections on Student Persistence," *Student Success* 8, no. 2 (July 2017): 5.

78. Barkley, *Student Engagement Techniques*, 86.

79. Barkley, *Student Engagement Techniques*, 14.

80. Eve Brank and Lindsey Wylie, "Let's Discuss: Teaching Students about Discussions," *Journal of the Scholarship of Teaching & Learning* 13, no. 3 (August 2013): 23–32; Elise Dallimore, July Hertenstein, and Marjorie B. Platt, "Creating a Community of Learning through Classroom Discussion: Student Perceptions of the Relationships among Participation, Learning, Comfort, and Preparation," *Journal on Excellence in College Teaching* 27, no. 3 (2016): 137–71; Amber Finn and Paul Schrodt, "Teacher Discussion Facilitation: A New Measure and Its Associations with Students' Perceived Understanding, Interest, and Engagement," *Communication Education* 65, no. 4 (October 2016): 445–62; Jennifer H. Herman and Linda B. Nilson, eds., *Creating Engaging Discussions: Strategies for "Avoiding Crickets" in Any Size Classroom and Online* (Sterling, VA: Stylus, 2018); Jay R. Howard,

Discussion in the College Classroom: Getting Your Students Engaged and Participating in Person and Online (San Francisco: Jossey-Bass, 2015); Catherine O'Connor et al., "The Silent and the Vocal: Participating and Learning in Whole-Class Discussion," *Learning and Instruction* 48 (April 2017): 5–13.

81. Rebecca Cox, *The College Fear Factor: How Students and Professors Misunderstand One Another* (Cambridge: Harvard University Press, 2009), 90, 98–99; Elise Larsen and A. Hameed Badawy, "The Student Faculty Chasm: Looking at Where Students and Faculty Expectations Meet and Change" (presentation, Annual Lilly Conference on College and University Teaching and Learning, Bethesda, MD, May 31, 2013).

82. Gayle Sulik and Jennifer Keys, "'Many Students Really Do Not Yet Know How to Behave!' The Syllabus as a Tool for Socialization," *Teaching Sociology* 42, no. 2 (2014): 154–55. See also R. Eric Landrum, "Faculty Perceptions Concerning the Frequency and Appropriateness of Student Behaviors," *Teaching of Psychology* 38, no. 4 (2011): 269–72.

83. Karen Van Orman, "Setting the Tone: What Your Policies Communicate to Students," (roundtable, Annual Lilly Conference on College and University Teaching and Learning, Bethesda, MD, June 3, 2017).

84. Ludy et al., "Student Impressions of Syllabus Design." See also Robert Harnish and K. Robert Bridges, "Effect of Syllabus Tone: Students' Perceptions of Instructor and Course," *Social Psychology Education* 14 (2011): 319–30.

85. Richmond, Boysen, and Gurung, *An Evidence-Based Guide to College and University Teaching*, 140–50.

86. Gabriel, *Teaching Unprepared Students*, 39–40; Grunet, Millis, and Cohen, *The Course Syllabus*, 35; James M. Lang, "The 3 Essential Functions of Your Syllabus, Part 2," *The Chronicle of Higher Education*, April 3, 2015, 1; Patrick Raymark and Patricia Connor-Greene, "The Syllabus Quiz," *Teaching of Psychology* 29, no. 4 (October 2002): 286–88.

87. David S. Ackerman and Barbara L. Gross, "My Instructor Made Me Do It: Task Characteristics of Procrastination," *Journal of Marketing*

Education 27, no. 1 (April 2005): 10; William Humphrey, Alison Shields, and Debra Laverie, "Txt me that: Encouraging Millennial Syllabus Compliance through SMS Reminders," *Proceedings of the Marketing Management Association* (Fall 2016): 13–17; Elizabeth McCrea and Steven Lorenzet, "Mind Mapping: An Experiential Approach to Syllabus Review," *Organization Management Journal* 15, no. 1 (January–March 2018): 34–43.

88. My thanks to A. Lori Neuhaus for this insight into student behavior. See also Komarragu, Musulkin, and Bhattacharya, "Role of Student-Faculty Interactions in Developing College Students' Academic Self-Concept, Motivation, and Achievement," 333.

89. Randall Nedegarrd, "Overcoming Imposter Syndrome: How My Students Trained Me to Teach Them," *Reflections: Narratives of Professional Helping* 22, no. 4 (Fall 2016): 52–59.

90. Matt Reed, "Valedictorians: Standouts—Or Not," *Confessions of a Community College Dean* (blog), *Inside Higher Ed*, May 25, 2017, https://www.insidehighered.com/blogs/confessions-community -college-dean/valedictorians.

91. Su L. Boatright-Horowitz and Chris Arruda, "College Students' Categorical Perceptions of Grades: It's Simply 'Good' vs. 'Bad,'" *Assessment & Evaluation in Higher Education* 38, no. 3 (May 2013): 253–59; Michael Gordon and Charles Fay, "The Effects of Grading and Teaching Practices on Students' Perceptions of Grading Fairness," *College Teaching* 58, no. 3 (Summer 2010): 93–98; Gregory Tippin, Kathryn Lafreniere, and Stewart Page, "Student Perception of Academic Grading: Personality, Academic Orientation, and Effort," *Active Learning Higher Education*, 12, no. 1 (2012): 51–61.

92. Sandra Gross Lucas, "Returning Graded Assignments Is Part of the Learning Experience," in Perlman, McCann, and McFadden, *Lessons Learned*, 266.

93. Alastair Iron, *Enhancing Learning through Formative Assessment and Feedback* (London: Routledge, 2008); Ou Lydia Lui, Joseph Rios, and Victor Borden, "The Effects of Motivational Instruction on College Students' Performance on Low-Stakes Assessment," *Educational Assessment* 20, no. 2 (April–June 2015): 79–94; Leanne Owen,

"The Impact of Feedback as Formative Assessment on Student Performance," *International Journal of Teaching and Learning in Higher Education* 28, no. 2 (2016): 168–75.

94.   Scott Bledsoe and Janice Baskin, "Recognizing Student Fear: The Elephant in the Classroom," *College Teaching* 62, no. 1 (Winter 2014): 34–41; Parker J. Palmer, *The Courage to Teach: Exploring the Inner Landscape of a Teacher's Life*, Tenth Anniversary Edition (San Francisco: John Wiley and Sons, 1998, 2007), 35–61.

95.   Peter Brown, Henry Roediger II, and Mark McDaniel, *Make It Stick: The Science of Successful Learning* (Cambridge: Harvard University Press, 2014), 226.

96.   In my discipline, see Andrew Stuart Bergerson et al., "Sharper, Clearer Outcomes: Using Stakeholder Focus Groups for Tuning History," *History Teacher* 49, no. 4 (August 2016): 561–86; Kadriye Ercikan and Peter Seixas, eds., *New Directions in Assessing Historical Thinking* (New York: Routledge, 2015); Anne Hyde, "Five Reasons History Professors Suck at Assessment," *Journal of American History* 102, no. 4 (March 2016): 1104–7; Jeffrey McClurken and Krystyn Moon, "Making Assessment Work for You," *Journal of American History* 102, no. 4 (March 2016): 1123–31.

97.   Hassan Sabere, *A Vertical and Horizontal Framework for Innovative Teaching: The Step-by-Step Framework to Excellence in Teaching* (Pittsburgh: Dorrance Publishing, 2017), 10; Shirley Scott, "Practising What We Preach: Towards a Student-Centered Definition of Feedback," *Teaching in Higher Education* 19, no. 1 (January 2014): 49–57; Maureen E. Squires, "Instructor Feedback on Student Work: Testing, Testing . . . One, Two . . . One, Two" (presentation, SUNY Plattsburgh Center for Teaching Excellence Annual Conference, Plattsburgh, NY, April 2013); Dylan Wiliam, "The Secret of Effective Feedback," *Educational Leadership* 73, no. 7 (April 2016): 10–15.

98.   Derek Bok, *Our Underachieving Colleges: A Candid Look at How Much Students Learn and Why They Should Be Learning More* (Princeton, NJ: Princeton University Press, 2006), 99, 121; Dana Dunn et al., eds., *Best Practices for Technology-Enhanced Teaching and Learning: Connecting to Psychology and the Social Sciences* (New York: Oxford University Press, 2011), 117; Emily Falk, *Becoming a*

New Instructor: A Guide for College Adjuncts and Graduate Students (New York: Routledge, 2012), 75; Robert J. Marzano, Debra J. Pickering, and Jane E. Pollock, *Classroom Instruction That Works: Research-Based Strategies for Increasing Student Achievement* (Alexandria, VA: Association for Supervision and Curriculum Development, 2001), 97, 157; Mihnea Moldoveanu and Maja Djikic, "Feedback: The Broken Loop in Higher Education—and How to Fix It," *Rotman Management,* Spring 2017, 62–67.

99.   For examples of assignments I use, visit geekypedagogy.com.

100. My thanks to Blake Odom for this metaphor.

101. Gabriel, *Teaching Unprepared Students,* 25; Barbara Iannarelli, Mary Ellen Bardsley, and Chandra J. Foote, "Here's Your Syllabus, See You Next Week: A Review of the First Day Practices of Outstanding Professors," *Journal of Effective Teaching* 10, no. 2 (2010): 29–41.

102. First impressions of a professor can significantly impact SET. See Stephanie Buchert et al., "First Impressions and Professor Reputation: Influence on Student Evaluations of Instruction," *Social Psychology of Education* 11, no. 4 (2008): 397–408; Dennis E. Clayson, "Initial Impressions and the Student Evaluation of Teaching," *Journal of Education for Business* 88 (2013): 26–35.

103. Self-identified nerd Jessica Bodner writes: "I do not know when to stop talking until it is too late and I have overshared or inadvertently displayed elitism. . . . Genuinely, I'm just overly excited about being able to share what I know with someone. . . . It is so dear to me that my sharing knowledge is sharing a piece of me." "A Nerd, a Geek, and Hipster Walk into a Bar," in *Age of the Geek: Depictions of Nerds and Geeks in Popular Media,* ed. Kathryn E. Lane (New York: Palgrave Macmillan, 2018), 25.

104. Jason J. Barr, "Developing a Positive Classroom Climate," IDEA Paper, October, 2016: https://files.eric.ed.gov/fulltext/ED573643.pdf. On "productive course climate," see Ambrose et al., *How Learning Works,* 180–87.

105. Lyons, McIntosh, and Kysilka, *Teaching College in an Age of Accountability,* 80–93.

106. Gabriel, *Teaching Unprepared Students,* 52.

107.   Wilson, Wilson, and Legg, "Building Rapport in the Classroom and Student Outcomes," 25–26.

108.   For example: "Thank you for your email. I'm very concerned that you will miss the first week of classes because we will be covering a lot of important material. In my experience, students who miss these classes are at a disadvantage for the rest of the semester, which has a negative impact on their grades. Is it possible for you to adjust your schedule to take this class next semester?"

109.   For citations on the first class meeting, see "Chapter 2 Bibliographic Essay," geekypedagogy.com.

110.   Iannarelli, Bardsley, and Foote, "Here's Your Syllabus, See You Next Week," 40.

111.   Svinick, McKeachie, et al., *McKeachie's Teaching Tips*, 25.

112.   Weimer, *Learner-Centered Teaching*, 149. See also Richmond, Boysen, and Gurung, *An Evidence-Based Guide to College and University Teaching*, 60–61; Janie Wilson and Kelli Taylor, "Professor Immediacy as Behaviors Associated with Liking Students," *Teaching of Psychology* 28, no. 2 (2001): 136.

113.   Jeannie D. DiClementi, "Empowering Students: Class-Generated Course Rules," *Teaching of Psychology* 32, no. 1 (2005): 18–21; L. Kimberly Epting et al., "Student Perspectives on the Distinction between Ideal and Typical Teachers," *Teaching of Psychology* 31, no. 3 (2004): 182.

114.   Lyons, McIntosh, and Kysilka, *Teaching College in an Age of Accountability*, 226–37.

115.   Elizabeth Bleicher, "The Last Class: Critical Thinking, Reflection, Course Effectiveness, and Student Engagement," *Honors in Practice* 7 (2011): 39–51; Christopher Uhl, "The Last Class," *College Teaching* 53, no. 4 (Fall 2005): 165–66; Margaret Walsh, "Five Tips for Wrapping Up a Course," *Faculty Focus*, December 2, 2009, https://www.facultyfocus.com/articles/effective-teaching-strategies/five-tips-for-wrapping-up-a-course.

116.   Richmond, Boysen, and Gurung, *An Evidence-Based Guide to College and University Teaching*, 18.

117.   Svinicki, McKeachie, et al., *McKeachie's Teaching Tips*, 148.

118.   James M. Lang, "Small Changes in Teaching: The Last 5 Minutes of Class," *The Chronicle of Higher Education*, April 2, 2016, A36–37; Lyons, McIntosh, and Kysilka, *Teaching College in an Age of Accountability*, 102–4; Cathy S. Mester, "Entrances and Exits: Making the Most of 60 Key Seconds in Every Class," *Association for Psychological Science*, December 2004, https://www.psychologicalscience.org/observer/entrances-and-exits-making-the-most-of-60-key-seconds-in-every-class.

119.   Jay Parini, *The Art of Teaching* (Cambridge: Oxford University Press, 2005), 48.

120.   Michelle D. Miller, *Minds Online: Teaching Effectively with Technology* (Cambridge, MA: Harvard University Press, 2016). For citations on teaching with social media, see "Chapter 2 Bibliographic Essay," geekypedagogy.com.

121.   Brookfield, *The Skillful Teacher*, 218–37; Anton O. Tolman, Andy Sechler, and Shea Smart, "Defining and Understanding Student Resistance," in *Why Students Resist Learning*, 6, 13.

122.   Tolman, Sechler, and Smart, "Defining and Understanding Student Resistance," 3–4.

123.   Anton O. Tolman, Janine Kremlig, and Ryan Radmall, "Creating a Campus Climate to Reduce Resistance," in Tolman and Kremling, *Why Students Resist Learning*, 192.

124.   Brown, *A Buddhist in the Classroom*, 25. See also Maryellen Weimer, "She Didn't Teach. We Had to Learn It Ourselves," *Teaching Professor* (blog), *Faculty Focus*, September 10, 2014, https://www.facultyfocus.com/articles/teaching-professor-blog/didnt-teach-learn.

125.   Cox, *The College Fear Factor*, 90, 105.

126.   Van Sickle, "Discrepancies between Student Perception and Achievement of Learning Outcomes in the Flipped Classroom," 29, 33.

127.   Hodges and Stanton, "Translating Comments on Student Evaluations into the Language of Learning," 284. See also Dominic Voge, "Discovering Students' Beliefs about Meaning May Be Key to Understanding Their Resistance to Adopting Active Approaches to Learning," *Research and Teaching in Developmental Education* 22,

no. 2 (Spring 2006): 95–100. For in-depth discussion of SET, see chapter 3.

128.   Gabriel, *Teaching Unprepared Students*, 78.

129.   Richard M. Felder and Rebecca Brent, "Navigating the Bumpy Road to Student-Centered Instruction," *College Teaching* 44, no. 2 (Spring 1996): 43.

130.   Berkeley, *Student Engagement Techniques*, 23.

131.   Ambrose et al., *How Learning Works*, 3.

132.   Brookfield, *The Skillful Teacher*, 10.

133.   Clayton R. Cook et al., "Evaluating the Impact of Increasing General Education Teachers' Ratio of Positive-to-Negative Interactions on Students' Classroom Behavior," *Journal of Positive Behavior Interventions* 19, no. 2 (April 2017): 67–77; Albert Heike, Helen Hazen, and Rebecca Theobald, "Classroom Incivilities: The Challenge of Interactions between College Students and Instructors in the U.S.," *Journal of Geography in Higher Education* 34, no. 3 (August 2010): 439–62; Zac Johnson et al., "College Student Misbehaviors: An Exploration of Instructor Perceptions," *Communication Education* 66, no. 1 (January 2017): 54–69; Kristen Knepp Frey, "Understanding Student and Faculty Incivility in Higher Education," *Journal of Effective Teaching* 12, no. 1 (February 2012): 33–46; Mark Silvestri and William Buskit, "Conflict in the College Classroom: Understanding, Preventing, and Dealing with Classroom Incivilities," in *Effective College and University Teaching: Strategies and Tactics for the New Professoriate*, ed. William Buskit and Victor Benassi (Thousand Oaks, CA: Sage Publications, 2012).

134.   Mary E. McNaughton-Cassill, "Is It Incivility or Mental Illness? Understanding and Coping with Disruptive Student Behavior in the College Classroom," *Journal of Effective Teaching* 13, no. 2 (2013): 94–108; Brian Van Brunt, *A Faculty Guide to Addressing Disruptive and Dangerous Behavior* (Hoboken, NJ: Taylor and Francis, 2013).

135.   Lynda Donathan, Misty Hanks, and Anthony Doston, "Minimizing Incivility in the Online Classroom," *Radiologic Technology* 89, no. 1 (September–October 2017): 88–91; Emily Hopkins et al., "Incivility in the Online Classroom: A Guide for Policy Development," *Nursing*

Forum 52, no. 4 (October–December 2017): 306–12; Laura A. Wankel and Charles Wankel, eds., *Misbehavior Online in Higher Education* (Cambridge, MA: Emerald Group, 2012).

136.   Gerald Amada, *Coping with Misconduct in the College Classroom: A Practical Model* (Prospect, CT: Biographical Publishing, 2015); Gurung A. Boysen, "Teacher Responses to Classroom Incivility: Student Perceptions of Effectiveness," *Teaching of Psychology* 39, no. 4 (October 2012): 276–79; Donelson R. Forsyth, *College Teaching: Practical Insights from the Science of Teaching and Learning* (Washington, DC: American Psychological Association, 2016), 201–50.

137.   Stephen W. Braden and Deborah N. Smith, "Managing the College Classroom: Perspectives from an Introvert and an Extrovert," *College Quarterly* 9, no. 1 (2006): https://eric.ed.gov/?id=EJ835334; Hagopian, "Rethinking the Structural Architecture of the College Classroom," 10; Heather Knowlton, "Affirming Ego through Out-of-Class Interactions: A Practitioner's View," *New Directions for Teaching and Learning* 135 (Fall 2013): 69; McGlynn, *Teaching Today's College Students*, 68.

138.   Reinhard Pekrum, "Emotions in Students' Scholastic Development," in Perry and Smart, *The Scholarship of Teaching and Learning in Higher Education*, 553–610.

139.   "Recognizing and making adjustments when a student feels sad, stressed, or threatened can remove roadblocks not solvable by cognitive strategies alone." Barkley, *Student Engagement Techniques*, 35. See also Ryan C. Martin, "Anger in the Classroom: How a Supposedly Negative Emotion Can Enhance Learning," *New Directions for Teaching and Learning* 153 (Spring 2018): 37–44.

140.   Brookfield, *The Skillful Teacher*, 8.

141.   Bledsoe and Baksin, "Recognizing Student Fear," 33.

142.   Rotenberg, *The Art and Craft of College Teaching*, 296.

143.   Ambrose et al., *How Learning Works*, 160–69; Brookfield, *The Skillful Teacher*, 25.

144.   Brookfield, *The Skillful Teacher*, 271–72.

145.   McGlynn, *Teaching Today's College Students*, 67.

146.   Katherine Broton and Sara Goldrick-Rab, "Going Without: An Exploration of Food and Housing Insecurity among

Undergraduates," *Educational Researcher* 47, no. 2 (March 2018): 121–33; Chad Klitzman, "College Student Homelessness: A Hidden Epidemic," *Columbia Journal of Law and Social Problems* 51, no. 4 (Summer 2018): 587–619; Bledsoe and Baskin, "Recognizing Student Fear," 33, 36.

147.   McGlynn, *Teaching Today's College Students*, 67.

148.   Rotenberg, *The Art and Craft of College Teaching*, 297.

149.   Stacey Tantleff-Dunn, Michael E. Dunn, and Jessica L. Gokee, "Understanding Faculty-Student Conflict: Student Perceptions of Precipitating Events and Faculty Responses," *Teaching of Psychology* 29, no. 3 (2002): 199, 200. Faculty behavior such as "seeming cold and uncaring, arriving late to class, disparaging students, presenting material too rapidly, and surprising students in terms of testing or grading practices" can contribute to student incivility. Meyers et al., "How Do Faculty Experience and Respond to Classroom Conflict?" 180–81.

150.   Braden and Smith, "Managing the College Classroom."

151.   Tantleff-Dunn, Dunn, and Gokee, "Understanding Faculty-Student Conflict," 199–201.

152.   Meyers et al., "How Do Faculty Experience and Respond to Classroom Conflict?" 180–81.

153.   Ann Bainbridge Frymier and Marian L. Houser, "The Teacher-Student Relationship as an Interpersonal Relationship," *Communication Education* 49, no. 3 (July 2000): 215.

154.   Tantleff-Dunn, Dunn, and Gokee, "Understanding Faculty-Student Conflict," 199. See also Wilson, Wilson, and Legg, "Building Rapport in the Classroom and Student Outcomes," 28.

155.   Fullerton, "What Students Say about Their Own Sense of Entitlement," *New Directions for Teaching and Learning* no. 135 (Fall 2013): 35.

156.   Lyons, McIntosh, and Kysilka, *Teaching College in an Age of Accountability*, 50.

157.   Rachel Slater, Patricia Veach, and Ziqui Li, "Recognizing and Managing Countertransference in the College Classroom: An Exploration of Expert Teachers' Inner Experiences," *Innovative Higher Education* 38, no. 1 (February 2013): 3–17.

158. Lyons, McIntosh, and Kysilka, *Teaching College in an Age of Accountability*, 106–7.

159. Judith Baer and Alexander Cheryomukhnin, "Students' Distress over Grades: Entitlement or a Coping Mechanism?" *Journal of Social Work Education* 47, no. 3 (Fall 2011): 565–77.

160. Brown, *A Buddhist in the Classroom*, 23.

161. Ambrose et al., *How Learning Works*, 13; Rotenberg, *The Art and Craft of College Teaching*, 296–97. This doesn't apply to situations that are physically dangerous or circumstances that require documentation, such as plagiarism.

162. For further citations on academic honesty, see "Chapter 2 Bibliographic Essay," geekypedagogy.com.

163. Donald G. Schoffstall, "Don't Assume a Student's Previous Knowledge," in *Teaching Mistakes from the Classroom* (Madison, WI: Magna Publications, 2010), 7–8. See also Susan C. Eliason, "When Expectations Collide," in *Teaching Mistakes from the Classroom*, 8–9; McGlynn, *Teaching Today's College Students*, 67.

164. Thomas F. Hawk and Paul R. Lyons, "Please Don't Give Up on Me: When Faculty Fail to Care," *Journal of Management Education* 32, no. 3 (June 2008): 326. See also Wayne Weiten, Diane F. Halpern, and Douglas A. Bernstein, "A Textbook Case of Ethics," in R. Eric Landrum and Maureen A. McCarthy, eds., *Teaching Ethically: Challenges and Opportunities* (Washington, DC: American Psychological Association, 2012).

165. Parini, *The Art of Teaching*, 68–69.

166. Paul Gibbs, ed., *The Pedagogy of Compassion at the Heart of Higher Education* (The Netherlands: Springer, 2017); Stephanie Guedet, "Feeling Human Again: Towards a Pedagogy of Radical Empathy," *Assay: A Journal of Nonfiction Studies* 2, no. 2 (Spring 2016): https://www.assayjournal.com/stephanie-guedet-8203feeling-human -again-toward-a-pedagogy-of-radical-empathy-22.html; Judith Jordan and Harriet Schwartz, "Radical Empathy in Teaching," *New Directions in Teaching and Learning* 153 (Spring 2018): 25–35; Saloshna Vandeyar and Ronel Swart, "Educational Change: A Case for a 'Pedagogy of Compassion,'" *Education as Change* 20, no. 3 (2016): 141–59.

Chapter 3

1. "There is more research on student ratings than any other topic in higher education." Ronald A. Berk, *Thirteen Strategies to Measure College Teaching: A Consumer's Guide to Rating Scale Construction, Assessment, and Decision Making for Faculty, Administrators, and Clinicians* (Sterling, VA: Stylus, 2006), 13.

2. For further discussion of SET, including gender and racial bias, see "Chapter 3 Bibliographic Essay," available for download at geekypedagogy.com.

3. Gail Tom, Stephanie Tom Tong, and Charles Hesse, "Thick Slice and Thin Slice Teaching Evaluations," *Social Psychology Education* 13 (2010): 129.

4. Fadia Nasser-Abu Alhija, "Introduction to the Special Issue 'Contemporary Evaluation of Teaching: Challenges and Promises,'" *Studies in Education Evaluation* 54 (September 2017): 1.

5. Two scholars who make a strong case for using the term "ratings" rather than "evaluations" are Ronald Berk, *Top 10 Flashpoints in Students Ratings and the Evaluation of Teaching: What Faculty and Administrators Must Know to Protect Themselves in Employment Decisions* (Sterling, VA: Stylus, 2013) and Nira Hativa, *Student Ratings of Instruction: A Practical Approach to Designing, Operating, and Reporting*, Second Edition (US: Oron Publications, 2014). I use the term "student evaluations of teaching" rather than "ratings" because although it is limited in important ways, and should never be the sole source of evidence for employment decisions, student feedback on teaching does constitute one type of evaluation. Additionally, in my view the word "rating" has taken on a new dimension when everything is "rated" online and in social media, making it more problematic to apply to student feedback today.

6. Some SoTL describes this process as "self-assessment." Leila Jahangiri and Tom Mucciolo, *A Guide to Better Teaching: Skills, Advice, and Evaluation for College and University Professors* (Lanham, MD: Rowman and Littlefield, 2012), 5–6.

7. Paul Ashwin et al., *Reflective Teaching in Higher Education* (New York: Bloomsbury Academic, 2015); BKCD Cahusac de Caux et al.,

"Reflection for Learning in Doctoral Training: Writing Groups, Academic Writing Proficiency and Reflective Practice," *Reflective Practice* 18, no. 4 (August 2017): 463–73; Kathryn Coleman and Adele Flood, eds., *Enabling Reflective Thinking: Reflective Practices in Learning and Teaching* (Champaign, IL: Common Ground Publishing, 2016); Tony Ghaye, *Teaching and Learning through Reflective Practice: A Practical Guide for Positive Action*, Second Edition (New York: Routledge, 2011); Margaret Gregson, Yvonne Hillier, et al., *Reflective Teaching in Further, Adult, and Vocational Education*, Fourth Edition (London: Bloomsbury Academic, 2015); Linda Lawrence-Wilkes, *The Reflective Practitioner in Professional Education* (New York: Palgrave Macmillan, 2014); Greg Light, Susanna Calkins, and Roy Cox, *Learning and Teaching in Higher Education: The Reflective Professional*, Second Edition (Thousand Oaks, CA: Sage, 2009); George Nalliveettil Matthew, "Reflective Classroom Practice for Effective Classroom Instruction," *International Education Studies* 5, no. 3 (June 2012): 205–11; Jodi Roffey-Barensten and Richard Malthouse, *Reflective Practice in the Lifelong Learning Sector*, Second Edition (Thousand Oaks, CA: Sage, 2017).

8.   Stephen Brookfield, *Becoming a Critically Reflective Teacher*, Second Edition (San Francisco: Jossey-Bass, 2017), 3–5.

9.   Richard E. Lyons, Meggin McIntosh, and Marcella L. Kysilka, *Teaching College in an Age of Accountability* (Boston: Allyn and Bacon/Pearson, 2003), 17–18; David Purcell, "Sociology, Teaching, and Reflective Practice: Using Writing to Improve," *Teaching Sociology* 41, no. 1 (January 2013): 5–19; Thomas Pusateri, "Teaching Ethically: Ongoing Improvement, Collaboration, and Academic Freedom," *Teaching Ethically: Challenges and Opportunities*, ed. R. Eric Landrum and Maureen A. McCarthy (Washington, DC: American Psychological Association, 2012), 9; Aaron S. Richmond, Guy A. Boysen, and Regan A. R. Gurung, *An Evidence-Based Guide to College and University Teaching: Developing the Model Teacher* (New York: Routledge, 2016), xv; Marcela Ossa Parra, Robert Gutiérrez, and María Fernanda Aldana, "Engaging in Critical Reflective Teaching: From Theory to Practice in Pursuit of Transformative Learning," *Reflective Practice* 16, no. 1 (February

2015): 16–30; Gary Wagenheim, "Professional Artistry Revealed: Business Professors' Use of Reflection in Their Teaching," *Reflective Practice* 15, no. 6 (December 2014): 836–50.

10. Kimberly LaPrade, Marjaneh Gilpatrick, and David Perkins, "Impact of Reflective Practice on Online Teaching Performance in Higher Education," *Journal of Online Learning and Teaching* 10, no. 1 (2014): 625–39.

11. Gerald Hess and Sophie Sparrow, "What Helps Law Professors Develop as Teachers? An Empirical Study," *Widener Law Review* 14 (January 2008): 163.

12. Marcia Pereira, "My Reflective Practice as Research," *Teaching in Higher Education* 4, no. 3 (July 1999): 339–55. See also Merylann J. Schuttloffel, "Reflective Practice," in *University Teaching: A Reference Guide for Graduate Students and Faculty*, Second Edition, ed. Stacey Lane Tice et al. (Syracuse: Syracuse University Press, 2005), 263–64.

13. Keith Kroll, ed., *Contemplative Teaching and Learning* (San Francisco: Jossey-Bass, 2010); Jing Lin, Rebecca Oxford, and Edward Brantmeier, eds., *Re-envisioning Higher Education: Embodied Pathways to Wisdom and Social Transformation* (Charlotte, NC: Information Age Publishing, 2013); Patricia Owen-Smith, *The Contemplative Mind in the Scholarship of Teaching and Learning* (Bloomington: Indiana University Press, 2017); Miriam Raider-Roth, "Taking the Time to Think: A Portrait of Reflection," *Teaching and Learning: The Journal of Natural Inquiry and Reflective Practice* 18, no. 3 (2004): 79–97; Arthur Zojonc, "Contemplative Pedagogy: A Quiet Revolution in Higher Education," *New Directions for Teaching and Learning* 134 (Summer 2013): 83–94. For criticism, see Kathleen Fisher, "Look Before You Leap: Reconsidering Contemplative Pedagogy," *Teaching Theology and Religion* 20, no. 1 (January 2017): 4–21.

14. Stephen Brookfield, *The Skillful Teacher: On Technique, Trust, and Responsiveness in the Classroom*, Third Edition (San Francisco: Jossey-Bass, 2015), 11.

15. Jane Halonen et al., "Are You Really Above Average? Documenting Teaching Effectiveness," in *Evidence-Based Teaching for Higher*

Education, ed. Beth M. Schwartz and Regan A. R. Gurung (Washington, DC: American Psychological Association, 2012), 134.

16.   Kaisu Mälkki and Sari Lindblom-Ylänne, "From Reflection to Action? Barriers and Bridges between Higher Education Teachers' Thoughts and Actions," *Studies in Higher Education* 37, no. 1 (February 2012): 33–50; Kim Orton, "Reflective Practice: What's the Problem?" *Education Today* 64, no. 3 (Autumn 2014): 25.

17.   Spurgeon Thompson, "The Unnecessary Agony of Student Evaluations," *The Conversation* (blog), *The Chronicle of Higher Education*, March 1, 2013, http://www.chronicle.com/blogs/conversation/2013/03/01/the-unnecessary-agony-of-student-evaluations.

18.   "Even the best professors have felt the distinctive, exquisite pain that comes from an unexpected harsh review from students. Faculty can take some comfort in the notion that harsh reviews are a fact of life even among the best faculty." Halonen et al., "Are You Really Above Average?" 136. See also Sid Brown, *A Buddhist in the Classroom* (Albany: SUNY Press, 2008), 107; Donelson R. Forsyth, *College Teaching: Practical Insights from the Science of Teaching and Learning* (Washington, DC: American Psychological Association, 2016), ix–x; Mary Lindahl and Micahel Unger, "Cruelty in Student Teaching Evaluations," *College Teaching* 58, no. 3 (Summer 2010): 71–76; Maryellen Weimer, *Inspired College Teaching: A Career-Long Resource for Professional Growth* (San Francisco: Jossey-Bass, 2010), 63.

19.   Joseph Mick La Lopa, "The Key Researchers and Their Research on Student Evaluations of Teaching," *Journal of Culinary Science and Technology* 9 (2011): 198. See also Mark Cohan, "Bad Apple: The Social Production and Subsequent Reeducation of a Bad Teacher," *Change*, November/December 2009, 32.

20.   Linda C. Hodges and Katherine Stanton, "Translating Comments on Student Evaluations into the Language of Learning," *Innovative Higher Education* 31 (2007): 279.

21.   As quoted by La Lopa, "The Key Researchers and Their Research on Student Evaluations of Teaching," 198.

22.   Michael Theall and Jennifer Franklin, "Looking for Bias in All the Wrong Places: A Search for Truth or a Witch Hunt in Student Ratings of Instruction?" *New Directions for Institutional Research* 109 (Spring 2001): 47. See also Marta Kawka and Kevin Larkin, "Classtrophobia: The Student as Troll in Student Course Evaluations (An A/r/tographical Video Rendering)," *JCT: Journal of Curriculum Theorizing* 32, no. 2 (2017): 84–107.

23.   Kristina M. W. Mitchell and Jonathan Martin, "Gender Bias in Student Evaluations," *P.S.: Political Science* (March 2018): https://doi.org/10.1017/S104909651800001X. See also Tobia Wolbring, "How Beauty Works: Theoretical Mechanism and Two Empirical Applications on Students' Evaluations of Teaching," *Social Science Research* 57 (May 2016): 253–72.

24.   Angela R. Linse, "Interpreting and Using Student Ratings Data: Guidance for Faculty Serving as Administrators on Evaluation Committees," *Studies in Educational Evaluation* 54 (September 2017): 98.

25.   Sylvia R. Lazos, "Are Student Teaching Evaluations Holding Back Women and Minorities? The Perils of 'Doing' Gender and Race in the Classroom," in *Presumed Incompetent: The Intersections of Race and Class for Women in Academia*, ed. Gabriella y Muhs Gutiérrez et al. (Boulder: University Press of Colorado, 2012), 177, 179. See also Andrea Meltzer and James McNulty, "Contrast Effects of Stereotypes: 'Nurturing' Male Professors Are Evaluated More Positively Than 'Nurturing' Female Professors," *Journal of Men's Studies* 19, no. 1 (Winter 2011): 57–64; Social Scientists Feminist Network Research Interest Group, "The Burden of Invisible Work in Academia: Social Inequalities and Time Use in Five University Departments," *Humboldt Journal of Social Relations* 39 (2017): 228–45.

26.   Shishu Zhang, David Fike, and Gladys DeJesus, "Qualities University Students Seek in a Teacher," *Journal of Economics and Economic Education Research* 16, no. 1 (2015): 43.

27.   Lazos, "Are Student Teaching Evaluations Holding Back Women and Minorities?" 178.

28.   Anne Boring, Kellie Ottoboni, and Philip B. Stark, "Student Evaluations of Teaching (Mostly) Do Not Measure Teaching

Effectiveness," *ScienceOpen Research* (January 2017): doi: 10.14293/S2199-1006; Deborah J. Merritt, "Bias, the Brain and Student Evaluations of Teaching," *St. John's Law Review* 82 (January 2008): 235–287; Julie Sprinkle, "Student Perceptions of Effectiveness: An Examination of the Influence of Student Biases," *College Student Journal* 42, no. 2 (June 2008): 276–93.

29.   Lazos, "Are Student Teaching Evaluations Holding Back Women and Minorities?" 179.

30.   Weimer, *Inspired College Teaching*, 63. See also Frank Donoghue, "Should Student Evaluations Be Anonymous?" *Innovations* (blog), *The Chronicle of Higher Education,* August 7, 2012, https://www.chronicle.com/blogs/innovations/should-student-evaluations-be-anonymous/33905.

31.   Sue Scheff, *Shame Nation: The Global Epidemic of Online Hate* (Naperville, IL: Sourcebooks, 2017). See also Stefanie S. Bosewell: "Ratemyprofessors is hogwash (but I care): Effects of Ratemyprofessors and University-administered Teaching Evaluations on Professors," *Computers in Human Behavior* 56 (March 2016): 155–62; Neneh Kowai-Bell et al., "Professors Are People Too: The Impact of Informal Evaluations of Professors on Students and Professors," *Social Psychology of Education* 15, no. 3 (2012): 337–51.

32.   Thompson, "The Unnecessary Agony of Student Evaluations." See also Gina Cicco, "Reflecting on Online Course Evaluations: Five Must-Do's for Faculty and Students," *Journal on School Educational Technology* 12, no. 1 (June–August 2016): 1–7; Michael P. Marzano and Robert Allen, "Online v. Face-to-Face Course Evaluations: Considerations for Administrators and Faculty," *MERLOT Journal of Online Teaching and Learning* 9, no. 1 (2013): 140–48; Anglica Risquez, "Online Student Evaluations of Teaching: What Are We Sacrificing for the Affordances of Technology?" *Assessment and Evaluation in Higher Education* 40, no. 1 (February 2015): 120–34. On students' ethical responsibilities and SET, see Jonathan Bassett et al., "Are They Paying Attention? Students' Lack of Motivation and Attention Potentially Threaten the Utility of Course Evaluations," *Assessment and Evaluation in Higher Education* 42, no. 3 (2017): 431–42.

33.   Berk, *Thirteen Strategies to Measure College Teaching*, 2. See
      also Stephen L. Benton and Kenneth R. Ryalls, "Challenging
      Misconceptions about Student Ratings of Instruction," IDEA Paper
      #58, April 2016, http://www.eric.ed.gov/contentdelivery
      /servlet/ERICServlet?accno=ED573670; Hativa, *Student Ratings
      of Instruction*, xx, 37; Weimer, *Inspired College Teaching*, 50.

34.   Weimer, *Inspired College Teaching*, 63.

35.   See also Brian Ray, Jacob Babb, and Courtney Adams Wooten,
      "Rethinking SETs: Retuning Student Evaluations of Teaching for
      Student Agency," *Compositions Studies* 26, no. 1 (Spring 2018):
      34–56.

36.   Geoff Schneider, "Student Evaluations, Grade Inflation, and
      Pluralistic Teaching: Moving from Customer Satisfaction to Student
      Learning and Critical Thinking," *Forum for Social Economics* 42, no.
      1 (2013): 122–35.

37.   Phrasing SET questions in the first person like this may foster more
      responsible, ethical student engagement with evaluation because it
      could discourage distancing and depersonalizing "ratings" of "the
      instructor."

38.   Students "are generally correct when they claim that something is
      amiss, but often less reliable when attempting to identify the precise
      cause of the problem." James Wilkinson, "Interpreting Feedback and
      Evaluations," The Derek Bok Center for Teaching and Learning, no
      date, https://bokcenter.harvard.edu/interpreting-feedback-and
      -evaluations.

39.   Claire B. Potter, "If I could stick my pen in my heart/and spill it all
      over the stage: Teaching Evaluations," *Tenured Radical* (blog),
      The Chronicle of Higher Education, January 11, 2011, http://www
      .chronicle.com/blognetwork/tenuredradical/2011/01/if-i-could-stick
      -my-pen-in-my-heartand.

40.   Brookfield, *The Skillful Teacher*, 273.

41.   As quoted in Sylvia R. Lazos, "Are Student Teaching Evaluations
      Holding Back Women and Minorities?" 170–71.

42.   Janine Kremling and Erikca DeAnn Brown, "The Impact of
      Institutional Culture on Student Disengagement and Resistance
      to Learning," in *Why Students Resist Learning: A Practical Model*

for Understanding and Helping Students, ed. Anton O. Tolman and Janine Kremling (Sterling, VA: Stylus, 2017), 69–70. See also Lin Zhu and Deepa Anagondahalli, "Predicting Student Satisfaction: The Role of Academic Entitlement and Nonverbal Immediacy," *Communication Reports* 31, no. 1 (January–April 2018): 41–52.

43.   One infamous study concluded that a bribe of chocolate would mitigate this. Robert J. Youmans and Benjamin D. Jee, "Fudging the Numbers: Distributing Chocolate Influences Student Evaluations of an Undergraduate Course," *Teaching of Psychology* 34, no. 4 (2007): 245–47.

44.   Simone Juhasz Silva, Mary Tripp Reed, and Natalie Doering, "Do Alumni Change Their Minds Regarding Student Evaluations of Teachers? On the Time Stability of Student Evaluations," *Academy of Business Research Journal* 2 (2013): 18–44.

45.   John Malouff et al. "Using the Results of Teaching Evaluations to Improve Teaching: A Case Study of a New Systematic Process," *College Teaching* 63, no. 1 (January/March 2015): 3–7.

46.   Hodges and Stanton, "Translating Comments on Student Evaluations into the Language of Learning," 279–80.

47.   Hodges and Stanton, "Translating Comments on Student Evaluations into the Language of Learning," 285.

48.   Pieter Spooren and Wim Christiaens, "I liked your course because I believe in (the power of) student evaluations of teaching (SET): Students' Perceptions of a Teaching Evaluation Process and Their Relationship with SET Scores," *Studies in Education Evaluation* 54 (2017): 43–49. See also Katharina Brandl, Jess Mandel, and Babbi Winegarden, "Student Evaluation Team Focus Groups Increase Students' Satisfaction with the Overall Course Evaluation Process," *Medical Education* 51 (2017): 215–27. Contrary to popular wisdom, rates of SET completion may be more motivated by positive aspects of a course rather than negative. Caroline M. Jaquett, Victoria G. VanMaaren, and Robert L. Williams, "Course Factors That Motivate Students to Submit End-of-Course Evaluations," *Innovative Higher Education* 42 (Spring 2017): 19–31.

49.   "Mid-semester evaluations reflect that the students are all still in the classroom trying to make the whole thing work;

end-of-the-semester evaluations all too often reflect that they are under pressure and cranky. They're done with the class and only wish to be on break." Brown, *A Buddhist in the Classroom*, 107. See also Lori Price Aultman, "An Unexpected Benefit of Formative Student Evaluations," *College Teaching* 54, no. 3 (2006): 251; Diane Cummings Persellin and Mary Blythe Daniels, *A Concise Guide to Improving Student Learning: Six Evidence-Based Principles and How to Apply Them* (Sterling, VA: Stylus, 2014), 59; L. Dee Fink, *Creating Significant Learning Experiences, Revised and Updated* (San Francisco: Jossey Bass, 2013), 201–2; Karron Lewis, "Using Midsemester Feedback and Responding to It," *New Directions for Teaching and Learning* 87 (2001): 33–44; Ann Veeck et al., "The Use of Collaborative Midterm Student Evaluations to Provide Actionable Results," *Journal of Marketing Education* 38, no. 3 (December 2012): 157–69; Janis Warner and Aneika Simmons, "Giving Voice to Students: A Preliminary Analysis of Informal Mid-Term Evaluations and Procedural Justice," *Academy of Educational Leadership Journal* 19, no. 1 (2015): 71–79; S. R. Wickramasinghe and W. M. Timpson, "Mid-Semester Student Feedback Enhances Student Learning," *Education for Chemical Engineers* 1, no. 1 (2006): 126–33.

50. My thanks to Michael Murphy for this reminder.

51. Alice Hoon et al., "Use of the 'Stop, Start, Continue' Method Is Associated with the Production of Constructive Qualitative Feedback by Students in Higher Education," *Assessment and Evaluation in Higher Education* 40, no. 5 (August 2015): 755–67.

52. Dawn Little, "Seeking and Responding to Student Feedback: Challenges and Opportunities" (presentation, Annual Lilly Conference on College and University Teaching and Learning, Bethesda, MD, June 2, 2017).

53. Lyons, McIntosh, and Kysilka, *Teaching College in an Age of Accountability*, 240.

54. Brookfield, *The Skillful Teacher*, 8, 268.

55. Brookfield, *The Skillful Teacher*, 15.

56. John R. Slate et al., "Views of Effective Faculty: A Mixed Analysis," *Assessment and Evaluation in Higher Education* 36, no. 3 (2011): 331.

57. Richmond, Boysen, and Gurung, *An Evidence-Based Guide to College and University Teaching*, 17.

58. Halonen et al., "Are You Really Above Average?" 131–33.

59. Brookfield, *The Skillful Teacher*, 214.

60. Dorothy Wallace, "The Hornet's Opinion," in *The Art of College Teaching: 28 Takes*, ed. Marilyn Kallet and April Morgan (Knoxville: University of Tennessee Press, 2005), 124–25.

61. Stephen Brookfield, "Classroom Critical Incident Questionnaire," no date, http://www.stephenbrookfield.com/ciq/; Regan A. R. Gurung and Beth M. Schwartz, *Optimizing Teaching and Learning: Practicing Pedagogical Research* (Malden, MA: Wiley Blackwell, 2009), 97–99. See also Maryellen Weimer, Joan L. Parrett, and Mary-Margaret Kerns, *How Am I Teaching? Forms and Activities for Acquiring Instructional Input* (Madison, WI: Atwood Publishing, 2002).

62. McGlynn, *Teaching Today's College Students*, 67–80. See also Jorge Ballina, "Where Are You From and Why Are You Here? Microaggressions, Racialization, and Mexican College Students in a New Destination," *Sociological Inquiry* 87, no. 2 (May 2017): 385–410; Ronald Berk, "Microaggressions Trilogy: Part 3. Microaggressions in the Classroom," *Journal of Faculty Development* 31, no. 3 (September 2017): 95–110; Guy Boysen, "Teacher Student Perceptions of Microaggressions in College Classrooms," *College Teaching* 60, no. 3 (2012): 122–29; Jessica Harris, "Multiracial College Students' Experiences with Multiracial Microaggressions," *Race, Ethnicity, and Education* 20, no. 4 (July 2017): 429–45; Justin Lerner and Anjali Fulambarker, "Beyond Diversity and Inclusion: Creating a Social Justice Agenda in the Classroom," *Journal of Teaching in Social Work* 38, no. 1 (January–March 2018): 43–53; Carola Suárez-Orozco et al., "Toxic Rain in Class: Classroom Interpersonal Microaggressions," *Educational Researcher* 44, no. 3 (April 2015): 151–60.

63. Natascha Chtena, "How to Deal with Negative Teaching Evaluations," *GradHacker* (blog), *Inside Higher Ed*, February 9, 2014, https://www .insidehighered.com/blogs/gradhacker/how-deal-negative-teaching -evaluations; Michele DiPietro and Marie Norman, "Using Learning Principles as a Theoretical Framework for Instructional

Consultations," *International Journal for Academic Development* 19, no. 4 (2014): 289; W. J. McKeachie "Good Teaching Makes a Difference—And We Know What It Is," in *The Scholarship of Teaching and Learning in Higher Education: An Evidence-Based Perspective*, ed. Raymond Perry and John Smart (The Netherlands: Springer, 2007), 471.

64.   Rory Pfund et al., "Is the Professor In? Faculty Presence during Office Hours," *College Student Journal* 47, no. 3 (Fall 2013): 524–28.

65.   Linse, "Interpreting and Using Student Ratings Data," 100.

66.   Berk, *Thirteen Strategies to Measure College Teaching*, 14. See also Hativa, *Student Ratings of Instruction*, 5; Henry Hornstein, "Student Evaluations of Teaching Are an Inadequate Assessment Tool for Evaluating Faculty Performance," *Cogent Education* 4, no. 1 (December 2017): http://dx.doi.org/10.1080/233118 6X.2017.1304016; Adrian Lyde, David Grieshaber, and George Byrnes, "Faculty Teaching Performance: Perceptions of a Multi-Source Method for Evaluation (MME)," *Journal of the Scholarship of Teaching and Learning* 16, no. 3 (June 2016): 82–94.

67.   Berk, *Thirteen Strategies to Measure College Teaching*, 15; Phyllis Blumberg, *Assessing and Improving Your Teaching: Strategies and Rubrics for Faculty Growth and Student Learning* (San Francisco: Jossey-Bass, 2014); Halonen et al., "Are You Really Above Average?" 139–40; Melissa Contreras-McGavin and Adrianna Kezar, "Using Qualitative Methods to Assess Student Learning in Higher Education," *New Directions for Institutional Research* 136 (2007): 63–79; Jennifer Franklin, "Interpreting the Numbers: Using a Narrative to Help Others Read Student Evaluations of Your Teaching Accurately," *New Directions for Teaching and Learning* 87 (2001): 85–100.

68.   "Because teaching is such a complex, multidimensional activity, the portfolio has as a primary strength the ability to integrate information from several areas rather than relying on a single measure." Harry Richards, Lee Seidel, and Michael Lee, "The Teaching Portfolio," in *University Teaching: A Reference Guide for Graduate Students and Faculty*, Second Edition, ed. Stacey Lane Tice et al. (Syracuse: Syracuse University Press, 2005), 271. See

also Donelson R. Forsyth, *College Teaching: Practical Insights from the Science of Teaching and Learning* (Washington, DC: American Psychological Association, 2016), 273–95; Anastasia Samaras and Rebecca Fox, "Capturing the Process of Critical Reflective Teaching Practices through E-Portfolios," *Professional Development in Education* 39, no. 1 (February 2013): 23–41. On course portfolios, see Daniel Bernstein et al., *Making Teaching and Learning Visible: Course Portfolios and the Peer Review of Teaching* (Bolton, MA: Anker Publishing Company, 2006). However, institutional requirements regarding portfolios for employment review may undermine their utility for fostering authentic reflection. See Elizabeth Jones, "Personal Theory and Reflection in a Professional Practice Portfolio," *Assessment and Evaluation in Higher Education* 35, no. 6 (October 2010): 699–710; Lilly Orland-Barak, "Portfolios as Evidence of Reflective Practices: What Remains 'Untold,'" *Educational Research* 47, no. 1 (March 2005): 25–44.

69.   "The quality of these relationships is not a frill or 'feel-good' aspect of schooling, it is an essential feature of learning. What allows this relationship to flourish is complex and calls upon the mental, physical, emotional, and relational resources of the teacher." Carol Rodgers and Miriam Raider-Roth, "Presence in Teaching," *Teachers and Teaching: Theory and Practice* 12, no. 3 (June 2006), 266.

70.   Bradley E. Cox, "A Developmental Typology of Faculty-Student Interaction Outside of the Classroom," *New Directions for Institutional Research* (Winter 2011): 63.

71.   Greg Reihman, "Making Sense of Student Evaluations," Lehigh University Center for Innovation and Teaching, Summer 2004, https://citl.lehigh.edu/student-evaluations.

72.   Cox, "A Developmental Typology of Faculty-Student Interaction Outside of the Classroom," 63.

73.   Hativa, *Student Ratings of Instruction*, 43; La Lopa, "The Key Researchers and Their Research on Student Evaluations of Teaching," 195; Philip B. Stark and Richard Freishtat, "An Evaluation of Course Evaluations," *ScienceOpen,* September 2014, https://www.stat.berkeley.edu/~stark/Preprints/evaluations14.pdf, 13.

74.   "Student Evaluations of Teaching," The Harriet W. Sheridan Center

for Teaching and Learning, Brown University, no date, https://cft .vanderbilt.edu//cft/guides-sub-pages/student-evaluations.

75.   Alecia Anderson et al., "Student Perceptions of Teaching Transparency," *Journal of Effective Teaching* 13, no. 2 (September 2013): 38–47; Mary-Ann Winkelmes, "Transparency in Teaching: Faculty Share Data and Improve Students' Learning," *Liberal Education* 99, no. 2 (Spring 2013): 48–55.

76.   Fink, *Creating Significant Learning Experiences*, 25.

77.   Merylann J. Schuttloffel, "Reflective Practice," 262.

78.   Jennifer A. Moon, *Learning Journals: A Handbook for Academics, Students and Professional Development* (Sterling, VA: Stylus, 1999), 23.

79.   As quoted in Dannelle D. Stevens and Joanne E. Cooper, *Journal Keeping: How to Use Reflective Writing for Effective Teaching, Professional Insight, and Positive Change* (Sterling, VA: Stylus, 2009), 21.

80.   As quoted in Stevens and Cooper, *Journal Keeping*, 21.

81.   Stevens and Cooper, *Journal Keeping*, 24.

82.   Evelyn M. Boyd and Ann W. Fales, "Reflective Learning: Key to Learning from Experience," *Journal of Humanistic Psychology* 23, no. 2 (Spring 1983): 100.

83.   Stevens and Cooper, *Journal Keeping*, 19, 38.

84.   David Boud, "Using Journal Writing to Enhance Reflective Practice," *New Directions for Adult and Continuing Education* 90 (Summer 2001): 11.

85.   Boud, "Using Journal Writing to Enhance Reflective Practice," 10.

86.   DiPietro and Norman, "Using Learning Principles as a Theoretical Framework for Institutional Consultations," 288. According to DiePietro and Norman, faculty often believe they are "reflecting" far more than they actually do (288).

87.   Alison Cook-Sather et al., *Learning from the Student's Perspective: A Sourcebook for Effective Teaching* (Boulder: Paradigm Publishers, 2009), 120.

88.   Carolin Kreber, *Authenticity in and through Teaching in Higher Education: The Transformative Potential of the Scholarship of Teaching* (New York: Routledge, 2013), 5.

89.   Marilyn Roberts, "Creating a Dynamic Syllabus: A Strategy for Course Assessment," *College Teaching* 61 (2013): 109.

90.   Anne Guarner, "Reflective Teaching Three Ways," *GradHacker* (blog), *Inside Higher Ed*, May 21, 2017, https://www.insidehighered.com /blogs/gradhacker/reflective-teaching-three-ways.

91.   For citations on writing a teaching philosophy, see "Chapter 3 Bibliographic Essay," geekypedagogy.com.

92.   Boud, "Using Journal Writing to Enhance Reflective Practice"; Moon, *Learning Journals*; Stevens and Cooper, *Journal Keeping*. See also Josh Boyd and Steve Boyd, "Reflect and Improve: Instructional Development through a Teaching Journal," *College Teaching* 53, no. 3 (2005): 110–14; Ruth Damian, "Teaching Strategies: Reflections on Professional Practice," *Teaching in Higher Education* 19, no. 3 (April 2014): 254–65; Jane Dyment and Timothy O'Connell, "When the Ink Runs Dry: Implications for Theory and Practice When Educators Stop Keeping Reflective Journals," *Innovative Higher Education* 39, no. 5 (November 2014): 417–29; Muriel Gallego, "Professional Development of Graduate Teaching Assistants in Faculty-like Positions: Fostering Reflective Practices through Reflective Teaching Journals," *Journal of the Scholarship of Teaching and Learning* 14, no. 2 (May 2014): 96–110; Matthew Liberatore, "Two Minutes of Reflection Improves Teaching," *Chemical Engineering Education* 46, no. 4 (2012): 271; David Purcell, "Sociology, Teaching, and Reflective Practice: Using Writing to Improve," *Teaching Sociology* 41, no. 1 (2013): 5–19; Damian Ruth, "Teaching Strategy: Reflections on Professional Practice," *Teaching in Higher Education* 19, no. 3 (April 2014): 254–65.

93.   Boud, "Using Journal Writing to Enhance Reflective Practice," 9.

94.   Weimer, *Essential Teaching Principles*, 63.

95.   Daniel D. Pratt, "Good Teaching: One Size Fits All?" *New Directions for Adult and Continuing Education* 93 (Spring 2002): 14.

96.   Ken Winograd, "The Functions of Teacher Emotion: The Good, the Bad, and the Ugly," *Teachers College Record* 105, no. 9 (2003): 1667.

97.   This discussion draws largely on Kerry Howells, *Gratitude in Education: A Radical View* (Rotterdam/Boston: Springer, 2012). For more on her work, visit kerryhowells.com.

98. "I consciously rebel against the simplistic ways in which the concept of gratitude is used in some of the contemporary discourse that dominates the so-called 'positivity industry.'" Howells, *Gratitude in Education,* 9. See also Liz Jackson, "Why Should I Be Grateful: The Morality of Gratitude in Contexts Marked by Injustice," *Journal of Moral Education* 45, no. 3 (2016): 276–90; Blaire Morgan, Liz Gulliford, and David Carr, "Educating Gratitude: Some Conceptual and Moral Misgivings," *Journal of Moral Education* 44, no. 1 (2015): 97–111; Robin May Schott, "Misplaced Gratitude and the Ethics of Oppression," *Metaphilosophy* 47, no. 4/5 (October 2016): 524–38.

99. For citations on the benefits of gratitude, see "Chapter 3 Bibliographic Essay," geekypedagogy.com.

100. Gratitude "impels us to act in a certain positive way towards another. In this sense, gratitude is more than emotion or way of thinking because it involves an action of some kind. Without this action, it is not gratitude but something else—perhaps appreciation or thankfulness." Howells, *Gratitude in Education,* 36.

101. Howells, *Gratitude in Education,* 7.

102. Howells, *Gratitude in Education,* 93.

103. "When we think of what we are grateful for, we take a step back from the situation and are more able to choose our response. . . . Focusing on what we can be grateful for can empower us to make different choices, choices more likely to bring about positive outcomes . . . [and] to do something about the situation, or if needed, be able to make a clear decision about whether or not it is time to move away." Howells, *Gratitude in Education,* 120.

104. Howells, *Gratitude in Education,* 99.

105. Roy Baumeister et al., "Bad Is Stronger Than Good," *Review of General Psychology* 5, no. 4 (December 2001): 323–70.

106. Donald G. Schoffstall, "On a Frustrating Day or in a Troubled Class, Remember We All Make a Difference," in *Teaching Mistakes from the Classroom* (Madison, WI: Magna Publications, 2010), 21.

107. Pat Whitfield, "A Self-Care Strategy for Beleaguered Academics," *The Chronicle of Higher Education,* May 29, 2018, https://www.chronicle.com/article/A-Self-Care-Strategy-for/243521.

108. Howells, *Gratitude in Education*, 105.

109. My thanks to Alison Neuhaus for this metaphor.

110. Stephen Lippman, Ronald E. Bulanda, and Theodore C. Wagenaar, "Student Entitlement: Issues and Strategies for Confronting Entitlement in the Classroom and Beyond," *College Teaching* 57, no. 4 (Fall 2009): 198. See also Lixin Jiang, Thomas Tripp, and Phan Hong, "College Instruction Is Not So Stress Free after All: A Qualitative and Quantitative Study of Academic Entitlement, Uncivil Behaviors, and Instructor Burnout," *Stress and Health* 33, no. 5 (December 2017): 578–89.

111. Howells, *Gratitude in Education*, 46, 54.

112. Howells, *Gratitude in Education,* 53.

113. Daniel Mansson, "Exploring College Students' Expressed Concern about Their Academic Performance," *College Student Journal* 50, no. 1 (Spring 2016): 121–29.

114. Tiina Soini, Kirsi Pyhalto, and Janne Pietarinen, "Pedagogical Well-Being: Reflecting Learning and Well-Being in Teachers' Work," *Teachers and Teaching: Theory and Practice* 16, no. 6 (December 2010): 735–51.

115. Zac D. Johnson and Sara LaBelle, "An Examination of Teacher Authenticity in the College Classroom," *Communication Education* 66, no. 4 (2017): 430.

116. Harry Hubbal, John Collins, and Daniel Pratt, "Enhancing Reflective Teaching Practices: Implications for Faculty Development Programs," *Canadian Journal of Higher Education* 35, no. 3 (2005): 57–81. See also Howells, *Gratitude in Education*, 93–95.

117. Kreber, *Authenticity in and through Teaching in Higher Education*, 164.

118. Cooper and Stevens, *Journal Keeping*, 28.

119. Cooper and Stevens, *Journal Keeping*, 29.

120. Robert Minter, "Faculty Burnout," *Contemporary Issues in Education Research* 2, no. 2 (2009): 1–8; Karyn Z. Spoles, "The Emotional Balancing Act of Teaching: A Burnout Recovery Plan," *New Directions for Teaching and Learning* 153 (Spring 2018): 99–107; J. Watts and N. Robertson, "Burnout in Teaching University Staff: A

Systematic Literature Review," *Educational Research* 53, no. 1 (2011), https://doi.org/10.1080/00131881.2011.552235; Weimer, *Inspired College Teaching*, 174–76.

Chapter 4

1.   Charissa Eaton et al., "Faculty Perception of Support to Do Their Job Well," *InSight: A Journal of Scholarly Teaching* 10 (2015): 35–42; Michelle Harris et al., eds., *Stories from the Front of the Room: How Higher Education Faculty of Color Overcome Challenges and Thrive in the Academy* (Lanham, MD: Rowman and Littlefield, 2017); Frank Hernandez, Elizabeth Murakami, and Gloria Rodriguez, eds., *Abriendo Puertas, Cerrando Heridas (Opening Doors, Closing Wounds): Latinas/os Finding Work-Life Balance in Academia* (Charlotte, NC: IAP Information Age Publishing, 2015); Mary Ellen McNaughton-Cassill, "Stress in the College Classroom: Not Just a Student Problem Anymore," *Transformative Dialogues: Teaching and Learning Journal* 10, no. 2 (June 2017): 1–8. For further citations on stress (particularly for underrepresented faculty), life-work balance in academia, and organized labor in higher education, see "Chapter 4 Bibliographic Essay," available for download at geekypedagogy .com.

2.   Daniel Bernstein, "Amplifying the Impact of Pedagogical Research: The Role of Teaching Centers and Writing Centers," in *Changing the Conversation about Higher Education,* ed. Robert Thompson (Lanham, MD: Rowman and Littlefield, 2013); Constance E. Cook and Matthew Kaplan, eds., *Advancing the Culture of Teaching on Campus: How a Teaching Center Can Make a Difference* (Sterling, VA: Stylus, 2011); Alvin Evans and Edna Chun, "Teaching and Learning Centers as Catalysts for Faculty Diversity Development," *Academic Leader* 33, no. 12 (December 2017): 7–8; Christopher Young, "Teaching and Learning Centers Serve All Faculty," in *Quick Hits for Adjunct Faculty and Lecturers: Success Strategies from Award-Winning Teachers*, ed. Robin K. Morgan, Kimberly T. Olivares, and John Becker (Bloomington: Indiana University Press, 2015).

3.   Patricia Cranton, "Continuing Professional Education for Teachers and University and College Faculty," *New Directions for Adult and Continuing Education* 151 (Fall 2016): 43–52.

4.   Robert Kennelly, "Creating More 'Elbow Room' for Collaborative Reflective Practice in the Competitive, Performative Culture of Today's University," *Higher Education Research and Development* 34, no. 5 (September 2015): 924–65. See also Linda Schaak Distad and Joan Cady Brownstein, *Talking Teaching: Implementing Reflective Practice in Groups* (Lanham, MD: Scarecrow Education, 2004); Emma Sherry and Donna De Hann, "Sharing Experiences of an International Teaching Collaboration: From Bemoaning Blogging to Reflective Practice," *Reflective Practice* 3, no 6 (December 2012): 805–19.

5.   Mark Cohan, "Bad Apple: The Social Production and Subsequent Reeducation of a Bad Teacher," *Change*, November/December 2009, 36.

6.   Daniel B. Davis, *Contingent Academic Labor: Evaluating Conditions to Improve Student Outcomes* (Sterling, VA: Stylus, 2017); Laurel Messina Duluk, *Building Blocks to Improve the Quality of Adjunct Faculty Teaching: A Handbook for Best Practices* (Sterling, VA: Stylus, 2017); Roy Fuller, Marie Kendall Brown, and Kimberly Smith, *Adjunct Faculty Voices: Cultivating Professional Development at the Front Lines of Higher Education* (Sterling, VA: Stylus, 2017); Andrea W. Webb, Tracy Wong, and Harry Hubball, "Professional Development for Adjunct Teaching Faculty in a Research-Intensive University: Engagement in Scholarly Approaches to Teaching and Learning," *International Journal of Teaching and Learning in Higher Education* 25, no. 2 (2013): 231–38.

7.   Steffen Pope Wilson and Katherine Kipp, "Simple and Effective Methods for Talking about Teaching," in *Lessons Learned, Volume 2: Practical Advice for the Teaching of Psychology*, ed. Baron Perlman, Lee I. McCann, and Susan H. McFadden (Washington, DC: American Psychological Society, 2004), 13–14. See also David Arnold, "Kill the Professor and Save the Teacher: History Professors and the Scholarship of Teaching and Learning, Part II,"

The American Historian, February 2017, 33; Stephen Brookfield, *Becoming a Critically Reflective Teacher* (San Francisco: Jossey-Bass, 2017), 115–34.

8.   On faculty learning communities, see Joyce Anderson et al., "Transforming the Classroom—and the World: Voices from a Culturally Inclusive Pedagogy Faculty Learning Community," *Transformative Dialogues: Teaching and Learning Journal* 7, no. 1 (March 2014): 1–18; Mary Jo Banasik and Jennifer L. Dean, "Non-Tenure Track Faculty and Learning Communities: Bridging the Divide to Enhance Teaching Quality," *Innovative Higher Education* 41, no. 4 (August 2016): 333–42; Andrew Furco and Barbara E. Moely, "Using Learning Communities to Build Faculty Support for Pedagogical Innovation: A Multi-Campus Study," *Journal of Higher Education* 83, no. 1 (January–February 2012): 128–53; Julia Moore and Joya Carter-Hicks, "Let's Talk! Facilitating a Faculty Learning Community Using a Critical Friends Group Approach," *International Journal for the Scholarship of Teaching and Learning* 8, no. 2 (July 2014): 1–17; Susan Sipple and Robin Lightner, eds., *Developing Faculty Learning Communities at Two-Year Colleges: Collaborative Models to Improve Teaching and Learning* (Sterling, VA: Stylus, 2013); Mariela Tovar, Rosalie Jukier, and Jennie Ferris, "Overcoming Pedagogical Solitude: The Transformative Power of Discipline-Specific Faculty Learning Communities," *To Improve the Academy* 34, no. 1/2 (June 2015): 319–44. On teaching squares, see Barbara Gross Davis, *Tools for Teaching*, Second Edition (San Francisco: Jossey-Bass, 2009), 478; Greg Light and Roy Cox, *Learning and Teaching in Higher Education: The Reflective Professional* (London: Paul Chapman, 2001), 264. On peer review, see Douglas Atkinson and Susan Bolt, "Using Teaching Observations to Reflect Upon and Improve Teaching Practice in Higher Education," *Journal of the Scholarship of Teaching and Learning* 10, no. 3 (November 2010): 1–19; Mallory Bradford et al. "With a Little Help from My Friends: How Faculty Peer Review Can Transform Mediocre Teaching Methods into Powerful Learning Experiences," *AURCO Journal* 20 (Spring 2014): 192–203; Peter Grainger et al., "Working in Triads: A Case Study of a Peer Review Process," *Journal of University Teaching*

and Learning Practice 12, no. 1 (2015): 1–25; Graham Hendry, Amani Bell, and Kate Thomson, "Learning by Observing a Peer's Teaching Situation," *International Journal for Academic Development* 19, no. 4 (2014): 318–29; Christopher Klopper and Steve Drew, eds., *Teaching for Learning and Learning for Teaching: Peer Review of Teaching in Higher Education* (Rotterdam: Sense, 2015); Mark Potter et al., "Peer Observation of Teaching: A Case for Culture Change," *Teacher-Scholar* 3, no. 1 (Fall 2011): 29–38.

9.   Michelle Boettcher, "But Did It Really Matter? Wakonse Lessons on Faculty Reflection in Community," *Transformative Dialogues: Teaching and Learning Journal* 10, no. 2 (June 2017): 1–15; Mark Colgan and Matt DeLong, "A Teaching Polygon Makes Learning a Community Enterprise," *Primus* 25, no. 1 (2015): 41–49; Martha McAlister, "Emerging Communities of Practice," *Collected Essays on Learning and Teaching* 9 (2016): 125–32; Jacquie McDonald, ed., *Communities of Practice: Facilitating Social Learning in Higher Education* (The Netherlands: Springer 2017); Stephanie Oliver and Gavan Watson, "What if Grassroots Don't Take Root? Reflections on Cultivating Communities of Practice," *Transformative Dialogues: Teaching and Learning Journal* 10, no. 1 (April 2017): 1–6; Fiona Smart, "Poetic Transcription with a Twist: An Approach to Reflective Practice through Connection, Collaboration and Community," *Innovations in Education and Teaching International* 54, no. 2 (2017): 152–61; Gail O'Connor Mellow et al., *Taking College Seriously: Pedagogy Matters! Fostering Student Success through Faculty-Centered Practice Improvement* (Sterling, VA: Stylus, 2015); Audriana M. Stark, "Communities of Practice as Agents of Future Faculty Development," *Journal of Faculty Development* 30, no. 2 (Spring 2016): 59–67.

10.   Daniel Bernstein et al., *Making Teaching and Learning Visible: Course Portfolios and the Peer Review of Teaching* (Bolton, MA: Anker Publishing Company, 2006), 5–6.

11.   Margaret J. Marshall, "Teaching Circles: Supporting Shared Work and Professional Development," *Pedagogy* 8, no. 3 (Fall 2008), 420. See also Jennifer Ashton, "Using Teaching Circles amongst Online Adjunct Faculty," *Journal of Instructional Research* 1 (2012):

11–15; Richard Blackwell, Joanna Channell, and John Williams, "Teaching Circles: A Way Forward for Part-Time Teachers in Higher Education?" *International Journal for Academic Development* 6, no. 1 (May 2001): 40–53; Michelle Freeman, "Teaching Circles: A Low-Cost, High-Benefit Way to Engage Faculty," *Teaching Professor* 25, no. 2 (February 2011): 3; Barbara Mezeske, "Teaching Circles: Low-Cost, High-Impact Faculty Development," *Academic Leader* 22, no. 1 (January 2006): 8.

12.   Marshall, "Teaching Circles," 423. See also David Boose, "The Scholarship of Teaching and Learning as a Subversive Activity," *Teaching and Learning Inquiry* 4, no. 1 (2016): 1–12.

13.   Marshall, "Teaching Circles," 420.

14.   Roxanna Harlow, "'Race Doesn't Matter, But . . . ' The Effect of Race on Professors' Experiences and Emotion Management in the Undergraduate College Classroom," *Social Psychology Quarterly* 66, no. 4 (2003): 359–62.

15.   Gary Perry et al., "Maintaining Credibility and Authority as an Instructor of Color in Diversity-Education Classrooms: A Qualitative Inquiry," *The Journal of Higher Education* 80, no.1 (January/February 2009): 101.

16.   Lucila Vargas, *Women Faculty of Color in the White Classroom: Narratives on the Pedagogical Implications of Teacher Diversity* (New York: Peter Lang, 2002), 14.

17.   Marshall, "Teaching Circles," 423. See also Stephen Brookfield, *The Skillful Teacher: On Technique, Trust, and Responsiveness in the Classroom*, Third Edition (San Francisco: Jossey-Bass, 2015), 60, 141–53; Donald Finkel, *Teaching with Your Mouth Shut* (Portsmouth, NH: Boynton/Cook Publishers, 2000), 134–47; Lindsey Higgins and Kerry Litzenberg, "Transferring Experience through Team Teaching: The Chance of a Lifetime," *College Teaching* 63, no. 3 (July–September 2015): 105–11. On team-teaching challenges, see Lauren Bryant et al. "Complicated Spaces: Negotiating Collaborative Teaching and Interdisciplinarity in Higher Education," *Journal of Effective Teaching* 14, no. 2 (2014): 83–101; Anne Marie Garran et al., "Team-Teaching Anti-Oppression with Diverse Faculty: Challenges

and Opportunities," *Social Work Education* 34, no. 7 (October 2015): 799–814; Grischa Liebel, Håkan Burden, and Rogardt Heldal, "For Free: Continuity and Change by Team Teaching," *Teaching in Higher Education* 22, no. 1 (January 2017): 62–77; Jennifer Lock et al., "The Lived Experiences of Instructors Co-Teaching in Higher Education," *Brock Education: A Journal of Educational Research and Practice* 26, no. 1 (2016): 22–35.

18.   Julie Blais, Christopher Motz, and Timothy Pychyl, "Mentored Teaching, or How I Learned to Stop Worrying and Love Teaching," *College Teaching* 64, no. 1 (2016): 1–9; Carolyn Hoessler et al., "Surviving and Thriving: Recommendations for Graduate Student-Teachers from Colleagues further along the Path," *Transformative Dialogues: Teaching and Learning Journal* 9, no. 2 (November 2016): 1–15; Brad Johnson, *On Being a Mentor: A Guide for Higher Education Faculty* (Mahwah, NJ: Lawrence Erelbaum Associates, 2007); Tonya Hammer, Heather Trepal, and Stacy Speedlin, "Five Relational Strategies for Mentoring Female Faculty," *Adultspan Journal* 13, no. 1 (April 2014): 4–14; Emily Smith et al., "Institutionalizing Faculty Mentoring within a Community of Practice Model," *To Improve the Academy* 35, no. 1 (January 2016): 35–71; Caroline Sotello Viernes Turner and Juan Carlos Gonzalez, eds., *Modeling Mentoring across Race/Ethnicity and Gender: Practices to Cultivate the Next Generation of Diverse Faculty* (Sterling, VA: Stylus, 2015); Lynn Wild, Anne Marie Canale, and Cheryl Herdklotz, "The Power of Many: Mentoring Networks for Growth and Development," *College and University* 2 (2017): 37–41.

19.   Jane S. Halonne et al., "Are You Really Above Average? Documenting Teaching Effectiveness," in *Evidence-Based Teaching for Higher Education*, ed. Beth M. Schwartz and Regan A. R. Gurung (Washington, DC: American Psychological Association, 2012), 141–42; Aaron S. Richmond, Guy A. Boysen, and Regan A. R. Gurung, *An Evidence-Based Guide to College and University Teaching: Developing the Model Teacher* (New York: Routledge, 2016), 36.

20.   Maryellen Weimer, *Inspired College Teaching: A Career-Long Resource for Professional Growth* (San Francisco: Jossey-Bass, 2010), 205. See

also Joselynn Fountain and Kathryn Newcomer, "Developing and Sustaining Effective Faculty Mentoring Programs," *Journal of Public Affairs Education* 22, no. 4 (Fall 2016): 483–506.

21. Donald Schoffstall, "On a Frustrating Day or in a Troubled Class, Remember We All Make a Difference," in *Teaching Mistakes from the Classroom* (Madison, WI: Magna Publications, 2010), 21.

22. For links to some of these sites, visit geekypedagogy.com.

23. Ernest Boyer, *Scholarship Reconsidered: Priorities of the Professoriate* (Princeton, NJ: Carnegie Foundation for the Advancement of Teaching, 1990) introduced the term "scholarship of teaching," marking a shift toward a new professional research field of SoTL.

24. Pat Hutchings, "The Scholarship of Teaching and Learning: From Idea to Integration," *New Directions for Teaching and Learning* 123 (Fall 2010): 63–72.

25. As quoted in Kathleen McKinney, *Enhancing Learning through the Scholarship of Teaching and Learning: The Challenges and Joys of Juggling* (San Francisco: Anker Publishing, 2007), 3.

26. See Paul Savory, Amy Nelson Burnett, and Amy Goodburn, *Inquiry into the College Classroom: A Journey toward Scholarly Teaching* (Boston: Anker Publications, 2007).

27. Arnold, "Kill the Professor and Save the Teacher," 33.

28. Arnold, "Kill the Professor and Save the Teacher," 33.

29. Randy Bass, "The Scholarship of Teaching: What's the Problem?" *Inventio* 1, no. 1 (February 1999): https://my.vanderbilt.edu/sotl/files/2013/08/Bass-Problem1.pdf.

30. Bass, "The Scholarship of Teaching." See also Marian McCarthy, "The Scholarship of Teaching and Learning in Education: An Overview," in *The Scholarship of Teaching and Learning in Education*, ed. Rowena Murray (Berkshire, U.K.: Open University Press, 2008).

31. Mary Taylor Huber and Pat Hutchings, *The Advancement of Learning: Building the Teaching Commons* (San Francisco: Jossey Bass, 2005), 14, 120.

32. Pat Hutchings, Mary Taylor Huber, and Anthony Ciccone, *The Scholarship of Teaching and Learning Reconsidered: Institutional Integration and Impact* (San Francisco: Jossey-Bass, 2011), xi.

33. Carolin Kreber, *Authenticity in and through Teaching in Higher*

Education: The Transformative Potential of the Scholarship of Teaching (New York: Routledge, 2013); Kimberly W. Williams, *Doing Research to Improve Teaching and Learning: A Guide for College and University Faculty* (New York: Routledge, 2015). See also Alexis Franzese and Peter Felten, "Reflecting on Reflecting: Scholarship of Teaching and Learning as a Tool to Evaluate Contemplative Pedagogies," *International Journal for the Scholarship of Teaching and Learning* 11, no. 1 (January 2017), https://doi.org/10.20429/ijsotl.2017.110108.

34. Brookfield, *Becoming a Critically Reflective Teacher*, 171.

35. Weimer, *Inspired College Teaching*, 43.

36. Nancy L. Chick, "Difference, Privilege, and Power in the Scholarship of Teaching and Learning: The Value of Humanities SOTL," in *The Scholarship of Teaching In and Across the Disciplines*, ed. Kathleen McKinney (Bloomington: Indiana University Press, 2013), 15–17.

37. Hutchings, Huber, and Ciccone, *The Scholarship of Teaching and Learning Reconsidered*, 9. One group of scholars identifies a "second wave" of SoTL that includes more diversity in its methodological approach. See Nancy L. Chick, Aeron Haynie, and Regan A. R. Gurung, "Signature Pedagogies in the Liberal Arts and Beyond," in *Exploring More Signature Pedagogies: Approaches to Teaching Disciplinary Habits of Mind,* ed. Nancy L. Chick, Aeron Haynie, and Regan A. R. Gurung (Sterling, VA: Stylus, 2012), 3–4.

38. Weimer, *Enhancing Scholarly Work on Teaching and Learning*, 40; Maryellen Weimer, "Tulips, Tinfoil, and Teaching," *Teaching Professor* (blog), *Faculty Focus*, December 6, 2017, https://www .facultyfocus.com/articles/teaching-professor-blog/tulips-tinfoil-and -teaching.

39. The idea of including student voices in SoTL is still a "radical concept," according to Megan M. Otis and Joyce Hammond, "Participatory Action Research as a Rationale for Student Voices in the Scholarship of Teaching and Learning," in *Engaging Student Voices in the Study of Teaching and Learning*, ed. Carmen Werder and Megan M. Otis (Sterling, VA: Stylus, 2010), 32. On this topic, see Allison Boye, Micah Meixner Logan, and Suzanne Tapp, "Learning from Each Other: Involving Students in Centers for Teaching and Learning," *Journal on Centers for Teaching and Learning* 3 (2011):

65–82; Chick, Haynie, and Gurung, "Signature Pedagogies in the Liberal Arts and Beyond," 8–9; Alison Cook-Sather, "Multiplying Perspectives and Improving Practice: What Can Happen When Undergraduate Students Collaborate with College Faculty to Explore Teaching and Learning," *Instructional Science* 42, no. 1 (January 2014): 31–46; Hutchings, Huber, and Ciccone, *The Scholarship of Teaching and Learning Reconsidered*, 40; Angela Miller, "Improving SoTL Programs: The Impact of a Student Sector," *InSight: A Journal of Scholarly Teaching* 8 (2013): 44–50; Richard Minhas, Deborah Long, and Peter Felten, "Power and Expertise: Student-Faculty Collaboration in Course Design and the Scholarship of Teaching and Learning," *International Journal for the Scholarship of Teaching and Learning* 2, no. 2 (2008): 1–9. A new journal, *International Journal for Students as Partners*, https://mulpress.mcmaster.ca/ijsap/about, addresses this gap in the scholarship.

40.   But not totally absent. See for example *Teaching Mistakes from the College Classroom* (Madison, WI: Magna Publications, 2010); Cohan, "Bad Apple." See also Michelle Jackson, "On Engaging Students: What I Learned from One of my Biggest Teaching Mistakes," *Transformative Dialogues: Teaching and Learning Journal* 10, no. 2 (June 2017): 1–5; Coralie McCormack, Thea Vanags, and Robyn Prior, "'Things fall apart so they can fall together': Uncovering the Hidden Side of Writing a Teaching Award Application," *Higher Education Research and Development* 33, no. 5 (September 2014): 935–48; Chris Palmer, "Reflections on Teaching: Mistakes I've Made," *Faculty Focus*, March 21, 2013, https://www.facultyfocus.com/articles/faculty-development/reflections-on-teaching-mistakes-ive-made; Kenneth Stewart, "Lessons from Teaching Millennials," *College Teaching* 57, no. 2 (Spring 2009): 111–18.

41.   Ken Bain, *What the Best College Teachers Do* (Cambridge: Harvard University Press, 2004), 19.

42.   Graham Broad, "The Things I Did Badly: Looking Back on My First Five Years of Teaching," in *Teaching Mistakes from the Classroom*, 4. See also Debra Schwietert, "Neglecting to Cultivate a Research-Based Teaching Practice," in *Teaching Mistakes from the Classroom*, 12.

43. Jane S. Halonne et al., "Are You Really Above Average?" 133.

44. Nothing better proves my assertion that nerds constitute a disproportionate number of academics than the fact that "Buffy studies" is a bona fide field of academic inquiry with its own scholarly journal (*Slayage*). For further discussion and citations on Buffy studies, see "Chapter 4 Bibliographic Essay," geekypedagogy .com.

45. Liz Grauerholz and Eric Main, "Fallacies of SOTL: Rethinking How We Conduct Our Research," in McKinney, *The Scholarship of Teaching In and Across the Disciplines*, 157–159.

46. To see my recommended multidisciplinary SoTL books, journals, and teaching conferences, visit geekypedaogy.com.

47. Marion Engin and Barnaby Priest, "Observing Teaching: A Lens for Self-Reflection," *Journal of Perspectives in Applied Academic Practice* 2, no. 2 (2014): 2–9.

48. Hutchings, Huber, and Ciccone, *The Scholarship of Teaching and Learning Reconsidered*, 37, 28.

49. Ken Winograd, "The Functions of Teacher Emotion: The Good, the Bad, and the Ugly," *Teachers College Record* 105, no. 9 (2003): 1669. Winograd is discussing primary school teaching but his point also applies to higher education.

50. Weimer, *Inspired College Teaching*, 105.

51. Huber and Hutchings, *The Advancement of Learning*, 18.

Chapter 5

1. Pat Hutchings, Mary Taylor Huber, and Anthony Ciccone, *The Scholarship of Teaching and Learning Reconsidered: Institutional Integration and Impact* (San Francisco: Jossey-Bass, 2011), 124–25.

2. Maryellen Weimer, *Inspired College Teaching: A Career-Long Resource for Professional Growth* (San Francisco: Jossey-Bass, 2010), 5, 193.

3. Marshall, "Teaching Circles," *Pedagogy* 8, no. 3 (Fall 2008): 428.

4. Michele DiPietro and Marie Norman, "Using Learning Principles as a Theoretical Framework for Instructional Consultations," *International Journal for Academic Development* 19, no. 4 (2014), 286, 290.

5.   Elizabeth F. Barkley, *Student Engagement Techniques: A Handbook for College Faculty* (San Francisco: Jossey-Bass, 2010), 30.

6.   DiPietro and Norman, "Using Learning Principles as a Theoretical Framework for Instructional Consultations," 284–85.

7.   T. Scott Bledsoe and Janice C. Baksin, "Recognizing Student Fear: The Elephant in the Classroom," *College Teaching* 62 (2014): 34.

8.   Anton O. Tolman, Andy Sechler, and Shea Smart, "Obstacles, Biases, and the Urgent Need to Understand the Social Cost of Resistance," in *Why Students Resist Learning: A Practical Model for Understanding and Helping Students*, ed. Anton O. Tolman and Janine Kremling (Sterling, VA: Stylus, 2017), 41.

9.   "The process of becoming an effective teacher is all trial and error, often quite painful and exhausting." Jay Parini, *The Art of Teaching* (Cambridge: Oxford University Press, 2005), 50–51.

10. Wiemer, *Inspired College Teaching*, 7. See also Sarah Burnell and Daniel Bernstein, "Overcoming Some Threshold Concepts in Scholarly Teaching," *Journal of Faculty Development* 26, no. 3 (September 2012): 14–18; DiPietro and Norman, "Using Learning Principles as a Theoretical Framework for Instructional Consultations," 287.

11. Dannelle D. Stevens and Joanne E. Cooper, *Journal Keeping: How to Use Reflective Writing for Effective Learning, Teaching, Professional Insight, and Positive Change* (Sterling, VA: Stylus, 2009), 21, 24. See also Aaron S. Richmond, Guy A. Boysen, and Regan A. R. Gurung, *An Evidence-Based Guide to College and University Teaching: Developing the Model Teacher* (New York: Routledge, 2016), who summarize: "Set learning goals → Facilitate learning → Assess outcomes → Make revisions" and repeat (110).

12. DiPietro and Norman, "Using Learning Principles as a Theoretical Framework for Instructional Consultations," 285.

13. Laurie Penny, "The Problem with Nerd Entitlement," *New Statesmen*, January 9–15, 2015, 14.

14. Mark Okrand, *Klingon for the Galactic Traveler* (New York: Pocket Books, 2014). See also the Klingon Language Institute at https://www.kli.org. For further discussion of scholarship on *Star Trek*,

see "Chapter 5 Bibliographic Essay," available for download at geekypedagogy.com.

15. For example, Kevin Jack Hagopian discusses how many of the pedagogical strategies outlined in Bain's *What the Best College Teachers Do* would not work for his introductory class of 450 students. "Rethinking the Structural Architecture of the College Classroom," *New Directions for Teaching and Learning* 135 (Fall 2013): 12.

16. "Whether a first-year assistant professor or a tenured full professor, one can always improve upon the effectiveness of teaching." Regan A. R. Gurung and Beth M. Schwartz, *Optimizing Teaching and Learning: Practicing Pedagogical Research* (Malden, MA: Wiley Blackwell, 2009), 169.

17. Jared W. Keeley, Emad Ismail, and William Buskit, "Excellent Teachers' Perspectives on Excellent Teaching," *Teaching of Psychology* 43, no. 3 (2016): 176.

18. Stephen W. Braden and Deborah N. Smith, "Managing the College Classroom: Perspectives from an Introvert and an Extrovert," *College Quarterly* 9, no. 1 (Winter 2006): http://collegequarterly.ca/2006-vol09 -num01-winter/braden_smith.html.

19. Parini, *The Art of Teaching,* 105.

20. Elizabeth Green, "Can Good Teaching Be Learned?" *New York Times Magazine*, March 7, 2010, 37.

21. To assess how well your own classes are creating the necessary conditions for productive struggle, see Josh Eyler, "What Is the Error Climate of Your Course?" July 6, 2016, Rice University Center for Teaching Excellence Blog, http://cte.rice.edu/blogarchive/2016/7/6 /what-is-the-error-climate-of-your-course.

22. Donald G. Schoffstall, "Don't Assume a Student's Previous Knowledge," in *Teaching Mistakes from the Classroom* (Madison, WI: Magna Publications, 2010), 8.

23. "You should spend at least as much time listening as speaking. Students want to communicate; give them the opportunity to do so." Richard E. Lyons, Meggin McIntosh, Marcella L. Kysilka, *Teaching College in an Age of Accountability* (Boston: Allyn and Bacon/Pearson, 2003), 105.

24.   Louis J. Gross, "It's Wednesday: Take Two," in *The Art of College Teaching: 28 Takes*, ed. Marilyn Kallet and April Morgan (Knoxville: The University of Tennessee Press, 2005), 119.

25.   Christopher Schaberg and Mark Yakich, "How Should a Professor Be?" *Inside Higher Ed*, September 2, 2015, https://www.insidehighered.com/advice/2015/09/02/essay-offers-advice-how-be-good-and-effective-professor.

26.   Weimer, *Inspired College Teaching*, 182.

27.   Parini, *The Art of Teaching*, 5–6.

28.   Brookfield, *The Skillful Teacher*, 215–216.

29.   "Academics are thinkers, objective problem solvers, critical analysts, and experts with highly specialized knowledge. It's not an environment that gives much credence to emotions [but] an ongoing commitment to teaching cannot be powered by the intellect alone. Content knowledge and rational thinking don't get faculty through the daily grind of preparing for classes, going to class, grading homework, exams, and papers, interacting with needy students, balancing the competing demands of teaching and research, serving on countless committees, and putting up with political antics of colleagues." Weimer, *Inspired College Teaching*, 182.

30.   Brookfield, *The Skillful Teacher*, 6, 265–66.

31.   Brookfield, *The Skillful Teacher*, 273.

32.   Barkley, *Student Engagement Techniques*, 3.

33.   Susan Ambrose et al., *How Learning Works: Seven Research-Based Principles for Smart Teaching* (San Francisco: Jossey-Bass, 2010), 217–24.

34.   Hutchings, Huber, and Ciccone, *The Scholarship of Teaching and Learning Reconsidered*, 64–65.

35.   Jennifer Fletcher and Hetty Yelland, "Engaging Learners," in *Fostering Habits of Mind in Today's Students: A New Approach to Developmental Education*, ed. Jennifer Fletcher, Adela Najarro, and Hetty Yelland (Sterling, VA: Stylus, 2015), 87.

36.   Robert Rotenberg, *The Art and Craft of College Teaching: A Guide for New Professors and Graduate Students*, Second Edition (Walnut Creek, CA: Left Coast Press, 2010), 50.

37. Marilla D. Svinicki, *Learning and Motivation in the Postsecondary Classroom* (San Franciso: Anker Publishing Company, 2004), 41.

38. Jennifer Fletcher, "Building Confidence," in Fletcher, Najarro, and Yelland, *Fostering Habits of Mind in Today's Students*, 124.

39. Dorothy Wallace, "The Hornet's Opinion," in Kallet and Morgan, *The Art of College Teaching*, 125.

40. Weimer, *Inspired College Teaching*, 12.

41. Marilla D. Svinick, Wilbert J. McKeachie, et al., *McKeachie's Teaching Tips: Strategies, Research, and Theory for College and University Teachers*, Fourteenth Edition (Belmont, CA: Wadsworth Cengage Learning, 2014), 5. See also Marshall, "Teaching Circles," 428.

42. David Pace, "The Amateur in the Operating Room: History and the Scholarship of Teaching and Learning," *The American Historical Review* 109, no. 4 (2004): 1171–1192.

43. Weimer, *Inspired College Teaching*, 183.

44. James E. Zull, *The Art of Changing the Brain: Enriching Teaching by Exploring the Biology of Learning* (Sterling, VA: Stylus, 2002), 60.

45. "Master teachers" always pursue "continuing education on pedagogy." Richmond, Boysen, and Gurung, *An Evidence-Based Guide to College and University Teaching*, 37. See also Carolin Kreber, *Authenticity in and through Teaching in Higher Education: The Transformative Potential of the Scholarship of Teaching* (New York: Routledge, 2013), who argues that discourse about teaching often focuses solely on student learning and neglects the learning we do as teachers (144–45).

INDEX